Søren Kierkegaard: Theologian of the Gospel

Editors: Todd Speidell,
Greg Marcar, and
Andrew Torrance

WIPF & STOCK · Eugene, Oregon

SØREN KIERKEGAARD
Theologian of the Gospel

Copyright © 2021 Wipf and Stock Publishers. All rights reserved. Except for brief quotations in critical publications or reviews, no part of this book may be reproduced in any manner without prior written permission from the publisher. Write: Permissions, Wipf and Stock Publishers, 199 W. 8th Ave., Suite 3, Eugene, OR 97401.

Wipf & Stock
An Imprint of Wipf and Stock Publishers
199 W. 8th Ave., Suite 3
Eugene, OR 97401

www.wipfandstock.com

PAPERBACK ISBN: 978-1-6667-0910-0
HARDCOVER ISBN: 978-1-6667-0911-7
EBOOK ISBN: 978-1-6667-0912-4

Contents

Abbreviations iii

Foreword
— **Paul Martens** ix

Preface
— **Todd Speidell** xi

Introduction
— **Andrew Torrance and Greg Marcar** xiii

Part I: Incarnational Theology and Ethics

1. Kierkegaard and the Trinitarian Grammar of Theology
— **Murray Rae** 1

2. Kierkegaard's Incarnational Realism
— **David J. Gouwens** 21

3. Kierkegaard's Paradoxical Christology
— **Andrew B. Torrance** 41

4. Kierkegaard on the Beauty of the Cross
— **Lee C. Barrett** 64

5. Busyness, Worry and the Prototypical Love of Christ: Another Look at the Character of

Kierkegaard's Ethics in *Works of Love*
— **G. P. Marcar** 83

Part II: Faith, Sin, and Offense

6. Kierkegaard: Father of Existentialism or Critic of Existentialism?
— **C. Stephen Evans** 110

7. The Theological Self in Kierkegaard's *Sickness unto Death*
— **Philip G. Ziegler** 129

8. Communion and the Remission of Sin: A Kierkegaardian Account
— **Joshua Cockayne** 145

9. Kierkegaard on Sin, Ambiguity, and Gospel Radicality: Towards a Response to George Pattison
— **Aaron P. Edwards** 168

10. The Difference the Incarnation Makes: The changing nature of faith and offence in the pseudonyms of Søren Kierkegaard
— **Stephen Backhouse** 191

11. The Inverse Dialectic of Jest and Earnestness in Kierkegaard's Theology
— **Sylvia Walsh** 224

Contributors 241

Abbreviations of Kierkegaard works

AUC *Attack Upon "Christendom," 1854-1855*, trans. Walter Lowrie (Oxford: Oxford University Press, 1944)

C *The Crisis and a Crisis in the Life of an Actress*, in *CD*, trans. Howard V. Hong and Edna H. Hong (Princeton: Princeton University Press, 1997), *KW* XVII.

CA *The Concept of Anxiety*, ed. and trans. Reidar Thomte in collaboration with Albert B. Anderson (Princeton: Princeton University Press, 1980)

CD *Christian Discourses. The Crisis and a Crisis in the Life of an Actress,* ed. and trans. Howard V. Hong and Edna H. Hong with Introduction and Notes (Princeton: Princeton University Press, 1997), *KW* XVII

CI *The Concept of Irony*, trans. and ed. Howard V. Hong and Edna H. Hong (Princeton: Princeton University Press, 1989), *KW* II

CUP *Concluding Unscientific Postscript*, ed. and trans. Howard V. Hong and Edna H. Hong with Introduction and Notes (Princeton: Princeton University Press, 1992), *KW* XII

DACF   *Discourses at the Communion on Fridays*, ed. and trans. Sylvia Walsh (Bloomington, IN: Indiana University Press, 2011)

EUD   *Eighteen Upbuilding Discourses*, ed. and trans. by Howard V. and Edna H. Hong (Princeton, NJ: Princeton University Press, 1990), *KW* V

FSE   *For Self-Examination. Judge for Yourself!* ed. and trans. Howard V. and Edna H. Hong (Princeton: Princeton University Press, 1990), *KW* XXI

FT   *Fear and Trembling*, ed. and trans. Howard V. Hong and Edna H. Hong (Princeton: Princeton University Press, 1983), *KW* VI

GS   *Gospel of Sufferings*, trans. A. S. Aldworth and W. S. Ferries (Cambridge: James Clarke & Co., 2015)

JC   *Johannes Climacus (or De Omnibus Dubitandum Est) and A Sermon*, trans. T. H. Croxall (Stanford: Stanford University Press, 1958)

JFY   *Judge for Yourself!*, in *For Self-Examination. Judge for Yourself!* ed. and trans. Howard V. and Edna H. Hong (Princeton: Princeton University Press, 1990), *KW* XXI

JP	*Søren Kierkegaard's Journals and Papers*, ed. and trans. Howard V. Hong and Edna H. Hong, assisted by Gregor Malantschuk (Bloomington and London: Indiana University Press, 1967-1978), 7 vols.
KJN	*Kierkegaard's Journals and Notebooks*, eds. Niels Jørgen Cappelørn, Alastair Hannay, David Kangas, Bruce H. Kirmmse, George Pattison, Vanessa Rumble, and K. Brian Söderquist (Princeton, NJ: Princeton University Press, 2015-2019), 11 vols.
KG	*Kjerlighedens Gjerninger: nogle christelige Overveielser i Talers Form* (C.A. Reitzel, 1862)
KW	*Kierkegaard's Writings*, trans. Howard V. Hong and Edna H. Hong (Princeton: Princeton University Press, 1978-98), vols. I-XXVI.
LD	*Letters and Documents*, trans. Hendrik Rosenmeier (Princeton: Princeton University Press, 2009), *KW* XXV
M	*The Moment and Late Writings*, ed. and trans. Howard V. Hong and Edna H. Hong (Princeton: Princeton University Press, 1998), *KW* XXIII

OT   *Opbyggelige taler i forskjellig aand*
            (Reitzels forlag, 1862)

P   *Prefaces. Writing Sampler,* ed. and trans.
            Howard V. Hong and Edna H. Hong
            (Princeton: Princeton University Press,
            1998), *KW* IX

PA   *The Present Age,* trans. Alexander Dru
            (London: Collins, 1962)

PhC   *Philosophical Crumbs,* trans. M. G. Piety
            (Oxford: Oxford University Press, 2009)

PC   *Practice in Christianity,* ed. and trans.
            Howard V. Hong and Edna H. Hong with
            Introduction and Notes (Princeton:
            Princeton University Press, 1991), *KW* XX

POH   *Purity of Heart Is to Will One Thing;*
            Spiritual Preparation for the Office of
            Confession (New York: Harper, 1956)

POV   *Point of View,* ed. and trans. Howard V.
            Hong and Edna H. Hong (Princeton:
            Princeton University Press, 1998), *KW*
            XXII

PF   *Philosophical Fragments and Johannes*
            Climacus, ed. and trans. Howard V. Hong
            and Edna H. Hong with Introduction and
            Notes (Princeton: Princeton University
            Press, 1985), *KW* VII

SKS   *Søren Kierkegaard Skrifter*, ed. Niels Jørgen Cappelørn, Joakim Garff, Jette Knudsen, Johnny Kondrup, Alastair McKinnon, and Finn Hauberg Mortensen (Copenhagen: Gads Forlag, 1997ff.), 28 vols.

SKP   *Søren Kierkegaards Papirer*, second enlarged edition ed. Niels Thulstrup (Copenhagen: Gyldendal, 1968–78), with index vols. 14–16 by Niels Jørgen Cappelørn

SLW   *Stages on Life's Way*, ed. and trans. Howard V. and Edna H. Hong (Princeton: Princeton University Press, 1988), *KW* XI

SUD   *The Sickness unto Death*, ed. and trans. Howard V. Hong and Edna H. Hong (Princeton: Princeton University Press, 1980), *KW* XIX

TDIO   *Three Discourses on Imagined Occasions*, ed. and trans. Howard V. and Edna H. Hong (Princeton: Princeton University Press, 1993), *KW* X

UDVS   *Upbuilding Discourses in Various Spirits*, ed. and trans. Howard V. and Edna H. Hong (Princeton: Princeton University Press, 1993), *KW* XV

WA   *Without Authority*, ed. and trans. Howard V. and Edna H. Hong (Princeton: Princeton University Press, 1997), *KW* XVIII

WL   *Works of Love*, ed. and trans. Howard V. Hong and Edna H. Hong (Princeton, NJ: Princeton University Press, 1995), *KW* XVI

WOL   *Works of Love*, trans. David F. Swenson and Lillian Marvin Swenson (Princeton, NJ: Princeton University Press, 1946)

—   *For Self-Examination; And, Judge for Yourselves; And, Three Discourses 1851*, trans. Walter Lowrie (Princeton, NJ: Princeton University Press, 1944)

Foreword

Paul Martens

Kierkegaard is not a theologian, or at least that is the familiar critique. Since the defense of his dissertation, academic theologians have been critical of the style within which he communicated his insight, and Kierkegaard returns the favor by openly mocking theology professors and pastors alike who depend on Christian doctrine for a living.

Yet, Kierkegaard is a theologian, unabashedly and unflinchingly so. This volume does not set out to prove that this is the case; this volume demonstrates the case performatively. It does not do so primarily in order to burnish Kierkegaard's orthodox Christian credentials (although many of the contributors would no doubt be quite happy if that was the result). Rather, it does so adventurously and unsystematically as it explores the implications of what it means for a self to stand before God (*coram deo*), what it means for humans as relational selves to find rest in the presence of a relational God.

The result, evidenced throughout this volume, is that Kierkegaard is something of a radical theologian, not an advocate of radical freedom aligned with post-WWII existentialism but a witness to the kind of radical self-giving love at the heart of the gospel. It is a theology rooted in a God revealed by kenotic love, by love that turns the world's expectations on their head, by love that is both offensive and absolute. It is a life-giving theology springing from and sustained by God's grace, and it is in this unified voice that this small collection makes a unique and compelling rendering of Kierkegaard's theology.

To that end, Luther, Barth, Bonhoeffer and T.F. Torrance are probably the most defining and provocative interlocutors in the following pages, though they play merely illustrative roles. And, in the same breath, it is worth noting that the range of engagement with Kierkegaard's corpus in this volume excellently reflects its breadth and depth, from the knight of faith in *Fear and Trembling* to the late attack on Danish Christendom while frequently lingering in *Philosophical Fragments*, *Sickness Unto Death*, *Practice in Christianity* and an array of upbuilding and Christian discourses.

Over the past decades, I have learned much from the senior scholars gathered here, and I am not alone—Steve Evans, Lee Barrett, David Gouwens, and Sylvia Walsh have been some of the most illuminating guides for a generation of theologically-inclined readers of Kierkegaard. This volume reveals that the next generation is going to be in good hands as well, and there is not much more I could say that would constitute higher praise than this.

Preface

Todd Speidell

The Scottish theologian T. F. Torrance first introduced me to the idea that Soren Kierkegaard was not an "existentialist" but was rather an incarnational realist who understood personal and subjective truth based on the objective reality of the self-giving God in Jesus Christ. Torrance contends that "a whole host of existentialist thinkers arose to interpret in their own way that 'truth is subjectivity,' i.e. in a sense the opposite to that which Kierkegaard contended": namely, that God is "Truth in the form of personal Being, that is Truth as active Subject," for only then can knowing subjects experience faith as they encounter the Truth in a way that human "existence is involved and transformed in conformity to it."[1] Kierkegaard did not intend his "leap of faith," Torrance continues, to "mean at all a leap in the dark, an irrational act," but he did mean that "our knowing of Him and our speaking of Him must be in a mode corresponding to His historical and His divine nature. We are thus unable to report the historical fact of Christ truthfully without reporting in the mode of faith..." and without renouncing abstract generalizations and doctrinal preconceptions, so that we may appropriately apprehend and acknowledge Truth in relationship to Jesus Christ.[2]

Many years later, I told Steve Evans that I was considering editing a volume on Kierkegaard as a Christian, incarnational theologian and asked him if he thought the "existentialist" label had any validity in regard to Kierkegaard, and he replied by submitting an

---

[1] Thomas F. Torrance, *Theological Science* (London: Oxford University Press, 1969), 4f.

[2] Ibid., 154, 178, 302. Also see Torrance's *Incarnation: The Person and Life of Christ* (Paternoster/IVP Academic, 2008) that Kierkegaard's "leap of faith" did not revolve around "the decision of faith itself" in a way that eradicates objective reality but is a personal response "to the mode of Christ's coming into being in history" (26, 286).

unpublished paper presentation: "Kierkegaard was NOT an Existentialist" (which became Chapter 6 of this book)![3] I'm also grateful to Steve for introducing me to the theological work about Kierkegaard by Murray Rae[4] and Andrew Torrance[5] and recommending that they both contribute essays to this volume and also recommend other Kierkegaard scholars who understand him on his own terms as a Christian theologian, not an existentialist philosopher. Greg Marcar and Andrew Torrance not only wrote excellent essays but also helped consider overall conceptual themes and address the multitudinous details of an edited volume.

I also wish to thank Jim Tedrick of Wipf and Stock Publishers for taking interest in this project. It is a good thing to have a publisher who makes a commitment to a theology of the Incarnation, especially here as it intersects with a thinker who is often and profoundly misunderstood as the founder of a philosophical school of "existentialism." I finally extend a word of gratitude to Dr. Kerry Magruder, Webmaster of the Thomas F. Torrance Theological Fellowship, who helped convert and transform a prior journal volume into a new and revised book with expert technological skill.

---

[3] Also see of related interest Paul Martens and C. Stephen Evans, eds., *Kierkegaard and Christian Faith* (Waco, TX: Baylor University Press, 2016).

[4] *Kierkegaard's Vision of the Incarnation* (Oxford: Oxford University Press, 1997) and *Kierkegaard and Theology* (London: T&T Clark, 2010).

[5] *The Freedom to Become a Christian: A Kierkegaardian Account of Human Transformation in Relationship with God* (London: Bloomsbury, 2016).

Introduction

Andrew Torrance and Greg Marcar

Kierkegaard's theological writings can be read as a commentary on the Gospel. He is committed to thinking out of the Gospel, which he presents as the centre and ground of the theological task. What do we mean by the Gospel? The Gospel, for Kierkegaard, is the good news of God with us. It is the message who is the Word become flesh, Jesus Christ, the one mediator between God and humankind. And it is the story of God's mighty act of redemption. To paraphrase one of Kierkegaard's journal entries, Christianity is the Gospel *par excellence*; it is the reality of God's only begotten Son doing everything—to the point of losing his life—to save humanity according to the Father's purposes from the beginning.[1]

Not only is the Gospel at the heart of Kierkegaard's theology, it is also, in turn, the ground of his anthropology. For him, the Gospel is the central witness to who God is for us and also to who we are called to be before God. No human is more intimately before God than the one in whom there is union between God and humanity: Jesus Christ. Therefore, no human more fully reveals what it means to be human. Accordingly, Kierkegaard is well known for presenting Jesus Christ as the divine prototype for humanity. For him, Christ stands as an example who invites us all to follow him, so that we might learn who we are in kinship with the one to whom we belong. At the same time, Kierkegaard is completely clear that we cannot help but fall short of our true calling; so, out of God's overwhelming love for us, Jesus Christ serves as redeemer. On the one hand, Jesus Christ calls us to follow him to the point of suffering, burdened by the struggle of taking up one's cross. Yet, on the other hand, no person is called to follow Christ to the point of despair. In a prayer on "Christ as prototype," Kierkegaard writes:

---

[1] *JP 3*, 2874 / *KJN 7*, 373

> ...when the striving one droops under the prototype, crushed, almost despairing, the Redeemer raises him up again; but at the same moment [Christ is] again the prototype so that we might be kept in the striving. O Redeemer, by your holy suffering and death you have made satisfaction for everyone and everything; no eternal salvation either can or shall be earned—it has been earned. Yet you left your footprints, you, the holy prototype for the human race and for every individual, so that by your Atonement the saved might at every moment find the confidence and boldness to want to strive to follow you.[2]

Throughout his writings, Kierkegaard presents a balanced vision of the Gospel that conveys both its high demands and also the peace and rest that comes from knowing and encountering the presence of God. While these two sides of the Gospel can appear to be in tension from our immediate perspective, Kierkegaard presents them as being entirely complementary to one another. The reason we do not directly experience this harmony is that we encounter God in a sinful context that is hostile to God's purposes. For this reason, God's creative purposes do not naturally unfold within the immanence of this world. So the Gospel message is needed to reveal to the world that God creates us for something more, something greater. He writes:

> The world, as is natural, speaks about this world, simply and solely about this world, does not know and does not wish to know that there is another world—another world would indeed be a perilous discovery for "this world." The Gospel speaks eternally about this other world, about eternity.[3]

But again, the Gospel does not simply call us to strive against the grain of this world by ourselves. Kierkegaard's stress on the costliness of discipleship is continually accompanied by a reference to the comfort of Jesus' words, "Come to me, you who are heavy laden, and I will give you rest" (Matt. 11:28). When emphasising the more challenging side of the Gospel's message, he is ever quick to qualify his emphasis by referring to its more uplifting side.

---

[2] *JFY*, 147.
[3] *JFY*, 150

INTRODUCTION

This volume gathers together a collection of essays that seek to represent the fact that Kierkegaard's theology of the Gospel is grounded in a Christological understanding of grace that calls us to a life of radical faith: a faith that involves taking up of one's cross and yet also bringing one's burdens to God to find rest in God's embrace. So while much of the first part of this volume focuses on how Kierkegaard's theology is shaped by the good news of the incarnation, the second part focuses on his understanding of what it means to be a self, particularly one that is corrupted by sin and seeks shelter from this condition in a life of faith. Yet, as one will notice from many of these essays, it is not at all straightforward to divide these sections up because these two sides of Kierkegaard's theology of the Gospel are so intertwined with one another. The Gospel is the good news of God-with-us: news that seeks to comfort and encourage us, but also transforms us in a way that is totally disruptive of the fallen ways into which this world has settled.

Chapter outline

As previously mentioned, this volume is divided into two sections. The first focuses on Kierkegaard's incarnational theology and ethics. The second further explores how—in light of the Gospel—Kierkegaard's thought recasts what it is to be and live as a human self, looking particularly at what it means for human beings to be corrupted by sin and delivered into a life of faith by way of a divine revelation which always contains the possibility of offense.

In the opening chapter, Murray Rae shows how Kierkegaard's thought is dependent on an orthodox trinitarian theology. While Kierkegaard's writings have very few explicit references to the Trinity, Rae shows that Kierkegaard's understanding of how persons are drawn into relationship with God is very much trinitarian. This is especially evident in the form of his prayers which are often addressed to Father, Son, and Spirit.

In chapter two, David Gouwens argues that Kierkegaard's theology is committed to theological and incarnational realism: one that is akin to that of T. F. Torrance. He argues that Kierkegaard's focus on the subjective "how" of faith does indeed affirm a "Christian knowledge" of a reality outside ourselves, as seen both in his epistemological realism in *Philosophical Fragments* and *Concluding Unscientific Postscript* and in his stress in *Practice in Christianity* and *Communion Discourses* on the believer's relation to Jesus Christ, in all his particularity, prompting offense or faith. While significant differences still obtain between their understandings of the "grammar" of Christian knowledge, Gouwens shows that Kierkegaard and share a realistic "grammar of Christian redemption" that sees "truth" in relation to God's self-giving in Jesus Christ.

In the third chapter, Andrew Torrance considers how Kierkegaard's paradoxical Christology seeks to draw attention to God's nearness to humanity and, particularly to the union that God establishes between God and humanity in Christ. By so doing, he looks at how Kierkegaard's paradoxical understanding of the God-human relationship can help us to understand two difficult issues in theology: (1) God's relationship to Christ's suffering; and (2) the changelessness of God. He ends by examining the more practical role that paradox played in Kierkegaard theology.

Chapter four focuses on Kierkegaard's theological account of the crucifixion, as an event that can paradoxically be seen to occasion joy. As Lee C. Barrett shows, for Kierkegaard, this joy is not simply due to the way in which this event brings forgiveness of sins (though this is a part of it), but it is also bound up to Kierkegaard's incarnational realism. As Barrett shows, Kierkegaard sees the cross as the manifestation of God's desire to be in communion with humanity, and therefore as the culmination of the lowliness of the incarnation. Because self-oriented humans cannot abide the prospect of radically other-regarding love, Christ inevitably provoked lethal hostility. Nevertheless, Christ accepted this persecution and suffering as the price that had to be paid for divine fellowship with humanity. The beauty of this costly divine self-giving can exult the human heart and inspire emulation.

In chapter five, G. P. Marcar explores the character and grammar of Kierkegaard's Christian ethics in the first series of *Works of Love*. Specifically, Marcar engages with the contention that

INTRODUCTION

Kierkegaard's thought is apathetic towards temporal socio-economic goods. This is initially done by viewing Kierkegaard's comments in *Works of Love* alongside his discussion of busyness, distraction, worry and comparison elsewhere. Through this examination, Marcar sets the vision of *Works of Love* against the intertextual backdrop of Kierkegaard's thought on the individual's relatedness to God, and the nature of the love which God mandates towards others. The linchpin of both these strands of thought, Marcar argues, is the figure of Jesus Christ: the self-revelation of God and "the prototype" for humanity. Such an approach connects Kierkegaard's ethics with his Christology and theological anthropology. Seen thus, Marcar maintains that Kierkegaard's Christian ethics does indeed reject temporal goods as unimportant.

In the first chapter of the second main section, chapter six, C. Stephen Evans asks, what is Kierkegaard's relation to existentialism? For Evans, the lack of clarity of the concept of "existentialism" makes this question difficult. He argues, if we interpret existentialism in Sartre's terms, Kierkegaard is better thought of as a critic of existentialism than as its "father." Kierkegaard rejects both the classical foundationalism that demands objective certainty as the basis for ethics, and the Sartrean "radical choice" of will that the failure of classical foundationalism prompted. Kierkegaard shows how passion and subjectivity can help an individual acquire a truth that can be lived but is not subjective in the sense of being relativistic or arbitrary.

In chapter seven, Philip Ziegler's explores the place and function of the *coram deo* motif in Kierkegaard's theological programme, drawing particularly on *The Sickness Unto Death*. He argues that this motif speaks to the fact that the human self is constituted and governed by its relationship to God such that true human subjectivity finds its decisive condition of possibility in the transcendent reality of God's sovereign claim and mercy. Kierkegaard's use of the *coram deo* motif reiterates the essential logic of Luther's theological anthropology, sharpening the explication of human sinfulness and radicalizing the reality of divine grace as the sole possibility of genuine human selfhood.

SØREN KIERKEGAARD: THEOLOGIAN OF THE GOSPEL

By comparing Kierkegaard's discussion of Communion in his *Discourses at Communion on Fridays* and the account of sin presented in *Thus Sickness Unto Death,* Joshua Cockayne argues in chapter eight that we can address a problem discussed in contemporary philosophy of religion: how can the seemingly mundane acts involved in the practice of the Eucharist can play a role in the remission of sin? In response to this question, he argues that, for Kierkegaard, what prevents a person from being united to God in this life is not a lack of God's forgiveness, but rather, a weakness and dividedness of the human will. Not only does the practice of Communion bring about an awareness of one's resistance to God, but it also serves to draw one closer to Christ. By making this point, Cockayne shows how the ordinary actions involved in the Eucharist can be interpreted as releasing human beings from the grip of sin.

It is often assumed that Kierkegaard became "less nuanced" in his more polemical later period, leading many scholars to an interpretative ambivalence over his fundamental theological convictions. In chapter nine, Aaron P. Edwards offers a critical response to George Pattison with a view to explicating Kierkegaard's convictions on sin, redemption, and the implications of doubt and ambiguity. He argues that, for Kierkegaard, the catastrophic sickness of sin cannot be undone without a drastically invasive redemption. To speak in such homiletical binaries, of course, is to sound "unnuanced." Edwards shows that any attempt to underplay Kierkegaard's radical account of sin is to misunderstand the inherent nuance that undergirds his homiletical assertions, which were based entirely on his understanding of the Gospel. However alarming Kierkegaard's voice may sound to contemporary academic theology, it is precisely by not removing his veil of kerygmatic radicality that we retain his most paradoxically nuanced contribution to modern Christian thought.

In the tenth chapter, Stephen Backhouse provides a close reading of three of Kierkegaard's most important pseudonyms: Johannes de Silentio, Johannes Climacus and Anti-Climacus. He shows that, for de Silentio, faith requires a person to exist as an individual above the universal. Civic morality, the code of ethics that applies to all and is understood by all, is purposefully suspended by God for each individual that relates to him. Thus, de Silentio sees the offense as that which goes against the universal laws of society, and as a result of faith. He then argues that Climacus reverses the relationship, introducing a greater offense that itself causes the lesser offenses found in civil life. This essential offense stands as the gateway to faith, it is not a result of faith. Climacus sees the essential offense as the Absolute Paradox's assault on certain forms of human reason. Only if reason cedes the throne to the Paradox at this time can there be a happy relationship, a situation that Climacus identifies as "faith" and its opposite as "offense." By contrast, Anti-Climacus hardly ever alludes to the offense against reason. He sees the offense as a matter of obedience to Jesus Christ, not assent to a paradox (Climacus) or an affront to civic morality (de Silentio). Anti-Climacus describes Christ as the "sign of contradiction" that gives rise to the two forms of "essential offense." These two forms are the ethical aversion faced when this lowly man claims to be God, and when God claims to be this lowly man. Only the one who is contemporaneous with the incarnate one will face the possibility of offense. Only by facing the offense can authentic faith result.

In the eleventh and final chapter, Sylvia Walsh explores the conceptual interplay of jest and earnestness within Kierkegaard's corpus. Through a thorough examination of both Kierkegaard's self-authored and pseudonymous works, Walsh argues that there is an inverse dialectic between jest and earnestness throughout Kierkegaardian thought, and that this dialectic is deeply intertwined with how Kierkegaard conceives the relationship between freedom and grace, human and divine agency.

Part I
Incarnational Theology and Ethics

1.

KIERKEGAARD AND THE TRINITARIAN GRAMMAR OF CHRISTIAN THEOLOGY

Murray Rae

Thomas F. Torrance was a trinitarian theologian. He was utterly committed to speaking of God only as the communion of persons, Father, Son and Spirit, because this is who God has revealed himself to be in Jesus Christ. To speak otherwise of God is to place at risk the church's confession that the God who is the Creator of all things has made himself known, has acted in Christ and through the Spirit to reconcile the world to himself, and calls us to live in faithful covenant relationship with him. "The doctrine of the Trinity," Torrance writes, "gives expression to the fact that through his self-revelation in the incarnation God has opened himself to us in such a way that we may know him in the inner relations of his divine Being and have communion with him in his divine Life as Father, Son and Holy Spirit."[1] To think Christianly, Torrance insists, is to think within the framework of thought articulated and safeguarded through the doctrine of the Trinity: "the doctrine of the Holy Trinity constitutes the fundamental grammar of Christian theology, for it is upon our knowledge of the Father, the Son and the Holy Spirit, One God, Three Persons, that all Christian faith and worship depend, and from it that they take their essential orientation and significance."[2]

Getting clear about what Christian faith consists in, both conceptually and existentially, was the principal concern of the nineteenth century thinker Søren Kierkegaard. The fundamental idea of his whole authorship, Kierkegaard declares is "what it means to

---

[1] Thomas F. Torrance, *Trinitarian Perspectives: Toward Doctrinal Agreement* (Edinburgh: T & T Clark, 1994), 1.

[2] Torrance, *Trinitarian Perspectives*, 4.

become a Christian."³ This involves conceptual clarity, to be sure, but for Kierkegaard, our knowledge of the truth is inseparably bound up with the form of life we live, with our mode of existence. The two cannot be separated. Without that lifelong "becoming"—that lifelong effort at obedience, and the repeated experience of grace and forgiveness when we fall short—one cannot "know" what Christianity consists in. Christian understanding, that is, cannot be reduced to the parroting of doctrinal formulae. Christianity must be lived in order to be understood.

Although Torrance discusses Kierkegaard at length only in one relatively short article,⁴ he refers to him frequently throughout his theological writings and always with appreciation. Torrance regards Kierkegaard as a great thinker of the Christian tradition who understood "more profoundly than all his predecessors and contemporaries" the threat to Christian faith posed by certain errant movements in the theology of Kierkegaard's day.⁵

Torrance appreciates especially Kierkegaard's recognition of the dangers inherent in the supposition that knowledge of God is to be founded on some capacity or other of our own, rather than upon the gracious self-disclosure of God in Jesus Christ. Writing of Kierkegaard's influence on Karl Barth, Torrance observes that it is "the Truth of God incarnate, encountering us objectively, which therefore calls in question the illusion that truth arises from within us, from the depths of our own memories."⁶ Kierkegaard was concerned, Torrance

---

³ Søren Kierkegaard, "The Point of View for my Work as an Author," published in *The Point of View*, ed. and trans. Howard V. and Edna H. Hong (Princeton: Princeton University Press, 1998), 92.

⁴ See "Kierkegaard on the Knowledge of God" in *The Presbyter* 1.3 (1943), 4-7.

⁵ Thomas F. Torrance, *Theology in Reconstruction* (London: SCM Press, 1965) 72. As a further indication of Torrance's high regard for Kierkegaard, note his repeated and approving quotation of Barth's attribution of his own theology to "an ancestral line which runs back through *Kierkegaard* to *Luther* and *Calvin* and so to *Paul* and *Jeremiah.*" See Thomas F. Torrance, *Karl Barth: An Introduction to His Early Theology*, 1910-1931 (London: SCM Press, 1962), 46; cf. 47, 53. Italics original.

⁶ Torrance, *Karl Barth*, 45.

further explains, "to find a mode of knowing appropriate to the fundamental nature of the Truth. The Truth with which we have to do in theology is the Being of God in space and time, the movement of the Eternal in our temporal existence, the Life of God in human history, in the concrete particularity of Jesus Christ."[7] Kierkegaard sought to recover an account of what it is to know the Truth in accordance with God's giving of himself to be known in the person of Jesus Christ. He sought an account that conforms to the "fundamental grammar" of Christian theology. Torrance clearly approves of Kierkegaard's efforts, and yet, Kierkegaard pursues his project with almost no reference to the doctrine of the Trinity. What sense can there be then in regarding Kierkegaard, as I propose we ought, as a trinitarian theologian? Is it legitimate to ascribe to Kierkegaard a trinitarian frame of thought when he has almost no use for classical trinitarian terminology and makes no attempt to develop a doctrine of the Trinity?[8]

The Primacy of Faith

The paucity in Kierkegaard's work of classical trinitarian formulations does not itself justify the conclusion that Kierkegaard is no trinitarian theologian. After all, as Torrance observes, "the Holy Scriptures do not

---

[7] Torrance, *Theology in Reconstruction*, 73. Torrance does not approve in this context of Kierkegaard's description of this mode of knowing as a "leap of faith," but this is for Torrance no more than a minor quibble. Elsewhere, Torrance invokes Kierkegaard's concept of the leap of faith without critical comment. See Thomas F. Torrance, *Incarnation: The Person and Life of Christ*, ed. Robert T. Walker (Downers Grove, IL.: IVP, 2008), 26.

[8] On the paucity of trinitarian terminology in Kierkegaard's writings, see David R. Law, *Kierkegaard As Negative Theologian* (Oxford: Clarendon Press, 1993), 182, n.1. But note also the contention of several commentators that the paucity of explicit attention to the Trinity belies Kierkegaard's trinitarian understanding of God. Sylvia Walsh, for instance, notes that "while [Kierkegaard] affirms the doctrine of the Trinity, it is not an organizing principle of his theology." See Walsh, *Kierkegaard: Thinking Christianly in an Existential Mode* (Oxford: Oxford University Press, 2009), 53. Per Lønning agrees that "The dogma of the trinity does not play a dominating role [in Kierkegaard's thought], but it can be accentuated clearly enough." Per Lønning, "Kierkegaard as a Christian Thinker," in *Kierkegaard's View of Christianity*, eds. Niels Thulstrup and Marie Mikulová Thulstrup (Copenhagen: C.A. Reitzels Boghandel, 1978), 163-81 [166].

give us dogmatic propositions about the Trinity, but they do present us with definite witness to the oneness and differentiation between the Father, the Son and the Holy Spirit, under the constraint of which the early Church allowed the pattern and order of God's triune Life to impose themselves upon its mind."[9] If this be true, then the lack of dogmatic trinitarian propositions in the writings of Søren Kierkegaard need not preclude the possibility that the "pattern and order of God's triune life" as testified to in Scripture has also imposed itself upon *his* mind so as to become the foundation of his theological work. That possibility will occupy our attention in the investigation that follows. Following Torrance's own prescription as cited above—"The doctrine of the Trinity gives expression to the fact that through his self-revelation in the incarnation God has opened himself to us in such a way that *we may know him* in the inner relations of his divine Being *and have communion with him* in his divine Life as Father, Son and Holy Spirit"[10]—I will proceed by investigating the extent to which Kierkegaard's account of our knowledge of and communion with God depends crucially upon a trinitarian theological framework.[11]

Before proceeding, let me reiterate the point already hinted at above: Kierkegaard has no interest in doctrinal formulations for their own sake. Kierkegaard's pseudonym, Johannes Climacus explains that the formulation and the understanding of doctrine is not the same thing as understanding what it means to be a Christian. Christianity is not a philosophical theory; it is a form of existence. It can be understood only insofar as it is lived. "Christianity itself," Climacus explains, "must indeed regard as false Christians those who merely know what

---

[9] Thomas F. Torrance, *The Christian Doctrine of God: One Being Three Persons* (Edinburgh: T & T Clark, 1996), ix.

[10] Torrance, *Trinitarian Perspectives*, 1 (my emphasis).

[11] There is insufficient scope within an article of this nature to undertake a comprehensive study of Kierkegaard's treatment of these themes through the whole of his extensive corpus. My strategy, therefore, will be to present selections from his work that demonstrate, I suggest, the trinitarian logic that undergirds the whole.

Christianity is."[12] Climacus refers here to those who treat Christianity as if it were merely a system of knowledge to be understood, and who know nothing of what it means actually to follow Christ, to venture out in faith. Arnold Come puts the matter well: according to Kierkegaard, "revelation occurs as an event in which I am involved in my total being in an activity in the life of Jesus as the Christ."[13] This does not mean, for Kierkegaard, that theological deliberation is of no use. In *The Concept of Anxiety*, for example, Kierkegaard, again through a pseudonym, speaks positively of "Dogmatics" but only when it begins "where it properly should begin,"[14] namely in the actuality of faith. Kierkegaard takes an Anselmian view of the task of theology. It is faith seeking understanding where faith is the lived life of Christian discipleship. He has no time, therefore, for the speculative approach of his own age (notably, that of Hegel) that prefers to skip over faith in favour of philosophical deliberation. "While it may be alright for a learned theologian to spend his whole life learnedly investigating the doctrine of Scripture and the Church, it would indeed be a ludicrous contradiction if an existing person asked what Christianity is in terms of existence and then spent his whole life deliberating on that—for in that case when should he exist in it."[15] This concern with actual existence helps to explain why, if Kierkegaard is trinitarian in his thinking, we find very little discussion of the doctrine of the Trinity as such. The problem that concerned Kierkegaard in his own day, was not doctrinal error; he did not seek a revised formulation of Christian doctrine. The problem, rather, was the confusion of Christian discipleship with loyalty to the values and social conventions of respectable Danish society, a society whose Christian character was (mistakenly) taken for granted. Christian faith, so it was supposed at the tail end of Christendom, involved nothing other than going along with

---

[12] See Søren Kierkegaard, *Concluding Unscientific Postscript to Philosophical Fragments*, ed. and trans. Howard V. and Edna H. Hong (Princeton: Princeton University Press, 1992), 371.

[13] Arnold Come, *Kierkegaard as Theologian: Recovering My Self* (Montreal: McGill-Queen's University Press, 1997), 16.

[14] Søren Kierkegaard, *The Concept of Anxiety*, ed. and trans. Reidar Thomte (Princeton: Princeton University Press, 1980), 10.

[15] Kierkegaard, *Concluding Unscientific Postscript*, 370.

the crowd. The unmasking of that error was the task to which Kierkegaard's life's work was devoted. He sought to get clear about what it means to follow Christ. The doctrine of the Trinity is of interest, accordingly, only insofar as its formulation arises out of and informs the life of faith. Sylvia Walsh correctly observes that, "For Kierkegaard, the individual's God-relationship is the lens through which the Trinity is encountered and known in human existence."[16]

Our Knowledge of God

That God exists and can be known was not a point of dispute in Kierkegaard's corpus. He felt under no obligation to defend belief in or argue for the existence of God, but was concerned instead with the question, *how* is God to be known?[17] Kierkegaard did not share the confidence of many of his contemporaries that human reason provided comprehensive and ultimately infallible access to all truth, including that Truth which concerns us ultimately, and which Christian faith confesses to be revealed in and through Christ. Nor was he enamoured with the Romantic counter-proposal that aesthetic sensibility was the basis upon which the edifice of theological understanding could be built, or with the presumption, gathering momentum during Kierkegaard's life, that historical-critical enquiry would clarify at last what it really means to say that God is revealed in Christ. Dissatisfaction with these proposals set Kierkegaard in opposition to the three most influential theologians of his era, G. W. F. Hegel, F. D. E. Schleiermacher, and, a generation later, D. F. Strauss. The fault in each of their systems of thought, Kierkegaard contended, lay in the assumption that knowledge of God rests crucially upon some capacity or other of our own—reason in the case of Hegel, aesthetic sensibility

---

[16] Sylvia Walsh, *Kierkegaard: Thinking Christianly in Existential Mode* (Oxford: Oxford University Press, 2009) 53.

[17] It is essential to note here that Kierkegaard is wary of the suggestion that we may have "knowledge" of God. His reticence, however, is due to the equation of "knowledge" with assent to true propositions about God. Kierkegaard does not deny that the relation of faith, by which the believer lives contemporaneously with Christ, has cognitive content.

in the case of Schleiermacher, and the newly developed historical criticism, in the case of Strauss.

Kierkegaard's opposition to the presumption that knowledge of God depends crucially on any of these human capacities rests on three considerations. The first is an astute awareness of the epistemic consequences of human finitude and sin. Our knowledge is, at best, partial and provisional; it is often compromised by partisan interests and its scope is constrained in some respects by our particular cultural location. The presumption that human reason is capable of establishing infallible access to the truth and that nothing lies beyond its gaze fails to take proper account of the limitations of the existing human being who does not view the world *sub specie aeterni*, as God does. The pretension to omniscience, which Kierkegaard detected in Hegel, merely reveals that Hegel had "forgotten what it means to exist" as a finite human being.[18]

The second consideration that leads Kierkegaard to reject the idea that knowledge of God rests crucially on our own epistemic capacities is "the infinite qualitative difference" between God and everything that is not God. God is of a different order of being than the creation, yet the theological proposals of Hegel, of Schleiermacher, and of Strauss variously annul that distinction. The Hegelian system does so by making creation, and especially human beings, a part of the history of God's self-realisation. The infinite qualitative difference between God and creation—the *antithesis*, in Hegel's terms—is revealed in Christ to be merely dialectical and is ultimately transcended (*aufgehoben*) through a *synthesis* of the divine and the human. For Hegel, the unity in Christ of the divine and the human is no unique synthesis pertaining only to Christ, as has been confessed by the Church's creedal tradition, but reveals what is true of us all. We all share in the divine life in virtue of our capacity for rational thought. Schleiermacher, for his part, collapses the distinction between God and creation by construing the divinity of Christ as a function of his humanity: "The Redeemer is like all men," Schleiermacher writes, "in virtue of the identity of human nature, but distinguished from them all

---

[18] See Kierkegaard, *Concluding Unscientific Postscript*, 249.

by the constant potency of his God consciousness, which was a veritable existence of God in him."[19] Divinity turns out to be, in Schleiermacher's Christology, nothing other than the fullest possible realization of a human capacity. Finally, Strauss removes the distinction between God and creation by proposing that theology must be undertaken within the bounds of immanent causality. Human society as a whole takes the place of Christ as the embodiment of divinity, while all talk of the supernatural is consigned to the realm of myth.

The third and most basic reason for Kierkegaard's opposition to the presumption of theological knowledge founded upon human capacity is the offense of Christ. The reality of God's appearance among us in the lowly figure of Jesus of Nazareth who becomes a servant, spends time with the outcast and the despised, and eventually, at Calvary, becomes despised and outcast himself, confounds our human estimations of who God *must* be, and of how God should behave. Jesus of Nazareth, the God-Man, is in person, so the New Testament proclaims, the primary and definitive locus of divine revelation.[20] Kierkegaard remains faithful throughout his authorship to an observation he made as a student: "Christian dogmatics, it seems to me, must grow out of Christ's activity, and all the more so because Christ did not establish any doctrine; he acted. He *did not teach* that there was redemption for men, but *he redeemed men.*"[21]

The Offense of Christ

And yet, Kierkegaard repeatedly observes, the very one who is our redeemer is also the cause of offense. He who comes as Savior among us; he who promises rest to all who are weary and heavy laden, appears among us as the most unlikely of Saviors. Our natural inclination, well

---

[19] F. D. E. Schleiermacher. *The Christian Faith* (Edinburgh: T & T Clark, 1928), 385.

[20] See, for instance, the first chapters of John's Gospel and of the Epistle to the Hebrews, although the theological claim is implicit throughout the New Testament.

[21] Kierkegaard, *Journals*, ed. and trans. Howard V. Hong and Edna H. Hong (Bloomington: Indiana University Press, 1967-78), 7 vols., I/412, I A 27, November 5, 1834.

supported by rational deliberation, is to look elsewhere for the presence of God. Kierkegaard notices, however, that our well-reasoned estimations of how God should behave typically contradict the New Testament declaration that "God was in Christ reconciling the world to himself" (2 Corinthians 5:19). The epistemic resources of flesh and blood—reason, imagination, historical enquiry—are found wanting; they are not the means by which God is recognised (cf. Matthew 16:17).[22] We need God's help, rather, to recognise the God who comes among us in servant form.

An "Invocation" offered by the pseudonym Anti-Climacus[23] at the beginning of Kierkegaard's book, *Practice in Christianity*, addresses Jesus thus:

> Would that we might see you as you are and were and will be until your second coming in glory, as the sign of offense and the object of faith, the lowly man, yet the Savior and Redeemer of the human race, who out of love came to earth to seek the lost, to suffer and die, and yet, alas, every step you took on earth, every time you called to the straying, every time you reached out your hand to do signs and wonders, and every time you defenselessly suffered the opposition of people without raising a hand—again and again in concern you had to repeat, "Blessed is the one who is not offended at me." Would that we might see you in this way and that we then might not be offended at you![24]

To see Jesus as he is, the lowly man who is also the Savior and Redeemer of the human race, is a matter of *prayerful* attentiveness. Attentiveness alone will not do it. We must seek God's help. That is the

---

[22] Kierkegaard refers to this passage in *Practice in Christianity*, ed. and trans. Howard V. and Edna H. Hong (Princeton: Princeton University Press, 1991), 128.

[23] Anti-Climacus is said by Kierkegaard to be "a Christian on an extraordinarily high level." *Journals*, VI/6433, X¹ A 517) *n.d.*, 1849. Kierkegaard thus presents Anti-Climacus as one who, on the basis of his extraordinary existential expression of Christianity, understands well what it is to be a Christian. Kierkegaard does not wish to present himself in that position.

[24] Kierkegaard, *Practice in Christianity*, 9-10.

advice implicit in the invocation with which Kierkegaard begins *Practice in Christianity*.

The pseudonymous author, Anti-Climacus, proceeds in *Practice in Christianity* to critique the presumption that the truth about Jesus, the "god-man," can be uncovered through historical enquiry. "Can it be demonstrated from history that Christ was God?," Anti-Climacus asks.[25] The question is directed toward the "Quest of the historical Jesus" as it would later be named, a Quest that in the 1840s was gathering considerable momentum. We need not investigate here the details of Kierkegaard's critique of the Quest; it is sufficient for our purposes to note Anti-Climacus' insistence that, "one cannot *know* anything at all about *Christ*; he is the paradox, the object of faith, exists only for faith." The kind of knowledge Anti-Climacus has in mind here is the ideal promoted in "the age of reason": knowledge is attained through dispassionate and objective enquiry; it keeps its object at arms length and takes the form of objectively true and demonstrable propositions. The reality of Christ, however, is not accessible by these means and cannot be constrained in this way. The God who is present with us through abasement, who suffers, and is crucified, eludes the grasp of rational and historical-critical deliberation. The only way to recognise God in the lowly figure of the suffering servant, the only way to see his glory, is through what Kierkegaard calls, the autopsy of faith.[26] Faith, Kierkegaard insists, is not a human capacity; nor is it a condition that we can generate for ourselves.

Another of Kierkegaard's pseudonyms, Johannes Climacus, insists that the condition of faith is pure gift, given by God himself: "the god gave the follower the condition, the condition to see [that the servant is God] and opened for him the eyes of faith."[27] Although Johannes Climacus presents this claim under the guise of a "thought experiment," it is clear that the position he elucidates is that of the New Testament. It is "my Father in heaven" Jesus explains, who reveals to

---

[25] Kierkegaard, *Practice in Christianity*, 26.

[26] Søren Kierkegaard, *Philosophical Fragments*, ed. and trans. Howard V. and Edna H. Hong (Princeton: Princeton University Press, 1985), 70.

[27] Kierkegaard, *Philosophical Fragments*, 65. The Danish word translated here as "follower" is *Discipel*.

Peter that Jesus is "the Messiah, the Son of the living God" (Matthew 16:16-17). Similarly in John's gospel, Jesus advises the disciples that when he departs he will send the paraclete (John 16:7) who will "take what is mine and declare it to you" (John 16:14). Jesus explains further that, "All that the Father has is mine" (John 16:15). There is a clear trinitarian structure to the disciples' apprehension of who Jesus is. All three persons of the Trinity are involved. This logic undergirds Kierkegaard's contention, expressed pseudonymously in the texts considered so far, that God is involved in our knowing of him.

Although Anti-Climacus insists, as noted above, that "one cannot *know* anything at all about *Christ*," faith does involve cognitive content; it is not of the kind, however, that lies within the constraints of Modernity's preferred epistemology. The kind of knowledge of Christ that Kierkegaard thinks *is* possible is unlike the kind of knowledge we may claim to have of propositional truths and much more like the kind of knowledge we may have of other persons. Amongst Kierkegaard's papers we find the following note, penned apparently in an early draft of *Philosophical Fragments*: "[I]f the situation…is such that the teacher gives the condition, then one of course cannot know without being known by him, and one knows him only in so far as one is known."[28]

That our knowledge of God is utterly dependent upon God is emphasised again in the Discourse published under Kierkegaard's own name, "To Need God is a Human Being's Highest Perfection." Kierkegaard explains that it is precisely in virtue of a person experiencing the need of God that one truly "comes to *know God.*"[29] Without God, the person is "capable of nothing at all."[30] Our need of God is multi-faceted but includes especially our need of God's assistance to recognise him in the person of Jesus Christ.

---

[28] The passage is cited in the editors' supplementary notes to *Philosophical Fragments,* 198.

[29] Søren Kierkegaard, *Eighteen Upbuilding Discourses*, ed. and trans. Howard V. and Edna H. Hong (Princeton: Princeton University Press, 1990), 321. Emphasis original.

[30] This phrase is repeated throughout the aforementioned *Discourse.*

The Divine Incognito

The servant form of God's presence with us in Christ exercises Kierkegaard a good deal. He stresses repeatedly that God appears incognito.

> And now the God-man! He is God but chooses to become this individual human being. This, as said before, is the most profound incognito or the most impenetrable unrecognizability that is possible, because the contradiction between being God and being an individual human being is the greatest possible, the infinitely qualitative contradiction. But it is his will, his free decision, and therefore it is an omnipotently maintained incognito.[31]

The appearance of Christ incognito is motivated, Kierkegaard says, by love. It is out of love for humanity that Christ appears as one of us. It is out of love that he suffers. It is out of love that he comes as a servant—as one who serves our need of forgiveness and reconciliation. This theme is developed in a number of places in Kierkegaard's corpus, notably in the parable of the king and the maiden in *Philosophical Fragments*.[32] Johannes Climacus ponders the situation of a king who loves a lowly maiden, but who is troubled by the vast inequality between them. The inequality is bound to frustrate the king's desire for a relation of mutual love. If the king were to appear to the maiden in all his splendour, she might forget herself in adoring admiration but this would not overcome the deep inequality between them, nor achieve the mutuality the king desires. Conversely, if he were to house the maiden in his palace and clothe her in royal finery, this would enable him to enjoy her company but only at the cost of a deception. The inequality cannot be overcome by a mere change of costume. "Who grasps the contradiction of this sorrow," Climacus asks: "not to disclose itself is the death of love; to disclose itself is the death of the beloved."[33] Conceiving the situation as analogous to God's love for humanity, Climacus then goes on to propose that the problem is overcome by a

---

[31] See especially, *Practice in Christianity*, 127-33.

[32] See Kierkegaard, *Philosophical Fragments*, 26-34.

[33] Kierkegaard, *Philosophical Fragments*, 30.

descent. "[The god] will appear, therefore, as the equal of the lowliest of persons. But the lowliest of all is one who must serve others—consequently, the god will appear in the form of a *servant*." Eager to avoid any suggestion of Docetism, however, Climacus continues: "But this form of a servant is not something put on like the king's plebian cloak, which, just by flapping open would betray the king…but it is his true form."[34] The extent of the god's adoption of the servant form is stressed by Johannes Climacus. He remarks a second time: "But the form of the servant was not something put on."[35]

> Therefore the god must suffer all things, endure all things, be tried in all things, hunger in the desert, thirst in his agonies, be forsaken in death, absolutely the equal of the lowliest of human beings—look, behold the man! The suffering of death is not his suffering, but his whole life is a story of suffering, and it is love that suffers, love that gives all and is itself destitute.[36]

A Trinitarian Theology

Kierkegaard's deliberations upon the reality of "the god" coming among us in servant form reveal his commitment to the creedal Christology of the Christian tradition. It is truly God who becomes incarnate among us in Jesus, and the form adopted—that of the servant—is no pretence, but a genuine adoption of our humanity. These rudiments of orthodox Christology give rise to and are essential elements of the doctrine of the Trinity. The recognition that in Jesus of Nazareth we have to do with God himself is the fundamental impetus toward the development of the doctrine of the Trinity. That Kierkegaard in *Philosophical Fragments*, and again in *Practice in Christianity*, supports these orthodox Christological claims, albeit pseudonymously,

---

[34] Kierkegaard, *Philosophical Fragments*, 31-2.

[35] Kierkegaard, *Philosophical Fragments*, 32.

[36] Kierkegaard, *Philosophical Fragments*, 32-3.

lends weight to the contention that Kierkegaard's theology presumes and is informed by a trinitarian understanding of God.[37]

What of the work of the Spirit in this account of God's self-disclosure? Does the Spirit have a part to play? We do not get much hint of this in *Philosophical Fragments* for Kierkegaard's point in that work is to establish the decisiveness of Christ in our learning of the Truth. The importance of the Spirit does become apparent elsewhere, however. At the beginning of *Works of Love*, for instance, Kierkegaard offers a prayer successively addressed to the Father, "God of Love, source of all love," to the Son, "our Savior and Redeemer" who "revealed what love is," and to the Spirit: "How could one speak properly of love if you were forgotten, you Spirit of love, who take nothing of your own but remind us of that love sacrifice."[38] The trinitarian form of God's self-disclosure is more readily apparent here: God in three persons is the source of love, the revealer of love, and the one who enables recognition of that love. The allusions in the prayer to Jesus' teaching on the role of the paraclete in John 14:26,[39] and in John 16:13,[40] confirm the Spirit's key role in enabling one's apprehension of the truth of Christ.

---

[37] John D. Glenn Jr. contends that "Trinitarian Christianity is not denied in the *Fragments*, but it is not essential to Climacus' approach to the Incarnation and the Atonement." John D. Glenn Jr., "Kierkegaard and Anselm," in Robert L. Perkins, ed., *International Kierkegaard Commentary:* Philosophical Fragments *and* Johannes Climacus (Macon GA., Mercer University Press, 1994) 223-43, 239. I suggest however, that, while the doctrine of the Trinity is certainly not explicit in the Fragments, the unmistakeable invocation of a dual nature Christology cannot be sustained outside a trinitarian frame of reference.

[38] Søren Kierkegaard, *Works of Love*, ed. and trans. Howard V. and Edna H. Hong (Princeton: Princeton University Press, 1995), 3. The prayer to the Spirit "who takes nothing on his own" alludes to John 16:3 which makes explicit the Spirit's role in guiding "you" into all truth.

[39] "But the Advocate, the Holy Spirit, whom the Father will send in my name, will teach you everything, and *remind* you of all that I have said to you." My emphasis.

[40] "When the Spirit of truth comes, he will guide you into all the truth; for *he will not speak on his own*, but will speak whatever he hears , and he will declare to you the things that are to come." My emphasis.

Elsewhere Kierkegaard appeals directly to the testimony of the Spirit:

> There is only one proof for the truth of Xtnty: the inner proof, *argumentum spiritus sancti*. This is already hinted at in 1 John 5:9. If we accept hum. [*sic*; read "human"] witnesses (this means all historical proofs and arguments) "the witness of God is greater," i.e., the inner proof is greater. And now, in v.10 "Whoever believes in the Son of God has this witness within."[41]

The witness of the Spirit is straightforwardly regarded here as "the witness of God" and that witness gives rise to belief in the Son of God. It should by now be clear that Kierkegaard's account of God's self-disclosure and of how one may learn the Truth, to use Climacus' terminology, is grounded in a trinitarian theological framework. God makes himself known through his Son, the "god-man," who comes among us as a servant and is recognised as such through the gift and guidance of the Spirit.

Communion with God

As suggested already, the knowledge of God given through revelation is not primarily a matter of propositional or cognitive information. It is rather, as Kyle Roberts explains, "a relational knowledge that effects a personal, spiritual transformation of the self."[42] Kierkegaard himself writes, "in becoming known by a person [God] wants to create in him a new human being."[43] Thus, in Kierkegaard's view, the divine work of making himself known is bound up with the work of making new persons of us. That transformation takes place, as it turns out, precisely through relationship or communion with God. We turn now to consider then, the extent to which God's work of creating "a new human being" is also predicated in Kierkegaard's mind upon a trinitarian

---

[41] *Kierkegaard's Journals and Notebooks*, eds. Niels Jørgen Cappelorn et al. (Princeton: Princeton University Press, 2012), vol. 6, 105.

[42] Kyle Roberts, *Emerging Prophet: Kierkegaard and the Postmodern People of God* (Eugene, OR., Cascade Books, 2013), 20.

[43] Kierkegaard, *Eighteen Upbuilding Discourses*, 325.

understanding of God. How are the Father, the Son and the Spirit respectively involved in the work of bringing about this new reality?

We may build here on what has already been discovered in *Philosophical Fragments*. In that work, Johannes Climacus considers the possibility that the process of learning the Truth necessarily involves a transformation of the individual. Within the terms of the thought experiment set up by Climacus the individual is posited as existing in untruth and as bereft of the condition to learn the Truth. Recall that Kierkegaard is concerned here with the Truth present in Jesus the god-man.

Pursuing further his alternative to the Socratic model, exemplified by Kierkegaard's theological contemporaries, Climacus proposes that, since we are bereft of it, we need to be given the condition for learning the Truth. The "condition" Climacus later discloses, is not reason but *faith*.[44] This involves, furthermore, a transformation of the learner. "Let us call this change *conversion*," Climacus suggests.[45] Indeed, the making of a new person, involves a *rebirth*.[46] But who can bring about such a change? It is not the learner him or herself; otherwise we return to the Socratic. The change must be brought about by one who can give the condition and along with it the Truth.[47]

> Let us call him a *savior*, for he does indeed save the learner from unfreedom, saves him from himself. Let us call him a *deliverer*, for he does indeed deliver the person who had imprisoned himself, and no one is so dreadfully imprisoned, and no captivity is so impossible to break out of as that in which the individual holds himself captive! And yet, even this does not say enough, for by his unfreedom he had indeed become guilty of something, and if that teacher gives him the condition and the truth, then he is, of course a *reconciler* who takes away the wrath that lay

---

[44] Kierkegaard, *Philosophical Fragments*, 59.

[45] Kierkegaard, *Philosophical Fragments*, 18. Italics original.

[46] Kierkegaard, *Philosophical Fragments*, 19.

[47] Kierkegaard, *Philosophical Fragments*, 17.

over the incurred guilt.[48]

Learning the Truth, Climacus explains, requires that we be reconciled by and with the one who is himself the Truth. Kierkegaard does not use the term, but he is speaking here of what Torrance refers to as communion. The life of the Christian is a life of reconciled relationship with God.

Philosophical Fragments provides the rudiments of a trinitarian theology in which reconciliation with God is brought about through the work of Jesus, the god-man, but we must look elsewhere in Kierkegaard's work for more explicit reference to the trinitarian structure of the work of reconciliation. A Journal entry from 1852 offers further insight: Kierkegaard here considers the words of Jesus presented in John 6:45: "No one can come to me unless the Father who sent me draws him." "As a rule," Kierkegaard says, "the relationship is presented thus: it is Christ who leads us to God; man needs a mediator in order to come to God. But this is not the way it is presented in the New Testament."[49] It begins with the Father, to whom, as children, we might imagine ourselves to exist in direct relationship. But with maturity, Kierkegaard explains, comes the realization of our infinite distance from God and thus also of our need for a mediator. "Then it is that God directs one to the Son, to the Mediator."[50] The Mediator makes atonement, to be sure, but Kierkegaard is equally keen to point out that, "The Mediator is also the prototype."[51] Christ makes atonement for us. "Yet, the 'Atoner' must not supplant the 'prototype'; the prototype remains with his demand that there be a striving to be like

---

[48] Kierkegaard, *Philosophical Fragments,* 17. Italics original.

[49] Kierkegaard, *Journals,* II/1432, X^5 A23 *n.d.*, 1852. The deliberations of this Journal entry have their genesis in a marginal note found in Kierkegaard's copy of the New Testament. Alongside John 6:45, he writes: "It is thus not the Son who attracts (people) to the Father, but the Father who refers (people) to the Son, and the Son refers again to the Spirit." Cited in Bradley Rau Dewey, "Kierkegaard and the Blue Testament," in *Harvard Theological Review* 60 (1967), 391-409; citation at 407-08. Commenting upon the marginalia, Dewey writes, "Perhaps Kierkegaard was trying to work out a version of the Trinity." 408.

[50] Kierkegaard, *Journals,* II/1432, X^5 A23 *n.d.*, 1852.

[51] Kierkegaard, *Journals,* II/1432, X^5 A23 *n.d.*, 1852.

him."[52] It is important to stress here that, for Kierkegaard, there can be no question of salvation by works. Salvation is entirely a matter of grace. But salvation involves a transformation of the individual; it issues in a new form of life which Kierkegaard repeatedly characterizes as "following" Christ in the way of lowliness, servanthood, and suffering. In a prayer, Kierkegaard writes:

> O Redeemer, by your holy suffering and death you have made satisfaction for everyone and everything; no eternal salvation either can or shall be earned—it has been earned. Yet you left your footprints, you, the holy prototype for the human race and for every individual, so that by your Atonement the saved might at every moment find the confidence and boldness to want to strive to follow you.[53]

When confronted with the call to follow Christ, our need of the Spirit's help again becomes clear. Kierkegaard explains: "[T]he prototype directs away from himself (just as the Father directed one to the Mediator), to the 'Spirit', as if he said: You cannot begin this striving naively; that would even be—as you yourself feel—presumptuous... No, you must have a Spirit to help you."[54]

Summarising the cooperation of the three persons in the work of reconciling us to God, Kierkegaard explains that, "it is the Father who directs to the Son, the Son who directs to the Spirit, and not until then is it the Spirit who leads to the Son and the Son who leads to the Father."[55] Kierkegaard makes it clear that the relationship established with the Father—the communion, to use Torrance's term—is mediated through the Son and the Spirit. The initiative of the Father, the mediation of the Son, and the enabling of the Spirit are thus to be regarded as essential elements in Kierkegaard's understanding of what it means to become and to be a Christian.

---

[52] Kierkegaard, *Journals*, II/1432, X^5 A23 *n.d.*, 1852.

[53] Kierkegaard, *Judge for Yourself!*, 147.

[54] Kierkegaard, *Journals*, II/1432, X^5 A23 *n.d.*, 1852.

[55] Kierkegaard, *Journals*, II/1432, X^5 A23 *n.d.*, 1852.

Conclusion

I have attempted to show in this essay that while explicit reference to the Trinity does not appear often in Kierkegaard's work, his account of how we may come to know God, of how we may be reconciled with him, and of how we may live in communion with him, depends crucially upon a trinitarian understanding of God. Kierkegaard's account of the Christian life is thoroughly Christocentric, to the point sometimes of obscuring the work of the Father and the Spirit, but the underlying logic is certainly trinitarian. It is true for Kierkegaard too, as it was for Thomas Torrance, that "the doctrine of the Holy Trinity constitutes the fundamental grammar of Christian theology..."[56]

There is much scope in Kierkegaard's work for further exploration of the contention that his theological deliberations are framed within an orthodox doctrine of the Trinity, but, within the constraints of this essay, one final point may be offered in support of this claim. Kierkegaard's life of prayer, as presented in his writings, frequently reveals a deeply trinitarian sensibility. The successive clauses of a prayer penned in his *Journals*, for instance, are addressed in turn to "Father in heaven," "our Lord Jesus Christ" and "God the Holy Spirit."[57] These invocations are replicated almost exactly in the prayers that precede each of the three discourses in *For Self-Examination*,[58] and they are echoed, as noted above, in the prayer that appears in the opening pages of *Works of Love*. T. F. Torrance certainly recognised that theology proceeds from doxology. He explains in the opening pages of *The Trinitarian Faith* that, "From the start the theology of the Church took the form, not of a set of abstract propositions, but of embodied truth in which the knowing and worshipping of God and the daily obedience of faith and life

---

[56] As cited above: Torrance, *Trinitarian Perspectives*, 4.

[57] Søren Kierkegaard, *Journals and Papers,* ed. and trans. Howard V. and Edna H. Hong, (Bloomington: Indiana University Press, 1967-78), 6 vols., 3/3423, VIII² B 1433 *n.d.,* 1848.

[58] See Søren Kierkegaard, *For Self-Examination. Judge for Yourself!* ed. and trans. Howard V. and Edna H. Hong (Princeton: Princeton University Press, 1990), 13, 56, 73.

interpenetrated one another."[59] Consistent with this theological tradition, the explicitly trinitarian prayers found in Kierkegaard's writings penetrate and shape the content of his searching explorations of how one becomes a Christian and of how the Christian life is to be lived.

---

[59] Torrance, *The Trinitarian Faith* (Edinburgh: T&T Clark, 1988), 6.

2.

KIERKEGAARD'S INCARNATIONAL REALISM:

THE GRAMMAR OF CHRISTIAN KNOWLEDGE

David J. Gouwens

Introduction

Vast differences obviously obtain between Thomas F. Torrance and Søren Kierkegaard as philosophical and theological thinkers. Whereas Kierkegaard focuses upon the concept of subjectivity as key to understanding ethics, religion, and Christian faith, Torrance orients himself to objectivity. Whereas Kierkegaard is often critical of "doctrine," Torrance commits himself to the importance of the dogmatic task. And whereas Kierkegaard critiques comprehensive philosophical or theological "systems," Torrance champions the ideal of "scientific theology" that seeks a comprehensive account of human knowledge, including both theology and the natural sciences.[1]

It would be understandable therefore to see Kierkegaard as a "subjectivist" and Torrance as an "objectivist." Against this simplistic view I want to explore some points of contact between Torrance and Kierkegaard that subvert a simple opposition between "objectivity" and "subjectivity," and in particular, I want to argue that both share a profound theological realism, especially in holding to a strong incarnational realism.

Torrance's "objectivism," first, is by no means positivist. His appropriation of Michael Polanyi's thought on "personal knowledge" in both theology and science affirms a "fiduciary" element in all human knowing: "in both theology and the natural sciences discovery begins with faith (belief), which leads to the truth, truth being a fundamental

---

[1] Myk Habets, *Theology in Transposition: A Constructive Appraisal of T. F. Torrance* (Minneapolis: Fortress Press, 2013), 27–65.

insight into the *real*, as it is independent of the knower."[2] Indeed, as Myk Habets notes, Carl F. H. Henry, who advocated a strongly propositional account of revelation, criticized Torrance for "subjectivism," blaming this on Kierkegaard's and Polanyi's dire influence. But as Habets observes, "Torrance understands Kierkegaard's 'truth as subjectivity' as in fact theological objectivity and realism, the subject's proper relation to the object."[3] For Torrance, this fiduciary "personal knowing" means that "Reality is to be known in faith through an existential encounter with the ultimate Reality—Jesus Christ the incarnate Word (*Logos*)."[4]

But is Torrance right about Kierkegaard? Is Kierkegaard's focus on "subjectivity" compatible with "theological objectivity and realism" rather than "subjectivism"? I want to argue in this paper that Kierkegaard is indeed a "realist," in two ways.

First, Torrance is correct that Kierkegaard is a "realist" in epistemology, and, specifically with regard to the incarnation, that Kierkegaard affirms "Christian knowledge" of a reality outside ourselves. Kierkegaard's theological "realism" is even more remarkable in that it arises from a focus not upon "objectivity" but upon the subjective "how" of faith. Moreover, Kierkegaard's stress on the particularity and reality of the incarnation provides him tools to criticize a range of modern reinterpretations of the incarnation. To support this argument, I will turn to *Philosophical Fragments* and

---

[2] Habets, *Theology in Transposition*, 63.

[3] Habets, *Theology in Transposition*, 101. On objectivity in relation to Kierkegaard, see for example, Thomas F. Torrance, *Theology in Reconstruction* (Eugene, OR: Wipf & Stock, 1996), 235.

[4] Habets, *Theology in Transposition*, 64, 64n145, citing Torrance's definition of the term "personal knowing" from Torrance, ed., *Belief in Science and in Christian Life: The Relevance of Michael Polanyi's Thought for Christian Faith and Life* (Edinburgh: The Handsel Press, 1980), 141–2.

Concluding Unscientific Postscript, authored by Kierkegaard's pseudonym Johannes Climacus.[5]

Second, in his later literature Kierkegaard develops further an incarnational realism, with "realism" now describing Kierkegaard's narrative portrayal of Christ. In some contrast to the Climacus texts, Kierkegaard's *Practice in Christianity*, authored by his Christian pseudonym Anti-Climacus, employs narrative to describe Christ's life as the "The Inviter," the incarnate God whose life and actions present the possibility of offense or faith.[6] The realism of this portrayal resides in its "horizontal" depiction of Christ's life, beyond the "vertical" affirmation of the eternal breaking into time that Johannes Climacus in *Philosophical Fragments* called "more than enough."[7]

In the conclusion, I will note some of the similarities and the differences in how Kierkegaard and Torrance understand the "grammar" of this incarnational realism.

Incarnation, Transcendence, Revelation, and Realism in *Philosophical Fragments* and *Concluding Unscientific Postscript*

In *Philosophical Fragments*, Kierkegaard's pseudonym Johannes Climacus conducts a thought-project: let us ask whether one's eternal happiness depends upon a moment in time. Climacus in chapter I contrasts Socrates to a nameless Teacher B. Whereas Socrates is merely a midwife who prompts his hearers to discover eternal happiness as the truth they have in themselves, the learner's relation to Teacher B proceeds on other assumptions: the learner is in untruth, and through

---

[5] Søren Kierkegaard, *Philosophical Fragments* and *Johannes Climacus*, ed. and trans. Howard V. Hong and Edna H. Hong with Introduction and Notes (Princeton: Princeton University Press, 1985); Søren Kierkegaard, *Concluding Unscientific Postscript*, ed. and trans. Howard V. Hong and Edna H. Hong with Introduction and Notes (Princeton: Princeton University Press, 1992).

[6] Søren Kierkegaard, *Practice in Christianity*, ed. and trans. Howard V. Hong and Edna H. Hong with Introduction and Notes (Princeton: Princeton University Press, 1991).

[7] Kierkegaard, *PF*, 104.

his own fault (let us call this *sin*); the learner is unfree and bound, so the teacher must give him the condition for becoming free and along with it the truth (let us call this teacher a *savior, deliverer, reconciler, judge*); therefore the moment is decisive (let us call it *the fullness of time*). The learner must become a person of a different quality (let us call him a *new* person, who experiences *conversion, repentance, rebirth*).[8]

As Robert C. Roberts notes, in *Philosophical Fragments*, Johannes Climacus, in remarkably brief compass, deftly outlines the heart of the Christian gospel, the "grammar of Christian redemption," with its interrelated concepts of sin, salvation, God and Savior, faith, and revelation. Indeed, central to Climacus' thought-experiment is the concept of a revelation of the God in time, beyond human conception or hope, a revelation that confounds human expectation and confronts any human being with the possibility of offense or of faith.[9]

Climacus' thought-experiment in *Philosophical Fragments* is a tour de force in addressing a host of theological issues arising in modernity: faith and reason, the logical status of religious belief, the nature of truth, the relation of faith and history, and the meaning of a transcendent revelation. Climacus' critique suggests that a range of purportedly Christian modern interpretations of the incarnation are essentially Socratic. As Roberts and Murray Rae both rightly discern, Climacus' portrayal of the incarnation undermines a range of speculative Christologies, including Hegel's translation of the incarnation into a metaphysical principle of essential divine-human unity and Feuerbach's left-wing Hegelian mythological interpretation of the incarnation as "all theology is anthropology."[10] Even Schleiermacher, who holds Christ as sole mediator, unsuccessfully attempts to combine two incompatible conceptions: the grammar of

---

[8] Kierkegaard, *PF*, 9–22.

[9] On "the grammar of Christian redemption," see Robert C. Roberts, *Faith, Reason and History: Rethinking Kierkegaard's "Philosophical Fragments"* (Macon, GA: Mercer University Press, 1986), 26ff. Roberts acknowledges his indebtedness for this concept to Ludwig Wittgenstein and Paul L. Holmer.

[10] Kierkegaard, *CUP*, 579.

Christian redemption and the grammar of the Socratic teacher.[11] The critique can extend also to more recent Christologies, for example, Rudolf Bultmann's demythologized Christology or John Cobb's process Christology.[12] What emerges in *Philosophical Fragments* is an account of the incarnation much closer to traditional Christian theological beliefs, and also with considerable critical weight.[13]

But even if Climacus' thought-project on the incarnation is identifiably traditional, offering ways to criticize various speculative or anthropocentric Christologies, does not his theme that "truth is subjectivity" undermine this claim that the incarnation is a transcendent revelation, at least in any "realist" sense, thus resulting in a noncognitive fideism? Many students of Kierkegaard do object to describing him as a realist.[14] Some will argue, with some strands of postmodernism, that for Kierkegaard the multivocity of language precludes any stable referentiality of language to "reality," with language an endless play of signifiers.[15] For others, such as Richard Rorty, "realism" entails a commitment to classical foundationalism, and hence an untenable claim to direct access with reality.[16] Others, more modestly, see Kierkegaard as advocating, over against Hegel, a Kantian skepticism about our knowledge of the noumenal, suggesting that for Kierkegaard believers should at best hold to belief in God as a

---

[11] Murray Rae, *Kierkegaard's Vision of the Incarnation: By Faith Transformed* (Oxford: Clarendon Press, 1997), 41–6 (hereafter *KVI*); Roberts, *Faith, Reason and History*, 30–3.

[12] Rae, *KVI*, 61n29; Roberts, *Faith, Reason and History*, 34–41.

[13] C. Stephen Evans, *Kierkegaard on Faith and the Self: Collected Essays* (Waco, TX: Baylor University Press, 2006), 138 and 344n7 (hereafter *KFS*).

[14] Evans cites in particular Roger Poole, *Kierkegaard: The Indirect Communication* (Charlottesville: University of Virginia Press, 1993), also mentioning Louis Mackey, Sylviane Agacinski, John Vignaux Smythe, and John D. Caputo. See Evans, *KFS*, 29, 336n2. From a particular Wittgensteinian perspective, one might add D. Z. Phillips.

[15] For an analysis of various advocates of this view, see Lee Barrett, "Doctrines and Undecidability: Kierkegaard on the Indeterminacy of Christian Teachings," *Toronto Journal of Theology* 26/1 (2010): 59–74. In addition to Mackey and Poole, Barrett discusses Steven Shakespeare, Michael Strawser, Mark C. Taylor, Benjamin Daise, and Pat Bigelow.

[16] Evans, *KFS*, 43.

regulative concept, bracketing any metaphysical or ontological claims about God's existence.[17]

Yet a number of scholars support the counterargument that Kierkegaard is a realist, even, according to C. Stephen Evans, that Kierkegaard is "uncompromisingly on the side of realism."[18] Exploring the "realism and antirealism" debate extensively, Evans argues that Kierkegaard clearly is not a "realist" if that means adopting "the Cartesian project of providing absolute foundations for knowledge," claiming "a kind of unmediated access to Reality," "possessing a truth that is final and certain."[19] Kierkegaard agrees with critics of this Cartesian project. So too, Kierkegaard is skeptical of proofs for God's existence, of claims to unmediated experience of God,[20] and of "evidentialist" efforts to ground belief in God in objective evidence.[21] But the options are not either to "claim unmediated access to Reality that gives us final truth" or else "that there is no such thing as objective truth about the real."[22] Kierkegaard's realism is more modest, holding "that there is such an objective final truth, but also…that for finite human beings, such a truth can only be an ideal to be approximated and striven for."[23]

The reality of God and the ideality of objective final truth are summed up well when Climacus writes in *Postscript*: "existence itself is a system—for God."[24] So too, Climacus' "truth is subjectivity" "does not dismiss the idea of objective truth" but "claims that for us existing human beings, such truth can only be an *approximation* (*CUP*, 189)."[25]

---

[17] George Pattison, "'Before God' as a Regulative Concept," in *Kierkegaard Studies Yearbook 1997*, ed. Niels Jørgen Cappelørn and Hermann Deuser (Berlin: Walter de Gruyter, 1997), 70–84.

[18] Evans, *KFS*, 9. See especially chapters 2, 3, 7, 8, 10, and 11.

[19] Evans, *KFS*, 55–6.

[20] Kierkegaard, *CUP*, 243–5, 600; Evans, *KFS*, 60.

[21] Evans, *KFS*, 63.

[22] Evans, *KFS*, 56.

[23] Evans, *KFS*, 56.

[24] Kierkegaard, *CUP*, 118; Evans, *KFS*, 57.

[25] Evans, *KFS*, 57.

Hence, Evans claims, Kierkegaard's famous thesis that "truth is subjectivity does not undermine this commitment to realism."[26] First, "truth is subjectivity" is limited to moral and religious truth; in the natural sciences and mathematics, for example, truth is clearly objectivity. Second, and more importantly, the thesis "truth is subjectivity" in *Postscript* "is not on the nature of objective propositional truth but on the question as to what makes a person's life true" and indeed presupposes that there is objective truth, even in moral and religious realms of discourse.[27] In a famous passage in *Postscript*, Climacus writes of the contrast between the Christian who "with knowledge of the true idea of God" "prays in untruth" while "someone who lives in an idolatrous land…prays with all the passion of infinity, although his eyes are resting upon the image of an idol"[28]: "[W]here, then," Climacus asks, "is there more truth? The one prays in truth to God although he is worshipping an idol; the other prays in untruth to the true God and is therefore in truth worshiping an idol."[29] Climacus here does not deny "the true God"; the question is how one relates truly ("prays in truth") whether to "the true God" or "the image of an idol."[30] Kierkegaard stresses how finite beings must always *strive* for the truth. This is especially true, again, of moral and religious truth. The significance of "subjectivity" for Kierkegaard is that "subjectivity is no second-best fallback position with respect to religious knowledge" but "is the ground of all genuine religious knowledge in all times" and that "religious knowledge is linked to subjectivity because there is an essential link between the attainment of religious insight and the development of religious character."[31]

Evans' point concerning this "essential link" illuminates a remarkable claim that Kierkegaard makes in his journals about

---

[26] Evans, *KFS*, 58.

[27] Evans, *KFS*, 58.

[28] Kierkegaard, *CUP*, 201.

[29] Kierkegaard, *CUP*, 201.

[30] Rae, *KVI*, 217, rightly notes: "The point of this example is clearly not the elevation of the idol to the status of the true God such that the truth is simply *what* we believe in with sufficient passion."

[31] Evans, *KFS*, 63.

Concluding Unscientific Postscript, that the entire book is aimed at showing that if one follows the path of subjectivity, the "how," one will, when encountering Christian faith, also be in a position to discern the "what," that "there is a How with the characteristic that when the How is scrupulously rendered the What is also given, that this is the How of 'faith.' Right here, at its very maximum, inwardness is shown to be objectivity."[32] Climacus, and Kierkegaard, are misunderstood if interpreted as reducing the "what" of faith (Christ as the incarnate God-in-time) to the "how" of faith. But they do highlight that any knowledge of the true God is grounded in subjectivity, that, as Evans puts it, God "has designed the world in such a way that…creatures can only come to know him if they are engaged in the struggle to become like him."[33] In a remarkable fashion, then, Kierkegaard's portrayal of "truth is subjectivity" never denies the reality of God and of the incarnation, but also insists that knowledge of this reality requires subjective struggle. Evans' account therefore is far from a "naive realism," but attends to the particular logic of reality claims in different realms of discourse. It is no surprise when Evans affirms how his reading of "realism" relates both to Jamesian pragmatism and Reformed epistemology.[34]

In a recent essay, M. G. Piety agrees that Kierkegaard's notion of "truth is subjectivity" does not result in noncognitive fideism, and that he does so in a manner surprisingly congruent with Patristic

---

[32] Søren Kierkegaard, *Søren Kierkegaard's Journals and Papers*, ed. and trans. Howard V. Hong and Edna H. Hong. Assisted by Gregor Malantschuk (Bloomington and London: Indiana University Press, 1967), vol. 4, entry 4550, p. 351; cf. Evans, *KFS*, 64.

[33] Evans, *KFS*, 63.

[34] On William James, see Evans, *KFS*, 51; on Evans and Reformed epistemology, especially Alvin Plantinga, see Evans, *KFS*, chapters 3, 7, 10–11. Paul L. Holmer says of the contextuality of reality claims: "'[R]eal' is not a name, and there are no irreducible reals…[W]e have to locate the 'real' in each context or each system of discourse in turn." Paul L. Holmer, *On Kierkegaard and the Truth*, ed. David J. Gouwens and Lee C. Barrett III (Eugene, OR: Cascade Books, 2012), 172.

theology.³⁵ Piety argues that for Kierkegaard "Christian knowing is not merely about having true beliefs; it is primarily a matter of living out Christian truth as a way of life," "articulating the role that knowledge plays in a life lived in relation to Christian truth as expressed maximally in God's grace, mercy, and love."³⁶ Arguing that Kierkegaard's epistemology holds important similarities with Irenaeus and Clement of Alexandria, Piety maintains that, for Kierkegaard, specifically "Christian knowledge is a product of revelation, and the specific revelation with which Kierkegaard is concerned can be characterized as an encounter with Christ, or as contemporaneity with Christ."³⁷ In this encounter with Christ as paradox, one learns what one cannot learn by oneself, that one is a sinner, outside the truth, but also that one's sins are forgiven.³⁸ It is only in the passion of faith, the "happy passion," that one receives this good news.³⁹

But is this "faith" really "knowledge of Christ"? Piety here employs the traditional distinction between "acquaintance knowledge" and "propositional knowledge," in which "the former is the source of the latter, just as our acquaintance with the objects of our experience is the source of our propositional knowledge of them."⁴⁰ Based on an important early journal entry by Kierkegaard on *Credo ut intelligam* and *Nihil est in intellectus quod non antea fuerit in sensu* [there is nothing in the intellect that has not previously been in the senses],⁴¹ she concludes that for Kierkegaard:

> a person meets Christ...in the moment of faith. This meeting yields an acquaintance "knowledge" of Christ.

---

³⁵ M. G. Piety, "Kierkegaard and the Early Church on Christian Knowledge and Its Existential Implications," chapter 11 in Stephen Minister, J. Aaron Simmons, and Michael Strawser, eds., *Kierkegaard's God and the Good Life* (Bloomington: Indiana University Press, 2017), 191–208 (hereafter *KEC*).

³⁶ Minister, et al., "Editors' Introduction," *Kierkegaard's God and the Good Life*, xvi.

³⁷ Piety, *KEC*, 193.

³⁸ Piety, *KEC*, 196.

³⁹ Kierkegaard, *PF*, 54.

⁴⁰ Piety, *KEC*, 193.

⁴¹ Kierkegaard, *JP*, vol. 2, entry 1098, p. 4.

> If there is Christian knowledge in the propositional sense, this acquaintance knowledge of Christ both precedes it and provides the foundation for it. To become acquainted with Christ is an experience that is related to the intellect in a manner analogous to the way *sensory* experience is related to the intellect.[42]

As with Clement, who held that "an 'august knowledge of the truth' may be built 'on the foundation of faith' (*Stromata* V, Chapter 1),"[43] so for Kierkegaard, Piety explains, "Knowledge of the truth…is a product of faith, or of a faithful life."[44] It is not that one first possesses propositional knowledge of Christ that is then "applied." Rather, Piety argues, Kierkegaard holds that "Christian truth, or the truth of Christianity, when viewed merely as knowledge (i.e., as an idea or concept) abstracted from any existential situation, is untruth."[45] True Christian knowledge occurs only when the belief that God became man in Christ is grasped, in Kierkegaard's words, as "the objective uncertainty maintained through appropriation in the most passionate inwardness,"[46] joined with, Piety says, "the wise person's insight that the only way one can properly relate to this 'knowledge' is subjectively, in the passion of faith."[47]

Striking about Piety's account is how this acquaintance knowledge of Christ entails the individual's *encountering* Christ, or "meeting" Christ.[48] While the incarnation, as the eternal truth that can be known only in consequence of believing that it has become

---

[42] Piety, *KEC*, 194.

[43] Piety, *KEC*, 202, 207n49.

[44] Piety, *KEC*, 203.

[45] Piety, *KEC*, 198.

[46] Piety, *KEC*, 200, quoting Søren Kierkegaard, *Concluding Unscientific Postscript*, trans. Alastair Hannay (Cambridge: Cambridge University Press, 2009), 17.

[47] Piety, *KEC*, 200. For more detailed discussion, see M. G. Piety, *Ways of Knowing: Kierkegaard's Pluralist Epistemology* (Waco, TX: Baylor University Press, 2010), 115–60 (hereafter *WOK*).

[48] Compare Thomas F. Torrance, *The Ground and Grammar of Theology* (Charlottesville: University Press of Virginia, 1980), 156–7.

historical, cannot be an object of "knowledge,"[49] the encounter with the God in time produces a capacity that a person could not by herself engender, the ability to see herself not only as guilty but as sinner. So too, Christ presents one with the possibility of offense or faith, and the person who then receives faith finds herself utterly and continuously reliant upon Christ in the "happy passion" that is faith.[50] This acquaintance knowledge itself, what the Patristics called "faith" (*pistis*) as opposed to the Gnostics' intellectualistic and elitist version of *gnosis*, is the foundation for the propositional knowledge that only faith can grasp.

Piety aptly summarizes Kierkegaard's account of this "faith seeking understanding," how faith's "objective uncertainty" merges with a subjective certainty, and how faith entails reality claims: "A person who has encountered God's love is thus able to understand both that he is a sinner and that his sins are forgiven. Not only is he able to understand these things; he is able to achieve certainty, in the psychological sense, that this conception of himself and his relation to God corresponds to reality."[51]

Incarnational Realism in Narrative Form in *Practice in Christianity*

Thus far we have seen how Kierkegaard's concern with "truth is subjectivity," far from leading to subjectivism or irrational fideism, can be seen as affirming an incarnational realism. More specifically, faith includes a "knowledge of Christ" in which the believer relates to a reality beyond herself.

This does not exhaust Kierkegaard's incarnational realism. In his later writings, such as *Practice in Christianity*, authored by Kierkegaard's Christian pseudonym Anti-Climacus, Kierkegaard explores further the grammar of Christian redemption, and in particular the concept of "offense," with a more detailed narrative account of the

---

[49] Piety, *KEC*, 199. See also Piety, *WOK*, 153–5, 171–7.
[50] Kierkegaard, *PF*, 54.
[51] Piety, *KEC*, 196.

person of Christ. This extended narrative account of Christ is absent in the earlier *Philosophical Fragments*, which uses "thin" narratives (the contrast between the Socratic teacher and Teacher B, and the poem of the king and the maiden) rhetorically to shed light on the distinctiveness of the "grammar of Christian redemption" over against Socratic faith.

Turning to *Practice in Christianity* one is struck by its fulsome narrative quality. In contrast to the "algebraic" portrayals of Christ in *Philosophical Fragments*, offense and contemporaneity are now amplified and given texture through extended explication of the narrative structure of the gospels. In *Practice in Christianity*, No. I, Anti-Climacus expounds upon Christ's invitation, "Come Here, All You Who Labor and Are Burdened, and I Will Give You Rest" (Matthew 11:28),[52] wherein that invitation evokes a variety of responses of "offense."[53] Then in *Practice in Christianity*, No. II, "Blessed Is He Who Is Not Offended at Me" (Matthew 11:6), Anti-Climacus rehearses through "Biblical Exposition and Christian Definition"[54] the different "categories of offense" the incarnation elicits: offense in relation to the loftiness "that an individual human being claims to be God, acts or speaks in a manner that manifests God" or offense in relation to the lowliness, "that the one who is God is this lowly human being, suffering as a lowly human being."[55]

Narrative comes to the fore in Anti-Climacus' discussion of the incarnation and offense or faith in *Practice in Christianity* for four reasons. First, narrative illuminates doctrinal theology, the belief in Jesus as the God-Man, with an implicit rejection, as Murray Rae notes, of both Ebionitism as offense in relation to the loftiness of Jesus and Docetism as offense in relation to the lowliness of Jesus.[56]

---

[52] Kierkegaard, *PC*, 40–56.

[53] Kierkegaard, *PC*, 62–7.

[54] Kierkegaard, *PC*, 71.

[55] Kierkegaard, *PC*, 82.

[56] Rae, *KVI*, 71.

Second, the narrative of Jesus secures the specificity of his person as God incarnate. As we have seen, Kierkegaard's account of the God-Man serves as a check against speculative or mythological interpretations (Hegelians, right-wing or left-wing), or interpretations seeing Christ as simply intensifying a universal human capacity (such as Schleiermacher's "God-consciousness"). The narrative exhibits Christ to be the unique and unsubstitutable incarnate one. Over against "profane history" that would attempt to demonstrate historically the truth of the incarnation, making it a matter of "knowledge," Anti-Climacus sets a "sacred history" that confronts us with "the story of his life in the state of abasement [and] also that he claimed to be God" prompting not knowledge but offense or faith.[57]

Third, narrative functions to show how this "sacred history" interrogates the hearer or reader, making clear that all who come to faith must go through this possibility of offense.[58] Rhetorically, Anti-Climacus' reading of the gospel narrative shows how this narrated paradoxical Christ must shock the sensibilities of anyone, in whatever century, who would have faith, clarifying the experiential dimension of encounter with Christ.

Fourth, the fulsome picture of Christ's "being the truth" in *Practice in Christianity* shows how this experience requires the "redoubling of truth within yourself," in a life that "expresses the truth approximately in the striving for it...just as the truth was in Christ a life, for he was the truth."[59] "Subjective truth" in relation to Christ is narrated truth in two senses, for it is the narrative of Christ's life that displays truth, and the disciple who strives to follow Christ "redoubles" that truth in the narrative of her or his own life.

---

[57] Kierkegaard, *PC*, 30; cf. 25, 64, 221; Joel D. S. Rasmussen, "Kierkegaard's Biblical Hermeneutics: Imitation, Imaginative Freedom, and Paradoxical Fixation," in Lee C. Barrett and Jon Stewart, eds., *Kierkegaard and the Bible: Tome II: The New Testament*. Kierkegaard Research: Sources, Reception and Resources, Volume 1, Tome II (Farnham, UK / Burlington, VT: Ashgate, 2010), 249–84; on Kierkegaard's concept of "sacred history," see 266–9.

[58] Kierkegaard, *PC*, 101.

[59] Kierkegaard, *PC*, 205; see Piety, *WOK*, 103.

SØREN KIERKEGAARD: THEOLOGIAN OF THE GOSPEL

As Sylvia Walsh has shown, in depicting this striving to "redouble" the truth within oneself, Kierkegaard operates with an "inverse dialectic," exploring how, for example, Christian faith finds "joy in the strife of suffering."[60] Kierkegaardian faith involves negative qualifications (the consciousness of sin, the possibility of offense, dying to the world or self-denial, and suffering) but through these negative qualifications Christian strivers live in positive qualifications (faith, forgiveness, new life, love, hope, joy, and consolation), all of which are enclosed within "the broader complementary dialectical framework of Christianity as incorporating both gospel and law, grace and works, mildness and rigor through a relation to Christ in his dual role as the Christian striver's redeemer and prototype for living Christianly."[61]

It is important to recognize how, despite Kierkegaard's emphasis on striving, Christ is not only prototype but redeemer. This is especially clear in Kierkegaard's communion discourses, which Walsh rightly sees as "the resting point" of Kierkegaard's entire authorship. The communion discourses show how "the thrust of the authorship as a whole is clearly toward reconciliation with God, which is accomplished through the death and atonement of Christ and made true in the life of each person individually by loving Christ much and remaining in communion with him in one's daily life."[62]

But there still may remain a suspicion that Kierkegaard's portrayal of Christian existence is finally simply the victory of one's own religious experience as a forgiven, reconciled person. Yet, as Andrew B. Torrance observes, citing Eberhard Jüngel, this is to ignore

---

[60] Søren Kierkegaard, *Christian Discourses* and *The Crisis and a Crisis in the Life of an Actress*, ed. and trans. Howard V. Hong and Edna H. Hong with Introduction and Notes (Princeton: Princeton University Press, 1997), 93–159.

[61] Sylvia Walsh, *Living Christianly: Kierkegaard's Dialectic of Christian Existence* (University Park, PA: The Pennsylvania State University Press, 2005), 14.

[62] Sylvia Walsh Perkins, "At the Foot of the Altar: Kierkegaard's Communion Discourses as the Resting Point of His Authorship," in Warner M. Bailey, Lee C. Barrett III, and James O. Duke, eds., *The Theologically Formed Heart: Essays in Honor of David J. Gouwens* (Eugene, OR: Pickwick Publications, 2014), 241–63, 260.

how Kierkegaard's "truth is subjectivity" must be dialectically related to Kierkegaard's equally important understanding that one's "subjectivity is *untruth*." "[T]he reality of God cannot be captured in a subjective human idea and so it is only in and through a relationship with the person of Jesus Christ—'the way, and the truth, and the life' *who lies beyond human subjectivity*—that a person stands related to the truth of the Christian faith."[63] "Beyond existentialism," Kierkegaard holds that "God reconciles the world to himself *in the person of Jesus Christ* and not in the faith of the individual human."[64]

> The paradox here is the paradox that, to some extent, confronts all forms of realism: Christians are called to *believe* that their faith in God is not simply a product of their own belief-forming imagination but is grounded in the reality of Christ; they are called to believe that they cannot believe without the one in whom they believe. Without Christ, they can only generate unchristian beliefs.[65]

Kierkegaard's focus upon the narrated sacred history of Christ in *Practice in Christianity*, and the expansive theological vision in the communion discourses of Christ as redeemer and prototype, highlight a final sense in which Kierkegaard's vision of the incarnation is "realistic." Once more in continuity with Irenaeus, this time on the rule of faith, for Kierkegaard "scripture defines the world, not the other way around."[66] With his central concern for the sacred history of Christ leading to a fully-drawn realistic Scriptural hermeneutics, Kierkegaard

---

[63] Andrew B. Torrance, "Beyond Existentialism: Kierkegaard on the Human Relationship with the God Who is Wholly Other," *International Journal of Systematic Theology* 16, no. 3 (July 2014): 295–312, 308, original italics.

[64] Andrew B. Torrance, "Beyond Existentialism," 300–1, original italics.

[65] Andrew B. Torrance, "Beyond Existentialism," 307. For extensive development of Kierkegaard's vision of the reality of God's personal transformative communion that draws forth human relationship, see Andrew B. Torrance, *The Freedom to Become a Christian: A Kierkegaardian Account of Human Transformation in Relationship with God* (London: Bloomsbury T&T Clark, 2016).

[66] Timothy Houston Polk, *The Biblical Kierkegaard: Reading by the Rule of Faith* (Macon, GA: Mercer University Press, 1997), 79. Compare Rasmussen, "Kierkegaard's Biblical Hermeneutics," 251–2.

witnesses finally, with an Augustinian breadth of vision, to the incarnation as defining reality itself, witnessing at once to the heart's restless desire-filled journey to God and to God's self-emptying journey out of love to each individual, a relation of mutual reciprocity between God and humanity.[67]

Conclusion: Kierkegaard, Torrance, and Incarnational Realism

Thomas F. Torrance and Søren Kierkegaard do not represent a simple opposition between "objective realism" and "subjective anti-realism." I have argued rather that they present complex understandings of objectivity and subjectivity, and that each is committed to "realism," the sense of "truth being a fundamental insight into the *real*, as it is independent of the knower."[68] Moreover, Kierkegaard and Torrance both hold also to an incarnational realism in that they both "direct our minds to the self-giving of God in Jesus Christ" as the source of truth.[69]

Focusing on Kierkegaard, I have argued that the key to understanding how he relates subjectivity and objectivity in Christian faith lies in this journal entry: "when the How is scrupulously rendered the What is also given, that this is the How of 'faith.' Right here, at its very maximum, inwardness is shown to be objectivity."[70] Hence, the "how" and the "what" are logically intertwined in non-reductionistic ways. For Kierkegaard's theological realism, "subjectivity" does not reduce theological affirmations to expressions of personal affective states. Yet any "knowledge of Christ" as the incarnate one is "truth" only within the context of passionate interest in the encounter with the incarnate one. Kierkegaard holds that Christian affirmations of the

---

[67] Lee C. Barrett, *Eros and Self-Emptying: The Intersections of Augustine and Kierkegaard* (Grand Rapids, MI: William B. Eerdmans, 2013).

[68] Habets, *Theology in Transposition*, 63.

[69] Alister E. McGrath, *Thomas F. Torrance: An Intellectual Biography* (Edinburgh: T&T Clark, 1999), 219, quoting Thomas F. Torrance, *God and Rationality* (London: Oxford University Press, 1971), 45.

[70] Kierkegaard, *JP*, vol. 4, entry 4550, p. 351.

reality of the incarnation find their logical home within the passions of faith, hope, and love as a response to Jesus Christ.[71]

Kierkegaard fills out this depiction of incarnational realism in a host of ways: an epistemological realism, a stress on the reality and prior actuality of Christ as the incarnate one who challenges all human understanding, affirmation of a specifically "Christian knowledge" that arises from an "acquaintance knowledge" in encounter with Christ, an extended temporal narrative of Christ's life that entails Christ's continuing presence as "redeemer" and "prototype" in both his work and his person, and Kierkegaard's realistic reading of Scripture—all of these together can counter common pictures of a "subjectivistic" or "anti-realist" Kierkegaard. Torrance was therefore correct in seeing "Kierkegaard's 'truth as subjectivity' as in fact theological objectivity and realism, the subject's proper relation to the object."[72]

In their critical incarnational realism, Kierkegaard and Torrance do share this overall "grammar of Christian redemption": for Kierkegaard the subjective "how" of faith in encountering Christ reveals the objective "what," and acquaintance knowledge of Christ leads to propositional Christian knowledge. Torrance similarly begins with "the evangelical and doxological level" of encountering Christ, but then uses this to explore "the theological level" (the economic Trinity) and then the "higher theological and scientific level" (the ontological or immanent Trinity).[73] Yet where Kierkegaard diverges from Torrance is at this point, for he assumes the doctrinal tradition, but

---

[71] I explore these themes of a non-reductionistic reading of Kierkegaard, and the centrality of faith, hope, and love as responses to Christ, in *Kierkegaard as Religious Thinker* (Cambridge: Cambridge University Press, 1996).

[72] Habets, *Theology in Transposition*, 101.

[73] Thomas F. Torrance, "The Basic Grammar of Theology," in *The Ground and Grammar of Theology* (Charlottesville, Virginia: University Press of Virginia, 1980), 146–78, 156–61.

does not develop it dogmatically.[74] In his expressly Christian literature he aims, rather, as a "poet of the religious," to enliven for his readers the possibilities of offense or faith.

An even more striking difference between them lies in the contrast between, on the one hand, Torrance's "scientific theology," including formulating multi-layered hierarchies of knowledge and reality,[75] and, on the other hand, Kierkegaard's "unscientific" reflections. Given Kierkegaard's suspicions of Hegelian speculative philosophy and theology for reducing "faith" to "science," he seeks to clarify the logical features of "subjective knowledge" in ethics, religion, and, in its own distinctive way, in Christian discourse. Hence, Kierkegaard does not question Christian knowledge of God. But he is especially alert to the dangers of confusing this knowledge with "objective" in the sense of "non-self-involving" knowledge in the manner, he believes, of Hegel and his own contemporary Hans Lassen Martensen. Rather, Kierkegaard stresses, the logic of Christian discourse, and hence the knowledge of God in Christ, finds its context of meaning in its challenge to the will and to the heart. His goal, rhetorically rather than systematically, is to display how this knowledge challenges our self-reliant "reason," offends us, and enlists our emotions, passions, and feelings as much as our reflection in responding in faith.

Moreover, Kierkegaard has no interest, as does Torrance, in formulating an integrated and hierarchical account of our knowledge of the world.[76] Kierkegaard champions, rather, as Piety puts it, a "pluralist epistemology," a "nonreductionist account of the complexities of human knowing."[77] Hence, while Kierkegaard is premodern in his

---

[74] Kierkegaard does employ economic trinitarian language. Paul Martens suggests also that Kierkegaard uses this language as a means of "imagining the Immanent Trinity." See Paul Martens, "Trinity: A Concept Ubiquitous Yet Unthematized," in Aaron P. Edwards and David J. Gouwens, eds., *T&T Clark Companion to the Theology of Kierkegaard* (London and New York: Bloomsbury T&T Clark, 2020), 177-85.

[75] Habets, *Theology in Transposition*, 51–65.

[76] McGrath, *Thomas F. Torrance*, 232.

[77] Piety, *WOK*, 4.

understanding of truth, in his nonreductionist epistemology he is strikingly postmodern.[78] Content to clarify the distinctiveness of the logic of knowledge-claims within different realms of knowledge in order to prevent conceptual confusion, he sees no need for hierarchical integration of diverse realms of discourse.

Underlying this contrast between them lie different understandings of "grammar."[79] While they share the basic "grammar of Christian redemption," Torrance's critical realist epistemology aims at a unified account of theological science and the natural sciences, whereas Kierkegaard's "grammatical" investigations—which in no way reject the legitimacy of the methods and claims to "objective knowledge" in such fields as science, mathematics, and history—stress the distinctive differences between types of knowledge-claims, above all how "subjective knowledge" is marked by "objective uncertainty," "approximation," and "striving" in relation to religious truth.[80]

Despite these important differences, however, if Kierkegaard is indeed not subjectivistic, anti-realist, or "existentialist," but in some sense a grammarian of faith, this opens the door to exploring further his place within the broad ecumenical Christian theological tradition, and thus how he may engage doctrinally-oriented theologians like Torrance. Although deeply critical of much systematic theology in his own day for obscuring the contours and dynamics of Christian existence, Kierkegaard, as is clear in his account of incarnational realism, has much to offer by way of critical interaction and dialogue with that tradition, as many students of Kierkegaard are increasingly discovering.[81] Thomas F. Torrance, despite his differences from Kierkegaard, certainly saw the value of engaging with him. My hope is

---

[78] Piety, *WOK*, 4, citing Evans, *KFS*, 42.

[79] On Torrance on grammar, see again Thomas F. Torrance, *The Ground and Grammar of Theology*. On Kierkegaard on grammar, see Paul L. Holmer's explorations in relation to Wittgenstein's comments on "theology as grammar." Paul L. Holmer, *The Grammar of Faith* (San Francisco: Harper & Row, 1978).

[80] Piety, *WOK*, 168.

[81] See Edwards and Gouwens, eds., *T&T Clark Companion to the Theology of Kierkegaard*.

that this essay will stimulate others to explore further possibilities for dialogue between Kierkegaard and Torrance.

3.

KIERKEGAARD'S PARADOXICAL CHRISTOLOGY

Andrew B. Torrance

In his introduction to Karl Barth's early theology, T. F. Torrance writes:

> What interests Barth in Kierkegaard's teaching was the emphasis upon the explosive force that the invasion of God in his Godness in time and human existence meant, which Kierkegaard sought to express by the paradox and dialectic. This is a point that has been often misunderstood in both Kierkegaard and Barth—for the emphasis upon the infinite qualitative difference between time and eternity…was not upon some abstract and distant Deity, but precisely upon the nearness, the impact of God in all his Majesty and Godness upon man—that is the significance of Jesus that had been lost, and which Barth as well as Kierkegaard sought to recover.[1]

A lot is going on in Torrance's mind when he writes this passage—much more than can be addressed in this essay. But there is one specific point on which I wish to focus: that Kierkegaard's use of the "infinite qualitative difference" and "the paradox" sought to draw attention to the nearness of God in Jesus Christ.

While Torrance is not entirely clear in the above passage, his point appears to be as follows. Kierkegaard's and Barth's shared emphasis on the infinite qualitative difference sought to stress, in Kierkegaard's words, that there is "nothing whatever" that human beings can do, in and of themselves, to relate themselves directly to

---

[1] Thomas F. Torrance, *Karl Barth: An Introduction to his Early Theology - 1910-31* (London: SCM Press, 1962), 44.

God.² Consequently, it must be "God who gives everything; it is he who makes a [human being] able to have faith, etc. This is grace, and this is the major premise of [Christianity]."³ For both of them, this is the reality of the situation that faces us. So, for example, to try to advance an account of the nearness of God by asserting a natural synthesis between God and creation would be confused. To discover the truth of God's nearness to creation, we must look to the only one in whom there is full union between God and creation: Jesus Christ. For Kierkegaard,

> That the human race is supposed to be in kinship with God is ancient paganism; but *that* an individual human being is God is Christianity, and this particular human being is the God-man.⁴

This is the significance of Jesus which, as Torrance notes above, "had been lost, and which Barth as well as Kierkegaard sought to recover."⁵ Furthermore, because the nearness of this union is unique to the person of Christ, and because we cannot comprehend how God can unite Godself with humanity, the God-humanity of Christ presents itself to us as an absolute paradox. As Kierkegaard writes, "the God-man is... absolutely the paradox"—a position that Barth would come to develop in his own theology.⁶ As such, the world of Christian theology should not treat Christology as a puzzle-solving exercise; the puzzle of Christ's God-humanity is not one to which we can offer a solution.

In short, "the infinite qualitative difference" serves as a term of caution against overly systematic attempts to develop a human understanding of the relationship between God and creation. Instead,

---

² Kierkegaard, *Kierkegaard's Journals and Notebooks,* vol. 5, eds. Niels Jørgen Cappelørn, Alastair Hannay, David Kangas, Bruce H. Kirmmse, George Pattison, Vanessa Rumble, and K. Brian Söderquist (Princeton, NJ: Princeton University Press), 244.

³ *KJN* 5, 244.

⁴ Kierkegaard, *Practice in Christianity*, ed. & trans. Howard V. and Edna H. Hong (Princeton: Princeton University Press, 1991), 82.

⁵ Torrance, *Karl Barth*, 44.

⁶ *PC*, 82. The main place that Barth develops a paradoxical Christology is in the second edition of his commentary on Romans. He is open about the fact that this development emerged under the influence of Kierkegaard.

for Kierkegaard, we should direct our attention to the paradoxical person of Jesus: the one "mediator" "who leads us to God."[7]

There is much to discuss on this issue with respect to the relationship between Kierkegaard and Barth and, indeed, the relationship between Kierkegaard and Torrance. That said, I will limit my focus in this essay to Kierkegaard himself. More specifically, I shall concentrate on his paradoxical Christology as a position that helps us to understand God's nearness to humanity. I begin by looking at what Kierkegaard has to say about the union between God and humanity in Christ. I then turn to look at how his paradoxical understanding of the God-human relationship helps him to understand two difficult issues in theology: (1) God's relationship to Christ's suffering; and (2) the changelessness of God. Following this theological reflection, I examine the practical role that paradox plays in his theology. Finally, I conclude by offering a brief account of how Kierkegaard's paradoxical Christology relates to the mediation of Christ—a connection that would be taken up in the Christocentric theologies of Barth and Torrance. What we shall find is that, despite his limited understanding of Kierkegaard, the above statement from T. F. Torrance shows a deep appreciation for Kierkegaard's theology on an issue that is often overlooked and, as Torrance puts it, misunderstood.

The Paradoxical Union of God and Humanity in Christ

For Kierkegaard, the systematic question of who Jesus Christ is is one that needs to be approached cautiously, with a hesitancy to make statements about his constitution that go beyond what we are capable of saying. Yet there are some things that he thinks we do need to say about Christology, and we see this throughout much of his later authorship. For example, while he maintains that Jesus Christ is fully God and fully human, he also insists that we must not confuse these two natures—he strongly resists the suggestion that the Incarnation involves a synthesis

---

[7] Kierkegaard, *Journals and Papers*, vol. 2, ed. & trans. Howard V. and Edna H. Hong (Bloomington: Indiana University Press, 1967-78), 1432.

between God and the world.⁸ Also, he denies that the Son needs to become less divine in order to become incarnate—which some kenotic Christologies risk suggesting. For Kierkegaard, there is no competitive relationship between humanity and divinity; there is no zero-sum game between Christ's divine and human nature, which assumes that his humanity in some way takes away from his divinity. Jesus Christ is one person, "true God and true man," "the lowly human being, yet God, the only begotten of the Father."⁹ He "is in lowliness and in loftiness one and the same." ¹⁰ So, when it comes to following Christ, there is no choice "between Christ in lowliness and Christ in loftiness, for Christ is not divided; he is one and the same."¹¹ Humanity and divinity are in union (*Eenhed*) in Christ.¹²

As mentioned in the introduction, Kierkegaard does not think we can know how this could be the case. The logic of the Incarnation is beyond human comprehension; it is absolutely paradoxical. In holding to this view, he finds himself in company with much of Christian

---

⁸ For Kierkegaard, the infinite qualitative difference between God and humanity "always remains." *JP* 2, 1349; see also *JP* 3, 3087 and *JP* 1, 236.

⁹ *PC*, 160, 75. As David Law points out, Kierkegaard sometimes associates this union with the term *Sammensætning* (translated "placing together," "compound," "composite"). Law, *Kierkegaard's Kenotic Christology* (Oxford: Oxford University Press, 2013), 218-9; *PC*, 81, 82, and 16. However, his use of this term should not be interpreted as suggesting a Nestorian tendency in Kierkegaard's thought. Rather, it is a way of making sure his Christology took a firm stand against Christologies that would confuse the divine and human nature. As Law also notes, "The Nestorian impression created by *Sammensætning* is in any case corrected by Anti-Climacus' use of the term *Eenhed*, which makes clear that Anti-Climacus holds that the two natures are not merely juxtaposed but are united in the Person of Christ" (219). (Anti-Climacus is one of Kierkegaard's pseudonyms. He represents an extraordinary Christian. Normally, it is best to draw a clear distinction between Kierkegaard and Anti-Climacus. This essay, however, has not done this to try to keep the discussion more straightforward. This is justifiable because Kierkegaard and Anti-Climacus seem to hold the same theological position when it comes to the topics discussed in this essay. Indeed, *Practice in Christianity* was originally drafted under Kierkegaard's own name.)

¹⁰ *PC*, 161.

¹¹ *PC*, 161.

¹² *PC*, 160.

orthodoxy. For example, Cyril of Alexandria writes: "[w]e see in Christ the strange and rare paradox of Lordship in servant's form and divine glory in human abasement."[13] To be clear, an emphasis on the paradoxical nature of Christology should not be taken to suggest a logical contradiction. Rather, it simply suggests that the notion of Christ's hypostatic union *appears* contradictory to us in our limited finite understanding. Accordingly, Kierkegaard's understanding of the God-man as absolute paradox seeks to emphasize the inability of human beings to possess their own systematic or representative understanding of the logic of the Incarnation.[14] As it is written in 1 Timothy 6:16, Christ "dwells in inapproachable light, whom no one has ever seen or can see." Or, in Kierkegaard's words: "God dwells in a light from which flows every ray that illuminates the world, yet no one can force his way along the paths in order to see God since the paths of light turn into darkness when one turns toward the light."[15] So, again, the divinity of Christ remains hidden from direct human perception.

At the same time, Kierkegaard's emphasis on the paradoxicality of Christ should not be taken to be wholly negative. When God assumes humanity, God reveals Godself to the world in a mode that human beings can receive in faith. This does not mean that God reveals everything about Godself in Christ. There will always be features of God's inner life that remain hidden to us—features that are wholly consistent with his revelation. This is because there are qualities that are essential to God that cannot be represented by created things. But what it does mean is that God provides the world with a finite object (the humanity of Jesus Christ) through which God can communicate Godself to creation according to its limits. It is in Christ

---

[13] Cyril of Alexandria, *On the Unity of Christ*, trans. John McGuckin (Crestwood: St Vladimir's Seminary Press, 1995), 101.

[14] *PC*, 82. It has been well established by C. Stephen Evans (and widely acknowledged in Kierkegaard scholarship) that, for Kierkegaard, the paradox is not a formal or logical contradiction, but just appears to be so to speculative forms of natural human reason. See Evans, *Passionate Reason* (Indianapolis: Indiana University Press, 1992), 97-104; *Kierkegaard's Fragments and Postscript* (New Jersey: Humanities Press, 1983), 212-22.

[15] Kierkegaard, *Works of Love*, ed. and trans. Howard V. Hong and Edna H. Hong (Princeton, NJ: Princeton University Press, 1995), 9.

that God is nearest to creation and through Christ that God positively communicates Godself to the world. By the work of the Holy Spirit, we can receive this communication in faith.[16]

To provide some more theological context for Kierkegaard's paradoxical theology and show how it finds expression in his broader theology, I shall now briefly consider how he holds together the suffering, omnipotence, and changelessness of the God-human.

The One Who Suffers Omnipotently

Reminiscent of Cyril of Alexandria's view of Mary as *Theotokos* (*θεοτόκος*),[17] mother of God, Kierkegaard affirms that once God allows Godself "to be born," God "has in a certain sense bound himself once and for all."[18] He writes:

> [The God-man's] unrecognizability is so omnipotently maintained that in a way he himself is in the power of his own incognito, in which lies the literal *actuality* of his pure human suffering, that this is not merely appearance but in a certain sense is the assumed incognito's upper hand over him. Only in this way is

---

[16] We do not find much reference to the Holy Spirit in Kierkegaard's writings. This is because of the way in which the Spirit had come to be associated with the Hegelian theologies of which he was so critical. That said, he does note that "[t]he Spirit brings faith, the faith—that is, faith in the strictest sense of the word, this gift of the Holy Spirit." *For Self-Examination*, in *For Self-Examination and Judge for Yourself!*, ed. and trans. Howard V. and Edna H. Hong (Princeton: Princeton University Press, 1990), 81. Also, he maintains that the Spirit must help us to know the Son, the Mediator, who directs us to the Father: God "becomes my Father in the Mediator by means of the Spirit." *JP* 2, 1432.

[17] Cyril asks: "How could we confess in the rule of faith that we believe in the Son of God who was born of the virgin Mary, if it wasn't the Son of God but the son of man who was born of the virgin Mary?" Serm. 186. 1, Sermons, vi, trans. Edmund Hill (New York: New City Press, 1995), 25.

[18] *PC*, 131. Earlier, Kierkegaard writes: "When God chooses to let himself be born in lowliness, when he who holds all possibilities in his hand takes upon himself the form of a lowly servant, when he goes about defenceless and lets people do to him what they will, he surely must know well enough what he is doing and why he wills it; but for all that it is he who has people in his power and not they who have power over him." *PC*, 34.

there in the profoundest sense earnestness concerning his becoming true man; this is also why he suffers through the utmost suffering of feeling himself abandoned by God. He is not, therefore, at any moment beyond suffering but is actually in suffering, and this purely human experience befalls him, that the actuality proves to be more terrible than the possibility, that he who freely assumed unrecognizability yet actually suffers as if he were trapped or had trapped himself in unrecognizability...[The divine incognito] was maintained to such an extent that [the God-man] himself suffered purely humanly under the unrecognizability.[19]

Kierkegaard describes this dynamic as

...a strange kind of dialectic: that he, omnipotent, binds himself and does it so omnipotently that he actually feels bound, suffers under the consequence of his loving and free decision to become an individual human being—to that degree there was earnestness in his becoming an actual human being.[20]

In these passages, Kierkegaard makes it clear that the God-man subjects himself to human suffering in a way that really is caught up in the suffering of creation. This is possible because with "everything divinely in his power," Christ is free "to suffer humanly, every moment divinely capable of changing everything."[21] In other words, the God-man suffers omnipotently—a perspective reminiscent of the Cyrilline view that the incarnate Word suffers impassibly.[22] For Cyril, as Paul Gavrilyuk writes,

...both qualified divine impassibility and qualified

---

[19] *PC*, 131-32.

[20] *PC*, 132.

[21] *JP* 4, 4610. Drawing on Matthew 26:53, Kierkegaard asserts "that [Christ], the abased one, at all times had it in his power to ask his Father in heaven to send legions of angels to him to avert this most terrible thing [his death]." *PC*, 177.

[22] For further discussion of the notion that Christ suffered impassibly, see Thomas Weinandy, "Cyril and the Mystery of the Incarnation," in Thomas Weinandy and Daniel Keating, eds., *The Theology of Cyril of Alexandria* (Edinburgh: T&T Clark, 2003), 49-53.

divine possibility were necessary for a sound theology of incarnation. That affirmation of the impassibility was a way of protecting the truth that the one who became incarnate was truly God. Admitting a qualified passibility secured the point that God truly submitted himself to the conditions of the incarnation.[23]

Like Cyril, the words of Philippians 2:5-11 resonate throughout Kierkegaard's depiction of Jesus Christ. For example, in one of his upbuilding discourses, he writes:

> He who was equal with God took the form of a lowly servant, he would command legions of angels, indeed could command the world's creation and its destruction, he walked about defenceless; he who had everything in his power surrendered all power and could not even do anything for his beloved disciples but could only offer them the very same conditions of lowliness and contempt...if this is not self-denial, what then is self-denial.[24]

What does Kierkegaard mean by self-denial here? He does not think that the Son (the one "who was equal with God") denies his essential divinity (or Godness) by taking the form of a lowly servant.[25] Rather, God chooses to express God's power through a powerlessness that we might not naturally associate with God. Moreover, for Kierkegaard,

---

[23] Paul Gavrilyuk, *The Suffering of the Impassible God* (Oxford: Oxford University Press, 2004), 150.

[24] Kierkegaard, *Upbuilding Discourses in Various Spirits*, ed. and trans. Howard V. and Edna H. Hong (Princeton: Princeton University Press, 1993), 224-5. Kierkegaard also writes, Jesus Christ "learned obedience and was obedient, obedient in everything, obedient in giving up everything (the glory that he had before the foundation of the world was laid), obedient in doing without everything (even that on which he could lay his head), obedient in taking everything upon himself (the sin of humankind), obedient in suffering everything (the guilt of humankind), obedient to subjecting himself to everything in life, obedient in death." Kierkegaard, *Christian Discourses*, ed. and trans. Howard V. and Edna H. Hong (Princeton, NJ: Princeton University Press, 1997), 85.

[25] Reflecting on John 12:32, Kierkegaard refers to the uplifted one as "God's only begotten Son, our Lord, who from eternity was with God, was God, came to the world, then ascended into heaven, where he now sits at the Father's right hand, glorified with the glory he has before the world was." *PC*, 222.

God cannot express God's power through an apparent "powerlessness" without assuming a new form. God reveals Godself in an act that is not characterized by the kind of transcendent glory that characterizes the other acts of God that we read about elsewhere in Scripture. When "divine glory…take[s] on a lowly form,"[26] God gives Godself to relate personally to human beings in a new way, such that there would seem to be a sense in which the Incarnation involves "something new for God."[27] Indeed, Kierkegaard is willing to go so far as to say that "God suffers" in and through the humanity of Jesus Christ.[28] What we see here, in the words of Cyril, is a paradoxical understanding of Jesus Christ as one "who as God transcends suffering, suffered humanly in his flesh."[29] For Kierkegaard, this is possible by way of an omnipotence that "can withdraw itself at the same time it gives itself away."[30]

The Changelessness of God

There are a number of things that Kierkegaard has to say about the nature of God without getting caught up in overly systematic debates about the extent of God's attributes, their mutual compatibility, their precise definition, etc. For him, such debates often go beyond the remit of human theologizing, which, he believed, should be extremely hesitant about advancing overly systematic doctrines of God or overly rigid descriptions of God's attributes—especially if such description risks getting in the way of affirming positions that he took to be central to Christian orthodoxy. It is with this attitude that he approaches the

---

[26] Kierkegaard, *Eighteen Upbuilding Discourses*, ed. and trans. by Howard V. and Edna H. Hong (Princeton, NJ: Princeton University Press, 1990), 303.

[27] Paul R. Sponheim, "Relational Transcendence in Divine Agency," in *International Kierkegaard Commentary: Practice in Christianity*, ed. Robert L. Perkins (Macon, GA: Mercer University Press, 2004), 53.

[28] *JP* 4, 4610. Kierkegaard also notes that "Christ entered into the world *in order to suffer*." Kierkegaard, *Concluding Unscientific Postscript to Philosophical Fragments*, ed. and trans. Howard V. and Edna H. Hong (Princeton: Princeton University Press, 1992), 597.

[29] Cyril of Alexandria, *De symbolo*, 24, in L. R. Wickham, *Cyril of Alexandria: Selected Letters* (Oxford: Clarendon, 1983), 123.

[30] *JP* 2, 1251.

changelessness of God. He is clear that there is an important sense in which we need to maintain divine changelessness. At the same time, he does not commit himself to a doctrine of this attribute that stops him, for example, from affirming what he wants to say about the way in which God involves Godself in the history of creation.

The place where Kierkegaard gives particular attention to divine changelessness is in his sermon on "The Changelessness of God," where he offers a reflection on James 1:17-21, particularly verse 17: "Every good and perfect gift is from above and comes down from the Father of lights, with whom there is no variableness or shadow or turning."[31] The message of this sermon closely corresponds to its title, and it would be hard to walk away from this sermon thinking that he was willing to call into question the immutability of God. For example, in the opening prayer of this sermon, he refers to God as the "Changeless One, whom nothing changes!"[32] He then goes on to write: "no variation touches [God], not even the shadow of variation; in unchanged clarity, he, the Father of lights, is eternally unchanged."[33]

At the same time, in his opening prayer, he writes: "you who in infinite love let yourself be moved, may this our prayer also move you to bless it so that the prayer may change the one who is praying into conformity with your changeless will, you Changeless One!"[34] Here, he does not suggest that God changes who God essentially is or what God essentially wills. Yet he does acknowledge that God allows Godself to be moved by human prayers. For Kierkegaard, God is always free to interact with what God creates—albeit without the kind of emotional changeableness that characterizes human interaction. In recognizing this, he does not hold a diminished view of God's immutability but simply allows Scripture to shape his understanding of God's

---

[31] Kierkegaard, *The Moment and Late Writings*, ed. and trans. Howard V. Hong and Edna H. Hong (Princeton: Princeton University Press, 1998), 263-82.

[32] *M*, 269.

[33] *M*, 272.

[34] *M*, 269.

immutability—even if this offends some peoples' immediate expectations about what God should be like.

Again, Kierkegaard does not develop a systematic account of how exactly we can align divine changelessness with the various accounts we have of God interacting with creation. Not possessing divine changelessness himself, and not having access to it, he does not think that the complexities of divine providence are within the purview of human understanding. Indeed, he was highly critical of those who sought to think abstractly about God's changelessness, who enter into a "a phantom-battle about the predicates of God."[35] When emphasizing God's changelessness, his primary concern was to recognize that God is unchangeably good, true, and loving etc. He did not view God's changelessness as "an abstract something"—like the changelessness of the sun.[36] If God exists in this way, then Kierkegaard does not think there could be a reciprocal relationship between God and human beings, involving both parties. For him, God is a free subject whose personal activity expresses God's changeless truth in a lively and animated way that prevents it from being conceptualized by human reason. And he also believes that Scripture presents God as one who, in God's changelessness, freely chooses to be responsive to creation.

So, in a certain respect, Kierkegaard would seem to think that God's interactions with creation make a difference to God—especially in the case of the Incarnation. Apart from creation, God does not share a relationship with that which is not God, and so clearly does find union with that which is not God. On the other side, apart from the Incarnation, creation is not fully united with God in the way that is established in Christ. This again means that there is something entirely unique to the person of Christ—that is, again, absolutely paradoxical to limited human reason. Yet Kierkegaard does not think that such change makes a difference to who God essentially is. This means that, paradoxically, the unchangeable God is able to bring about change in his relationship with creation.

---

[35] *JP* 2, 1348.

[36] *JP* 2, 1348.

The Role of Paradoxical Christology

As I considered in the previous two sections, Kierkegaard's paradoxical theology allows him to maintain views about God's relationship to creation that are beyond what we can comprehend with our limited minds. However, given his commitment to the paradoxicality of Christianity, this did not concern him in the least. Before turning to consider the role of Kierkegaard's paradoxical Christology, it is important to be clear that the role that paradox plays in his thought was not simply functional but was also theological—it is grounded in his understanding of who God is and who we are before God. At the same time, while his approach was not primarily influenced by a concern for addressing the problems he saw in Denmark, he did see this theology as providing a firm basis for enabling him to diagnose and address some of the key problems he saw in his surrounding culture.

What were the problems he faced? In his later writings, Kierkegaard sought to challenge the kind of abstract speculation about Jesus Christ that distracted persons from relating to Christ in a way that would lead them into lives of discipleship. For him, this was not only a problem in his immediate context. It was one that hinders much of the history of Christological reflection, right from the very beginning when some Pharisees were blinded by their theologistic analysis of Jesus Christ—an analysis that was undergirded by the reigning theological orthodoxies. In Kierkegaard's own day, this problem expresses itself in a proclivity to think about Christianity in purely abstract terms that distract Christians from responding to Christ's call to discipleship.[37] This contributed to the illusion that the heart of Christianity was to be found in doctrinal statements, which turned Christianity into a religion for the elite and the bourgeois. Not only did this move take Christianity out of the hands of the poor and marginalized of society; it turned Christianity against them—it turned Christianity into a luxury that was barely within their means. He writes:

> Theory and doctrine are a fig leaf, and by means of this fig leaf a professor or clergyman looks so portentous that it is terrifying. And just as it is said of the

---

[37] *KJN* 1, 247.

> Pharisees that they not only do not enter into the kingdom of heaven themselves but even prevent others from entering, so also the professor prevents the unlearned man by giving him the idea that it depends on doctrine and that consequently he must try to follow along in a small way. This, of course, is to the professor's interest, for the more important the doctrine becomes, the more important the professor becomes as well, and the more splendid his occupation and the greater his reputation. Generally speaking, the professor's and pastor's spiritual counselling is a hoax, for it is calculated to prevent people from entering the kingdom of heaven.[38]

For Kierkegaard, there is a tendency in Christian scholarship to become so preoccupied with transposing Christian truths "into the sphere of the intellectual" that they ignore the "Truth" who stands right in front of them, calling them to leave their nets and follow him.[39] For him, this points to a failure to recognize the essence of Christianity. As he saw it, where there is no Christian living, there is no Christian understanding. "[W]hen the truth is the way, being the truth is a life—and this is indeed how Christ speaks of himself: I am the Truth and the Way and the Life."[40] Therefore, if a particular kind of theological discourse risks being detrimental to the liveliness of a person's discipleship, then something has gone very wrong.

At various points in his writings, Kierkegaard became so caught up in his critique of the intellectualization of Christianity that he became critical of any amount of reflection on Christian doctrine. Indeed, in one journal entry, he goes so far as to write: "I do not have a stitch of doctrine—and doctrine is what people want. Because doctrine is the indolence of aping and mimicking for the learner, and doctrine is the way to sensate power for the teacher, for doctrine collects men."[41] From what we have seen (and could see), he clearly has more than a stitch of doctrine, and he would not want to advance a theology that fell

---

[38] *JP* 4, 3870.

[39] *JP* 4, 4953.

[40] *PC*, 207.

[41] *JP* 6, 6917.

out of line with Christian orthodoxy. Nevertheless, he does not think that further theological digging and probing should have been the priority that it was for theologians in Denmark. For him, in his particular context, there was no immediate need for so much attention to be given to "progress" on this front—in many respects, he seems to think that we would be fine with nothing more than a kind of mere Christianity, to use Richard Baxter's phrase.[42] Indeed, in his view, the ongoing speculative pursuit of theological progress was leading to digression.

One of the prime targets that Kierkegaard had in his sights, was the systematic Christology of Hegelianism. To oversimplify matters, this project attempts to make progress in Christology by trying to work out the logic of the Incarnation by way of philosophical mediation (*Mediering*) or reconciliation (à la Hegel)—a form of mediation that sought to hold the divine and human together within a single system of human understanding.[43] Under this project, for Kierkegaard, the person of Jesus Christ came to be reduced to (or subsumed under) a systematic doctrine for intellectual stimulation. For him, this could not be more backward. Rather than seeing Christology as a witness that directs our attention to Jesus Christ, the person of Jesus Christ was being treated as a person who directs our attention to speculation over Christological puzzles—a pursuit that kept systematic theologians in business. This led him to emphasize that "it is not a doctrine that [Jesus Christ] communicates to you—no he gives you himself."[44] He also writes:

> The Savior of the world, our Lord Jesus Christ, did not come to the world in order to bring a doctrine; he never lectured. Since he did not bring a doctrine, he did not try by way of reasons to prevail upon anyone to accept the doctrine, nor did he try to authenticate it by proofs. His teaching was really his life, his existence...[O]ne does not become a Christian by hearing something about Christianity, by reading something about it, by

---

[42] While this phrase originated with Richard Baxter, it received new popularity through C. S. Lewis' *Mere Christianity*.

[43] See *PC*, 136.

[44] Kierkegaard, *Without Authority*, ed. and trans Howard V. and Edna H. Hong (Princeton: Princeton University Press, 1997), 187.

> thinking about it, or, while Christ was living, by seeing him once in a while or so by going and staring at him all day long. No, a *setting* [*Bestedelse*] (*situation*) is required—venture a decisive act; the proof does not precede but follows, is in and with the imitation that follows Christ.'[45]

For Kierkegaard, God speaks a person into creation, and that person bespeaks God. We are to love and follow this person, and it is by so doing that we come to know God. In this relationship, Jesus Christ must not be reduced to a set of human ideas or principles, which would allow us to miss out on the essential truth of who he is.[46] Kierkegaard's particular focus on the person of Jesus Christ is not something that theologians often associate with him and it has come to be more commonly associated with Dietrich Bonhoeffer and his emphasis on the importance of the "who" question.

In his lectures on Christology, Bonhoeffer stresses that when we approach Jesus Christ, we must resist the temptation to replace the person of Jesus Christ with our own Christologies—ideas that are contained within human systems of understanding. When Christology displaces Christ, our commitment to Christ fixates on "how" questions that become trapped within the immanent sphere of human understanding. We focus on such questions as "how is it possible for Jesus Christ to exist?" As a result, Christ becomes an object that is defined by human demands, rather than the one who himself demands the transformation of human beings. This makes it too easy for us to become caught up in pursuing and conforming to our own Christologies; concepts and principles that do not transform our lives in the way that the person of Jesus Christ does. Accordingly, Bonhoeffer stresses that we need to approach Jesus Christ by asking "who are you?," which is a question that recognizes the "otherness of the

---

[45] Kierkegaard, *Judge for Yourself!*, in *For Self-Examination and Judge for Yourself!*, ed. and trans. Howard V. and Edna H. Hong (Princeton: Princeton University Press, 1990), 191.

[46] *JP* 2, 1904.

other."[47] As we ask this question, we are called to look beyond ourselves to the risen and ascended Jesus Christ.

The connection between Bonhoeffer's Christology and Kierkegaard's is a result of the decisive impact that Kierkegaard had on Bonhoeffer. When Bonhoeffer emphasizes the "who" question, he is channeling Kierkegaard.[48] By so doing, he gave Kierkegaard's Christology a voice that it had not found from Kierkegaard himself, which is why this emphasis is normally associated with Bonhoeffer.[49] Why was it that Kierkegaard was unable to give this position a greater hearing? Why did his message find so much more gravitas under the conveyance of Bonhoeffer? There are many possible reasons for this, but there is one in particular that is worth mentioning here. Arguably, Kierkegaard's greatest weakness was his tendency to overstate his case; and, as we have already seen, this was a particular problem when it came to his critique of Christian doctrine. The disdain he had for theology in Denmark, particularly in his later life, did him no favors, and made it hard for him to be taken seriously. Simultaneously, and partly because of his particular tack, Kierkegaard's theology was overshadowed by the likes of Hans Lassen Martensen who, Kierkegaard comments, "sits there arranging a system of dogmatics" "[w]hile the whole of existence is disintegrating."[50]

---

[47] Dietrich Bonhoeffer, *Berlin, 1932–1933* (Bonhoeffer Works, Vol. 12), ed. L. Rasmussen, trans. I. Best and D. Higgins (Minneapolis: Fortress Press, 2009), 303; see also 300-8.

[48] Dietrich Bonhoeffer, *Christ the Center*, trans. Edwin Robertson (New York: Harper & Row, 1978), 27. Notably, the more recent translation of Bonhoeffer's lectures on Christology (cited above) does not show Bonhoeffer's reference to Kierkegaard because, as Christiane Tietz explains in her excellent chapter on Kierkegaard and Bonhoeffer, "this new edition follows only one student's notes instead of being a compilation of several like the earlier edition was." Christiane Tietz, "Dietrich Bonhoeffer: Standing 'in the tradition of Christian Thinking,'" in Jon Stewart, ed., *Kierkegaard's Influence on Theology—Tome I: German Protestant Theology* (Farnham: Ashgate, 2012), 47 n.14.

[49] Also, on a related note, it was not only Kierkegaard's emphasis on the person of Jesus Christ that had such a major impact on Bonhoeffer, his emphasis on the importance of following and imitating Jesus Christ was a cornerstone for Bonhoeffer's *The Cost of Discipleship*.

[50] *KJN* 6, 151.

What does this have to do with the role of Kierkegaard's paradoxical Christology? First, at risk of being repetitive, it is worth reiterating that Kierkegaard's Christology relies heavily on Christian tradition. Indeed, his very use of paradoxical Christology calls into question the extent of his critique of Christian doctrine.[51] At the same time, his paradoxical Christology also stresses the inability of human understanding to grasp the logic of the Incarnation: to know how we might hold together the propositions "Jesus Christ is fully human" and "Jesus Christ is fully God." It therefore calls for a halt to overly speculative approaches to Christology—to what we might call the quest for the incarnate Jesus (a quest to discover the hidden intricacies of the Incarnation).[52] For him, the logic of the Incarnation is to be believed and confessed, by faith: "the divine and the human have to be believed together, something only faith is capable of doing."[53] Christology, therefore, is not a venture in problem-solving: a project wherein scholars try to make the Incarnation fit into a human system of logic. He writes:

> To *believe* is to believe the divine and human together in Christ. To *comprehend* him [God] is to comprehend his life humanly. But to comprehend his life *humanly* is so far from being more than believing that it means to lose him if there is not believing in addition, since his life is what it is for faith, the *divine*-human. I can understand *myself* in *believing*...but comprehend faith or comprehend Christ, I cannot. On the contrary, I can understand that to be able to comprehend his life in every respect is the most absolute and also the most blasphemous misunderstanding.[54]

---

[51] We learn to embrace Christ in all his paradoxicality by aligning ourselves with the Symbol of Chalcedon, which affirms that Jesus Christ is "to be acknowledged in two natures, inconfusedly, unchangeably, indivisibly, inseparably." In the person of Jesus Christ, there is distinction in unity and unity in distinction: the *two* natures, divine and human, are "concurring in *one* Person," "God the Word, the Lord Jesus Christ." "Symbolum Chalcedonense," in Philip Schaff, ed., *The Creeds of Christendom*, vol. 2 (Grand Rapids: Baker, 1998), 62.

[52] *JP* 2, 1340.

[53] *JP* 4, 4610.

[54] *WA*, 65 (emphasis original).

Christology, for Kierkegaard, is the study of the first-order logic (or Logos) who makes sense of our humanity by reconciling us into faithful relationship with God. Once a person is halted from trying to exceed one's ability to systematize Christ for themselves—by recognising the absolute paradoxicality of Jesus Christ—then one is able to focus on the more important task at hand: following and imitating Jesus Christ, and thereby growing in one's loving and faithful devotion to Christ.

One of the problems and ironies with paradoxical presentations of Jesus Christ, however, is that they can incite the very speculation they seek to subvert—paradoxes are, after all, apparent contradictions that are prone to be disputed. The curious and controlling nature of fallen human reason is such that it is stubborn about letting go of its desire to see theological matters explained in terms that satisfy human systematic frameworks—that satisfy our "how" questions.[55] As such, paradoxical Christology has a tendency to beg "how" questions about the union between Christ's divinity and humanity. The history of such projects, Kierkegaard notes, has been fraught with confusion:

> In the first period of Christendom, when even aberrations bore an unmistakeable mark of one's nevertheless knowing what the issue was, the fallacy with respect to the God-man was either that in one way or another the term "God" was taken away (Ebionitism and the like) or the term "man" was taken away (Gnosticism). In the entire modern age, which so unmistakeably bears the mark that it does not even know what the issue is, the confusion is something different and far more dangerous. By way of didacticism, the God-man has been made into the speculative unity of God and man *sub specie aeterni* [under the aspect of eternity] or made visible in that nowhere-to-be-found medium of pure being, rather than that the God-man is the unity of being God and an individual human being in a historically actual situation. Or Christ has been abolished altogether,

---

[55] Kierkegaard, *Philosophical Fragments* in *Philosophical Fragments and Johannes Climacus*, ed. and trans Howard V. and Edna H. Hong (Princeton: Princeton University Press, 1985), 42-3.

> thrown out and his teaching taken over, and finally he is almost regarded as one regards an anonymous writer: the teaching is the principle thing, is everything.[56]

As this passage suggests, systematic approaches to Christology have led to: (1) zero-sum games between Christ's human and divine nature; (2) the development a "speculative unity of God and man" that directs our attention to an overarching realm within which God and humanity are united; (3) the setting aside of the person of Christ to focus on his teachings. What is Kierkegaard's fourth option? On the one hand, for him, we cannot teach persons to comprehend Christ in the way that we can teach persons how to solve philosophical problems.[57] "[Christ] knows that no human being can *comprehend* him, that the gnat that flies into the candlelight is not more certain of destruction than the person who wants to try to comprehend him or what is united in him: God and man."[58] On the other hand, we do need to come to *know* him because "he is the Savior, and for no human being is there salvation except through him."[59]

What Kierkegaard's paradoxical Christology seeks to direct our attention towards is the person rather than a doctrine—someone to love and respect, not simply observed and speculated over. So he does not simply seek to direct our attention to a paradox; again, his insistence on the paradox seeks to halt conversations that speculate over what we cannot (and should not try to) comprehend. Faith in Christ "does not consist in choosing either one side of the contrast [his lowliness/humanity or his loftiness/divinity] but in choosing a unity of both sides."[60] It consists in believing and trusting in a person and giving him the kind of attention that was given to him by his apostles:

> In the conversation of the apostles one continually gets the impression that they had been personally in the

---

[56] *PC*, 123.

[57] *PC*, 77.

[58] *PC*, 77.

[59] *PC*, 77.

[60] *PC*, 161.

> company of Christ, had lived with him as with a human being. Therefore their speech is very human, although they never do forget the infinite qualitative difference between the God-man and other human beings.[61]

By prioritizing the person of Christ, Kierkegaard directs our attention to one who can be known personally within the limits of our creaturely mode of reference, so that we can relate to him in a way that is comparable to the way in which the apostles relate to Jesus Christ. To be clear, this is not simply to turn attention to Christ's teaching because, for Kierkegaard, what makes the teaching so important is the one from whom they come, and, therefore, the one to whom they witness.[62] Kierkegaard notes that if "someone says that Christ's life is extraordinary because of the results, then this is again a mockery of God because Christ's life is the in-itself-extraordinary."[63] He then adds: "The emphasis does not fall upon the fact that a human being has lived. Only God can attach that much importance to himself, so that the fact that he has lived is infinitely more important than all the results that are registered in history."[64]

The Paradoxical Mediator

> ...there is one God, there is also one mediator between God and humankind, Christ Jesus, himself human. (1 Timothy 2:5)

---

[61] *JP 2*, 1385.

[62] As such, I would argue it is an overstatement for David Law to write: "Kierkegaard's primary concern is with Christ's existential significance. He simply accepts the Christ-event as a brute fact and then attempts to work out the existential consequences of this fact. The decisive issue is not 'Who or what is Christ?' but 'What does Christ mean to me?' Consequently, issues such as the relation between Christ's divinity and humanity, etc., recede into the background." David Law, *Kierkegaard as Negative Theologian*, 183. One can appreciate what Law is trying to say here—that Kierkegaard did not commit much of his energy to developing a nuanced systematic Christology. However, as I have tried to show, Kierkegaard is quite clear that who Jesus Christ is, the God-man, is of decisive significance.

[63] *JP 2*, 1385.

[64] *PC*, 32.

It is hard to think of another verse from Scripture that does a better job of capturing Kierkegaard's Christological vision than 1 Timothy 2:5. Yet he never cites this verse and he only rarely refers to the mediation of Jesus Christ. Why is this? There are a number of major theological themes that receive surprisingly little attention in Kierkegaard's writings and, much of the time, it is because of the way that these themes had come to be associated with the Hegelian philosophy of which he was so critical. The Holy Spirit, the Trinity, the mediation of Christ, participation in Christ, reconciliation (and we could go on) receive very little mention in his writings because of the way they connoted Hegelian theology. The particular difficulty with these terms was that they were being used by Hegelianism to synthesize "God" with humanity. Such synthesizing, for Kierkegaard, was a cornerstone of the cultural Christianity of Denmark. It not only allows but encourages the Gospel to be chopped and changed to fit its particular milieu.

One of the ways that Kierkegaard pushes back against the synthesizing of God and humanity was by insisting "that there is an infinite qualitative difference between God and man."[65] Moreover, he goes so far as to suggest that there is a sense in which "we cannot speak of fellowship with God, and man cannot endure the fellowship, cannot endure continually having only the impression of God's presence."[66] This statement can seem quite out of place for Kierkegaard—who was highly committed to emphasizing the decisiveness of a loving relationship with God. One could put these words down to rhetorical flourish, especially since they appear in the form of a journal entry. However, it would also be possible to interpret this passage in a way that is entirely consistent with his theological vision. For Kierkegaard, direct or immediate fellowship with God, in all God's transcendent glory, really is beyond the scope of what is possible for human beings (in and of themselves). The infinite qualitative difference "always remains."[67] So the relationship with God requires the mediation of the

---

[65] *JP 2*, 1416.

[66] *JP 2*, 1416.

[67] *JP 2*, 1349.

Son. Drawing on John 6:45, he writes: "God directs us to the Son, to the Mediator" and pronounces: "In the Mediator I can be a father to you."[68] By assuming human flesh, the eternal Son mediates God to humanity, thereby allowing human beings to know God according to the limits of their finitude. In this way, "the glory is not directly known as glory but, just the reverse, is known by inferiority, debasement."[69] In Christ, the glory of God is mediated to the lowliness of the world—to a world that is unable to contain God in God's transcendent glory.

Through the mediation of Christ, persons are delivered into a life of fellowship with God in whom the infinite qualitative difference no longer functions as an alienating difference. The person of Christ enables there to be correspondence between God and human beings across the divide. In Christ, God creates a real yet mediated relationship between human beings and God as beings who are infinitely qualitatively different from one another but who are also fully united with one another in Christ.[70] For Kierkegaard, we relate to God by sharing in a faithful relationship with the *person* of Jesus Christ: the God-human, in whom there is *both* mediation between God and humanity *and* reconciliation from the sin that totally alienates us from God.

Again, however, Kierkegaard hesitates to use the language of the mediation to talk about God's relationship to creation. Instead, he primarily chose to talk about Christ's mediatorial role in terms of his paradoxicality. Rather than simply focusing on the way that Christ creates unity between God and humanity, which risks Hegelian connotations, he presents Jesus Christ as one who incomprehensibly and unsettlingly brings God and humanity together, without confusing the creator-creature distinction. For him, it was a paradoxical Christology that was best able to draw attention to this message. The presentation of Jesus Christ as absolute paradox sought to bring a halt to the systematic and depersonalizing attempts to comprehend the logic

---

[68] *JP* 2, 1432.

[69] *JFY*, 161.

[70] See *JP* 2, 1383, *JP* 3, 3646, *JP* 5, 6076; *The Sickness unto Death*, ed. and trans. Howard V. Hong and Edna H. Hong (Princeton: Princeton University Press, 1980), 113-24; and *PC*, 139-40.

of Jesus Christ and, instead, focus attention on the person who invites us to come and follow him. However, as soon as the language of paradox has served this purpose, it should be dropped from discussion. From then on, the discussion should be left to be attentive to the primary theologian (or God-talker): Jesus Christ, God's Word made flesh. It is in this way, to return to our opening quote from Torrance, that come to know "the nearness, the impact of God in all his Majesty and Godness upon man."[71]

---

[71] Torrance, *Karl Barth*, 44.

4.

KIERKEGAARD AND THE BEAUTY OF THE CROSS

Lee C. Barrett

In the popular imagination Kierkegaard is often remembered as the epitome of gloom. A widely-read introduction to Kierkegaard from the mid-twentieth century propagated this characterization by dubbing him "the melancholy Dane."[1] Even serious theologians and philosophers have sometimes shared this view. Karl Barth famously lamented that Kierkegaard, who was a "school" through which every serious theologian must pass, was sadly deficient in Christian joy.[2] Hans Frei remarked that Kierkegaard was a depressed Pelagian who regarded the cultivation of anxiety and despair as meritorious acts.[3] Even more severely, Theodor Adorno critiqued Kierkegaard for being a joyless negator of life who dissolved the real world into a somber solipsistic interiority.[4]

So it may seem wildly counterintuitive to propose that at the core of Kierkegaard's theology is a conviction that individuals can experience exquisite and expansive joy.[5] Even more surprising may be the suggestion that for Kierkegaard the crucifixion of Jesus can elicit a response of spiritual exultation. To justify this claim we must examine Kierkegaard's numerous reflections on the significance of the cross, especially his evocations of its hidden and paradoxical beauty. "Beauty" in this context does not refer to Kierkegaard's category of the "aesthetic," which he usually associated with the pleasures of

---

[1] See H. V. Martin, *The Melancholy Dane* (London: Epworth Press, 1950).

[2] Karl Barth, "Dank und Referenz," *Evangelische Theologie*, vol. 23, 1963, 337-42.

[3] Conversation with the author, February, 1980.

[4] Theodor Adorno, *Kierkegaard. Konstruktion des Ästhetischen* (Tübingen: Mohr, 1933), 34-36.

[5] For a similar argument, see Carl Hughes, *Kierkegaard and the Staging of Desire* (New York: Fordham University Press, 2014).

contemplating harmonious or intriguing objects, and with the pursuit of interesting or self-gratifying experiences. Rather, here "beauty" is used more broadly to suggest a phenomenon that elicits yearning, rapt fascination, and delight in the sheer existence of the adored object.

First, it must be admitted that Kierkegaard often emphasizes the stark horror of the crucifixion. Frequently he uses the story of Jesus' execution to stir up in the reader a devastating sense of guilt, unworthiness, and contrition. Meditation upon the cross should provoke a despairing dissatisfaction with the shape and direction of one's own moral and spiritual life. This goal of afflicting the individual with painful self-knowledge is often overt in Kierkegaard's many calls to become aware of Christ's contemporaneity with the reader.[6] The crucifixion is not a past event to be treated with curiosity or aesthetic admiration, nor is it a theological puzzle to be solved. Rather, Kierkegaard exhorts the reader to view the cross as a mirror that exposes the depths of her own depravity.[7] Often he encourages the individual to visualize herself as a member of the crowd that clamored for Jesus' execution, or at least as one of the multitude who lacked the courage to protest it, and therefore as being personally responsible for his death.[8] The cross exposes the grim reality that each one of us is the sort of person who would have colluded in Jesus' execution. In these contexts Kierkegaard is careful to accentuate the repellant ugliness of the crucifixion before he gestures toward its attractive beauty.

The cross functions to repel the individual and terrify her conscience in yet another way. Whenever Kierkegaard asserts that we are called to follow after Christ our Prototype, he then reminds the reader that this path that we are to follow is the path of extravagant love, which is necessarily the way of the cross. We are required to suffer ostracism, persecution, and misunderstanding, just as Christ did

---

[6] Søren Kierkegaard, *Practice in Christianity*, trans. Howard Hong and Edna Hong (Princeton: Princeton University Press, 1991), 174-9.

[7] Søren Kierkegaard, *Without Authority*, trans. Howard Hong and Edna Hong (Princeton: Princeton University Press, 1997), 55-89.

[8] Søren Kierkegaard, *For Self-Examination* and *Judge for Yourself!*, trans. Howard Hong and Edna Hong (Princeton: Princeton University Press, 1990), 64.

on the cross. This prospect is so daunting that it can crush the individual under the weight of abject fear, which then engenders further remorse and guilt. Kierkegaard stressed this theme relentlessly because he feared that the message of salvation by grace in contemporary Lutheranism had become an excuse for indolence. Given the spiritual complacency of the Danish church, Kierkegaard recommended that the Epistle of James should be "drawn forward," so that the intimidating requirement of following Jesus on the narrow path of suffering would be accentuated.[9] James' injunction to perform works of love should lead to the candid admission that one's own self does not come close to approximating this ideal. Again, this call to a deflating form of self-knowledge does not sound much like an invitation to joy.

In these contexts Kierkegaard, like other devout Lutherans, uses the cross negatively in order to prepare the individual to experience gratitude for the forgiveness of sins accomplished through the crucifixion.[10] Here the crucifixion itself does not seem like an occasion for joy, but rather appears to be a necessary preliminary to the real joy, which is gratitude for the forgiveness of sins and the possibility of reconciliation with God. The cross, which can help the sinner to cultivate a disposition of repentance, is a means to the end of atonement; it is the atonement itself that is joyful. The anguish of Good Friday is only instrumentally related to the joy of Easter morning, as that joy's necessary precondition.

Admittedly Kierkegaard himself often does talk this way, using traditional sacrificial language to describe Christ's work on the cross. He agrees with the main trajectory of the Western Christian doctrinal tradition that the purpose of the crucifixion was that Jesus must suffer and die in order to remove the guilt of lost sinners.[11] But Kierkegaard showed little interest in developing a "theory of the atonement" to explain how the death of an innocent person could bring about the exoneration of the guilty parties. He did not attempt to grasp the

---

[9] Kierkegaard, *For Self-Examination*, 24.

[10] Craig Hinkson, "Luther and Kierkegaard: Theologians of the Cross," *International Journal of Systematic Theology* 3, no. 1 (2001): 27-45.

[11] Kierkegaard, *Practice in Christianity*, 10.

mechanics of God's reconciliation with humanity, as had Anselm, Aquinas, Luther, and Calvin. He shows little interest in explaining how Jesus' death satisfied God's honor, changed the legal situation of humanity *vis à vis* God, or paid a debt owed to God. For Kierkegaard the real mystery is not the cognitive puzzle about how the substitution of Jesus for sinners worked metaphysically. Rather, for Kierkegaard Jesus' suffering and pain in securing the forgiveness of sins should be the central focus. It is this demonstration of suffering love, not the rationale for it, which has the power to stir the heart.

For Kierkegaard the cross does not just afflict and condemn, and then offer the possibility of forgiveness. Rather, in itself the cross can be an occasion for joy. He exhibits this joy in his style of writing, as he waxes lyrical about the beauty of the crucifixion. He also makes this theme of the attractiveness of the cross basic to the logic of his thought about the Christian life. His understanding of the mysterious enticements of the cross cannot be appreciated without considering the role of the crucifixion in his authorship as a whole.

In general, Kierkegaard's work is oriented toward the prospect of a joy that the world can neither give nor take away.[12] He exclaims that "Christian consolation is joy" because this joy predates suffering and is not a response to earthly suffering or a compensation for it.[13] Eternity's joy, which is linked to love and is described as the "highest," far outweighs earthly joy. Similarly, in a communion discourse Kierkegaard exhorts his readers to "rejoice (what infinite joy of love!) in his (God's) love."[14] One of his series of discourses on the lilies and the birds ends with an exuberant call to learn joy from these unlikely

---

[12] Christopher Nelson, "The Joy of It," in *International Kierkegaard Commentary: Christian Discourses* and *The Crisis and A Crisis in the Life of an Actress*, ed. by Robert Perkins (Macon, GA: Mercer University Press, 2004), 161-85. See also John Lippitt, "Kierkegaard's Virtues?" in *Kierkegaard's God and the Good Life*, ed. by Stephen Minister, J. Aaron Simmons, and Michael Strawser (Bloomington: Indiana University Press, 2017), 95-113.

[13] Søren Kierkegaard, *Works of Love*, trans. Howard Hong and Edna Hong (Princeton: Princeton University Press, 1995), 64.

[14] Søren Kierkegaard, *Christian Discourses*, trans. Howard Hong and Edna Hong (Princeton: Princeton University Press, 1997), 284.

instructors.[15] In diverse contexts he enthuses about the blessedness of reconciliation,[16] and characterizes the Christian life as an intimation of eternal joy.[17] Paradoxically, the cross serves as a focal point and stimulus for this joy. In order to understand how a ghastly atrocity could be an occasion for joy, Kierkegaard's remarks about the crucifixion must be situated in the context of his more general statements about God's purpose in becoming incarnate.

In his different voices Kierkegaard implies that the goal of the Incarnation was not just the accomplishment of the forgiveness of sins and humanity's reconciliation with God, but was even more basically the enactment of God's desire for fellowship with humanity. This is most clear in the pseudonym Climacus' parable of the king who sought to be united with a peasant maiden.[18] The impediment to the union was the egregious difference in their social stations, which led the king to fear that the maiden would never be able to understand his love for her. Climacus writes, "Likewise the king could have appeared before the lowly maiden in all his splendor, could have let the sun of his glory rise over her hut, shine on the spot where he appeared to her, and let her forget herself in adoring admiration. This perhaps would have satisfied the girl, but it could not satisfy the king, for he did not want his own glorification but the girl's, and his sorrow would have been grievous because she would not understand him...."[19] The maiden would simply have been dazed by a display of royal power and magnificence. Climacus concludes that the union could only be achieved by the descent of the king rather than by the ascent of the maiden. The king must divest himself of royal glory and share her life as a peasant in order to make mutual comprehension, genuine reciprocity, and trust possible. Climacus insists that this divestment must not be a sham; the monarch must really leave behind his royal prerogatives and not merely

---

[15] Kierkegaard, *Without Authority*, 39.

[16] Kierkegaard, *Christian Discourses*, 268; *For Self-Examination*, 15.

[17] Kierkegaard, *Without Authority*, 44.

[18] Søren Kierkegaard, *Philosophical Fragments* and *Johannes Climacus*, trans. Howard Hong and Edna Hong (Princeton: Princeton University Press, 1985), 26-32.

[19] Ibid., 29.

hide his magnificence under a beggar's cloak. Climacus explains, "For this is the boundlessness of love, that in earnestness and truth and not in jest it wills to be the equal of the beloved, and it is the omnipotence of resolving love to be capable of that which neither the king nor Socrates was capable, which is why their assumed characters were still a kind of deceit."[20]

It is significant that the parable is drawn from the domain of romance and foregrounds the theme of interpersonal union. The presenting problem is not the possible sinfulness of the maiden, and certainly not that of the king. Instead, the focus is on the impediment to mutuality, the glaring disparity in their stations in life. The ultimate goal of the action is not the forgiveness of a guilty party, but is rather the reciprocity and solidarity of both parties. The desired interpersonal relationality necessarily involves an understanding of the partner's motivations, passions, and character.

The story transparently serves as a parable of the Incarnation. Just as Kierkegaard's tale is the narrative of a king who became a peasant, so also Christianity is the story of the God who became a human. Climacus implies that solidarity with humanity, and not just the atonement for sin, is the main purpose of the Incarnation. This divine decision is even more remarkable than the king's desire for union with the maiden. Unlike the king, God does not need to correct an antecedent lack. God's compassion and desire for mutuality are utterly gratuitous.

In many contexts Kierkegaard repeats this concentration on God's desire for relationality in his own voice, often in the communion discourses. He suggests that the sheer presence of Christ with the believer is the primary blessing that Christianity offers. He asserts that human beings have an often unrecognized and unacknowledged yearning for fellowship with God.[21] The presence of this longing for fellowship is not something which the individual gives to oneself, but is

---

[20] Ibid., 32.
[21] Kierkegaard, *Christian Discourses*, 251, 64. See Pia Søltoft, "Erotic Wisdom: On God, Passion, Faith, and Falling in Love," in *Kierkegaard's God and the Good Life*, ed. by Stephen Minister, J. Aaron Simmons, and Michael Strawser (Bloomington: Indiana University Press, 2017), 31-45.

a gift of God. Kierkegaard accentuates this theme of fellowship by praising the joy of being known by Jesus in the intimate way that a shepherd knows his sheep by name.[22] For Kierkegaard the "only joyful thought" is that the individual is loved by God and in a right relationship with God.[23] Similarly, he declares that the only unconditional joy is daring to believe that "God cares for you."[24]

Kierkegaard's focus on Jesus as the God who came to earth is evident in his identification of Jesus' personhood with God the Son. He does not hesitate to apply the language of divinity to Jesus, describing him as "he who was lord of Creation."[25] Similarly he writes that Christ always knew that he was the incarnation of love.[26] By so saying, Kierkegaard was following the "two natures in one person" formula of the Council of Chalcedon. "Person" in this context suggested an entity's principle of self-subsistence, while "nature" suggested the characteristics that are common to a species and determine its classification. The Lutheran confessional documents emphasized the point that the eternal Logos is the personal core of Jesus to which the divine and human attributes, the "natures," must be ascribed. This was articulated in the doctrine of "*anhypostasia*," which asserted that although Jesus possessed human nature, he did not possess a human person. Reflecting this tradition, Kierkegaard refers to Jesus simply as "God." Because of this identification, the Incarnation must be seen as the enactment in time of God's essential self-giving.

This ascription of human attributes to the divine person generates severe conceptual problems. Assuming that the attributes of humanity include finite limitations, even the capacity to suffer, how could these liabilities be attributed to a divine person who is metaphysically perfect? If the divine and human were truly united, how could Jesus experience anything that was authentically human? This

---

[22] Kierkegaard, *Christian Discourses*, 273.

[23] Søren Kierkegaard, *Upbuilding Discourses in Various Spirits*, trans. Howard Hong and Edna Hong (Princeton: Princeton University Press, 1990), 274.

[24] Kierkegaard, *Without Authority*, 43.

[25] Kierkegaard, *Upbuilding Discourses in Various Spirits*, 224.

[26] Kierkegaard, *Practice in Christianity*, 198.

problem inspired Lutheran theologians to elaborate the theme of *kenosis*, the second person of the Trinity's voluntary divestment or suspension of divine potencies, suggested by Philippians 2.[27] To clarify this, they drew a sharp distinction between Christ's state of humiliation during the Incarnation, and his state of exaltation before and after the Incarnation. In spite of this doctrinal consensus, Lutherans did disagree about the question of whether Christ, while retaining the possession of the divine metaphysical perfections in his state of humiliation, refrained from their use, or only concealed their use. This seemingly arcane conceptual puzzle had divided the schools of Tübingen and Giessen in the seventeenth century, and had been revived by Gottfried Thomasius during Kierkegaard's life-time.

Kierkegaard was aware of this Christological speculation from the lectures by H. N. Clausen that he encountered during his student days.[28] Like Clausen, he found the metaphysical theories advanced to explain *kenosis* to be unintelligible and to distract from the more serious business of living the Christian life. But Kierkegaard fully embraced Lutheranism's historic focus on Christ's state of humiliation and the conviction that Christians during their earthly lives know Christ primarily through his humiliation, not his exaltation. Like many of his Lutheran predecessors he often quoted or paraphrased Philippians 2, writing "He who was equal with God took the form of a lowly servant."[29] His Pietist roots reinforced his resistance to metaphysical speculation about the doctrine of *kenosis* while concentrating on its edifying purposes.[30] Kierkegaard exhorts, "Have faith that Christ is God—then call upon him, pray to him, and the rest will work itself out for you."[31] Instead of embroiling himself in the controversy between Tübingen and Giessen, Kierkegaard preferred to simply assert that God

---

[27] For a thorough account, see David Law, *Kierkegaard's Kenotic Christology* (Oxford: Oxford University Press, 2013).

[28] Søren Kierkegaard, *Kierkegaard's Journals and Notebooks*, ed. Niels Cappelørn et. al., (Princeton: Princeton University Press, 2000), vol. 3, 37-39.

[29] Kierkegaard, *Upbuilding Discourses in Various Spirits*, 224.

[30] Christopher Barnett, *Kierkegaard, Pietism, and Holiness* (Farnham, UK: Ashgate, 2011), 66-73.

[31] Kierkegaard, *Kierkegaard's Journals and Notebooks*, 4, 329.

the Son is so powerful that he could bind himself to his incognito, the form of a servant.[32] God can do this without ceasing to be God, without abdicating divinity. Here Kierkegaard's edifying focus fell on the "earnestness" of God the Son's self-imposed and genuine participation in human life. Paradoxically, this abasement is an expression of the omnipotence of divine love, for renouncing omnipotence is itself an act of omnipotence.

The theme of *kenosis* enabled Kierkegaard, like other Lutherans, to assert that ostensibly negative human experiences, including suffering, could be ascribed to the divine person. The state of humiliation allowed Christ to participate in and therefore to empathize with all the tribulations and agonies of the human condition. Therefore the pain of Jesus can be described as the pain of God, a theme not uncommon in the Lutheran "theology of the cross." Intensifying this tradition, Kierkegaard even proposes that it is God who through the God-man says, "My God, my God, why have you forsaken me?"[33]

For Kierkegaard, God's willingness to submit to the conditions of finitude is the ultimate paradox. The real paradox here is not the ostensible speculative puzzle concerning the confluence of the infinite and the finite, but is rather the claim that God would divest God's own self of power and glory in order to be in fellowship with humanity. The concept of God's *kenosis* is so outlandish and counter-intuitive that it could not naturally arise in any human being's heart. According to Kierkegaard, no one could have anticipated that God, instead of wanting to be adored as a cosmic potentate, would instead seek fellowship with lowly human beings. In fact, the divine *kenosis* and drive toward mutuality is so unexpected and unthinkable that it could only be revealed. As Climacus observes, "(For) if the god gave no indication, how could it occur to a man that the blessed god could need him?"[34]

The shock of the Incarnation, disorienting as it is, involves much more than the condescension of the omnipotent God and God's

---

[32] Kierkegaard, *Practice in Christianity*, 132.

[33] Kierkegaard, *Kierkegaard's Journals and Papers*, 5, 348.

[34] Kierkegaard, *Philosophical Fragments*, 36.

participation in the limitations of finitude in general. The dissonance is exacerbated by the kenotic pattern of the specific human life in which the Incarnation was enacted. The truly amazing (and potentially offensive) thing was not just that God became human, but that God did so as a lowly and abased human being. In several places in his authorship Kierkegaard retells the story of Jesus in such a way that the various forms of Christ's lowliness are emphasized.[35] For example, Jesus was born in poverty, in an obscure province of the Roman Empire. He refused to pursue worldly power, and thereby incited the wrath of the mob that longed for a politically triumphant messiah.[36] He was ostracized by his own family and rejected by his own village. His closest followers repeatedly failed to understand the nature of his message and mission. Furthermore, he experienced physical deprivation, hunger, and torture.

Kierkegaard highlights the fact that Christ's most severe form of suffering was due to his faithfulness to his "incognito." Because true solidarity with humanity required that Christ's divine power and glory be concealed in the form of lowliness, just as the king's majesty had been concealed, his divinity was in no way obvious. The personhood of God enacted in the life of Christ could not be immediately perceived by his contemporaries or deduced from such empirical evidence as the performance of miracles.[37] Because of this incognito, Christ could not directly manifest his love in a way that his followers could comprehend; he could not use his omnipotence to heal all their woes and rectify all their injustices. Consequently the claim that God was in Christ could be denied and rejected, even by eye-witnesses. Christ's most severe pain was his recognition that his efforts to be in fellowship with humanity might backfire by causing offense and becoming a stumbling block to many. But out of love God accepted the risk of being misunderstood and having the divine desire for fellowship frustrated.[38] The magnitude of divine self-abnegation is evidenced by

---

[35] Kierkegaard, *Practice in Christianity*, 85-144.
[36] Kierkegaard, *Judge for Yourself!*, 176-8.
[37] Kierkegaard, *Practice in Christianity*, 27.
[38] Kierkegaard, *Without Authority*, 63-4.

the fact that God makes God's own self vulnerable to disappointment and rejection.

God's assumption of lowliness contradicts all ordinary expectations about how a *metaphysically* perfect God should act. The humble life of Jesus is an offense to all natural concepts of transcendent power operating by sheer force. Kierkegaard critically observes that this common view of divine potency is actually rooted in the human lust for power.[39] Ordinary understandings of God's nature are a projection of what human beings would like to be. The alleged metaphysical perfections of God are actually qualities that people covet for themselves.[40] Because people are vulnerable and weak, they imagine a god who is free of their liabilities and chooses to assure their prosperity and felicity through an exercise of might. Because of this, the prospect of divine lowliness is an intolerable offense, for a lowly and abased God cannot guarantee earthly health, felicity, and power.

It is in the context of the offensiveness of the divine lowliness and the divine incognito that the crucifixion of Jesus must be interpreted. The crucifixion was the apogee of humanity's habitual hostility to divine *kenosis*. The pseudonym Anti-Climacus summarizes Jesus' life by writing, "…continual mistreatment finally ends in death."[41] In his own voice Kierkegaard laments that Jesus' abasement culminates in the horror of crucifixion.[42] Consequently, the cross can serve as a symbol of Christ's entire life. To emphasize this Kierkegaard cautions that Jesus should not be imagined as the indulgent and undemanding companion of popular piety. The sentimentalized and domesticated Jesus, epitomized by the infant with the holy family, should not be the focus of worship.[43] Moreover, aesthetic admiration of Jesus' glory must be avoided.[44] Rather, Jesus should first and foremost

---

[39] Ibid., 60-2.

[40] Kierkegaard, *Judge for Yourself!*, 174-82.

[41] Kierkegaard, *Practice in Christianity*, 168.

[42] Kierkegaard, *Christian Discourses*, 277.

[43] Kierkegaard, *Without Authority*, 55.

[44] Kierkegaard, *Judge for Yourself!*, 121.

be remembered as the crucified one, rejected and murdered by the very species that he was trying to help.

Kierkegaard explains that the hostility of humanity toward Jesus turns lethal because human beings cannot tolerate the spectacle of self-giving love. It is bad enough that Jesus embraced lowliness and eschewed comfort, security, and power, but it is even worse that he did so in order to love others with no thought for his own well-being. Kierkegaard mourns that the apostles "had the dreadful experience that love is not loved, that it is hated, that it is mocked, that it is spat upon, that it is crucified in this world..."[45] In relating the story of Jesus' persecution, Anti-Climacus states, "And he, the abased one, he was love...."[46] He elaborates by telling a story of a child who was shown a picture of the crucifixion and then told that the executed man was the most loving individual who ever lived.[47] He continues, "Tell the child that he (the crucified man) was love, that he came to the world out of love, took upon himself the form of a lowly servant, lived for only one thing—to love and to help people...."[48] In an ethical-religious essay, another pseudonymous author narrates a similar story of a child and a picture of the Crucified One,[49] and then clarifies that "He was crucified precisely because he was love, or to develop it further, because he refused to be self-loving."[50] Christ willed the Incarnation in order to enact God's love for human beings even though he knew that it would put him on the cross.[51] Out of love Christ announced that he was the enactment of God's self-abasing nature and voluntarily accepted the inevitable consequence of being killed by a virulently hostile humanity. The ascription of such extreme other-regarding and self-sacrificial love to God clashes with humanity's drive for self-aggrandizement and self-protection. The exposure that the selfless ways of God and the self-interested ways of the world are incompatible incites outraged

---

[45] Kierkegaard, *For Self-Examination*, 84.

[46] Kierkegaard, *Practice in Christianity*, 170-1.

[47] Ibid., 174-5.

[48] Ibid., 176.

[49] Kierkegaard, *Without Authority*, 55.

[50] Ibid., 59.

[51] Kierkegaard, *For Self-Examination*, 60.

humanity to eliminate Jesus, the source of this unsolicited and unwanted truth. For Kierkegaard this complicity in the execution of Jesus should not be restricted to some group of uniquely evil malefactors. Again and again he exhorts the individual to see herself as being present at the crucifixion as a willing accomplice.[52]

But the cross does much more than expose human selfishness and thereby cause humanity to be offended. Even more importantly the story of the crucifixion has a mysterious attractive power. Anti-Climacus makes this explicit, for after narrating the story of the crucifixion he directly asks the reader "Is this sight not able to move you?"[53] A few pages later he observes, "This is how it moved the apostles, who knew nothing and wanted to know nothing but Christ and him crucified—can it not so move you also?"[54] The spectacle of God's suffering love on the cross reveals the extent to which God was willing to go in order to be in fellowship with humanity. This vision of God's love is so dramatic that it has the power to move the human heart to love God in return. Kierkegaard writes that Christ "performs love's miracle, so that—without doing anything—by suffering he moves everyone who has a heart."[55] Anti-Climacus adds that Christ's radical act of love rivals the manifestation of divine beneficence evident in the act of creation.[56] The crucifixion, horrific as it was, should nevertheless evoke amazement, gratitude, and joy.

According to Kierkegaard the story of the crucifixion does not just evoke emotions in the way that an inert aesthetic object like a painting might; rather, the narrative actively draws the individual to Christ. The experience of joy is not a self-generated response to a passive portrayal of the crucifixion. Rather, Kierkegaard stresses the agency of the Crucified One that precedes every human response, actively reaching out to the individual. It is the prior compelling power of the depiction of Christ on the cross that initiates and sustains the

---

[52] See, for example, Kierkegaard, *Christian Discourses*, 278.

[53] Kierkegaard, *Practice in Christianity*, 171.

[54] Ibid., 178.

[55] Kierkegaard, *Christian Discourses*, 280.

[56] Kierkegaard, *Practice in Christianity*, 176.

attraction. For Kierkegaard, it is crucial to recognize that it is Christ in his abasement, not in his loftiness, who has the ability to issue the invitation to come to Him and rest.[57] The cross is associated with the open and welcoming arms of Jesus, for it is the Crucified One who has the power to draw the individual. Appropriately, Kierkegaard's final discourse in a series for Friday communion services concludes with Christ the abased one stretching out His arms at the Eucharistic table.[58]

The paradoxically attractive power of the cross is a function of the beauty of self-sacrificial love. Christ's refusal to seek anything for Himself and to empty Himself for the sake of others is sublime, for those who have eyes to see. The human heart, if it does not succumb to offense, can thrill at the spectacle of God's voluntary submission to suffering and death in order to enact God's solidarity and love. The cross was the climax of the kenotic purpose of God to sacrifice everything in order to be in communion with a humanity that had an allergic reaction to selfless love. The sufferings and death of Christ manifest the glorious and enthralling extent of God's commitment to be in fellowship with humanity, no matter what the cost. As Kierkegaard's tales of the boy who was shown a picture of the crucifixion suggest, it is the sheer attractive power of the vision of a self-emptying love so intense that it would embrace suffering and death that draws the heart.

These considerations reframe Kierkegaard's treatment of the theme of the incognito. The divine glory is not just hidden in Christ's lowliness, as if the loftiness and the lowliness were genuine opposites. Rather, the opposition is only apparent, for the divine glory precisely is the beauty of self-giving love willing to assume the form of lowliness. The life of Christ reaching its climax in the cross is the true glory of divine love. Kierkegaard writes, "But just as the essentially Christian always places opposites together, so the glory is not directly known as glory but, just the reverse, is known by inferiority, debasement—the cross that belongs to everything that is essentially Christian is here also."[59] Revelation through concealment is a function of the fact that

---

[57] Kierkegaard, *Christian Discourses*, 265.
[58] Ibid., 300.
[59] Kierkegaard, *Judge for Yourself!*, 161.

exaltation occurs precisely through abasement. The cross shows that the sublimity of divine love can only be manifested as lowliness and suffering.[60] Put starkly, the exaltation of Christ is his abasement; the two states are not strictly sequentially related.

Attraction to the sheer beauty of Christ's self-giving spawns many related types of joy and solace, all of which Kierkegaard frequently describes. For example, he devotes considerable attention to the multiple ways that the woes that a follower of Christ encounters can be reframed so that they become pathways to joy, rather than mere tragedies. The suffering Christ can function as a comforter to those in anguish because on the cross he shared the pain which they experience.[61] The empathy of the suffering Christ gives hope to all those who are heavy laden.[62] Particularly in *Upbuilding Discourses on Various Occasions* Kierkegaard comforts struggling Christians who are daunted by the prospect of persecution by enabling them to find a sense of blessedness even in the midst of tribulation. Encountering opposition and persecution can assure the questioning pilgrim that that she is indeed on the right path, for that path is the way of the cross.[63] Even when the follower of Christ is afflicted with misunderstanding, ostracism, and alienation, that follower can be consoled. The suffering disciple knows that God's desire is to enable humanity to mature toward the bliss of loving selflessly, even though that nurture is painful. Furthermore, human sagacity's inability to discern the purpose of suffering, and the doubts about God's goodness that tragedy provokes, can be reconceived as the joyful darkness in which prudential considerations vanish. It is more joyful to assume that God is loving, even in the midst of apparent afflictions, that to search for a theodicy to exculpate God from accusations of negligence or malevolence. Moreover, suffering educates the individual to let go of preferential self-will, for this renunciation of ego-centrism is an essential

---

[60] Ibid., 234-9.

[61] Kierkegaard, *Christian Discourses*, 266.

[62] Kierkegaard, *Without Authority*, 185-6.

[63] Kierkegaard, *Upbuilding Discourses in Various Spirits*, 226-7.

component of true joy.⁶⁴ In all of these instances suffering is transmuted into joy by seeing it as being potentially Christomorphic and cruciform.

Kierkegaard elaborates another kind of joy in the cross by reframing traditional Lutheran doctrines of the atonement and the theme of the relief that the crucifixion provides for the anguished conscience.⁶⁵ On the cross Jesus' forgiveness of his enemies was a revelation of the depth of God's mercy, showing that even the crowd that crucified Jesus was not beyond the scope of God's compassion.⁶⁶ Kierkegaard's communion discourses exult in the incomprehensible compassion exhibited in the forgiveness of sins and the stunning magnitude of mercy. Kierkegaard insists that the individual's sense of reconciliation is due to the attractive power of the cross, for we cannot do anything to become receptive to the offer of forgiveness. Kierkegaard writes, "If at the Communion table you want to be capable of the least little thing yourself, even merely to step forward yourself, you confuse everything, you prevent the reconciliation, make the satisfaction impossible."⁶⁷ We cannot even repent properly by our own powers; our contrition is elicited by the spectacle of the cross. Our response to Christ's atoning work should simply be to rejoice and be silent. Unlike many Lutheran theologians, Kierkegaard was more interested in the beauty of forgiveness and reconciliation than in the escape from divine punishment and the logistics of atonement.

Furthermore, the spectacle of the crucifixion has a joyfully transformative impact on the individual's mode of relating to her neighbors. Christ functions for Kierkegaard not only as the Redeemer but also as the Prototype, as the revelation of humanity as God intended it to be.⁶⁸ From his Pietist roots Kierkegaard absorbed an intense

---

⁶⁴ Kierkegaard, *Upbuilding Discourses on Various Occasions*, 335.

⁶⁵ Kierkegaard, *Without Authority*, 158-9.

⁶⁶ Søren Kierkegaard, *Eighteen Upbuilding Discourses*, trans. Howard Hong and Edna Hong (Princeton: Princeton University Press, 1990), 338.

⁶⁷ Kierkegaard, *Christian Discourses*, 298-99.

⁶⁸ See Sylvia Walsh *Living Christianly: Kierkegaard's Dialectic of Christian Existence* (University Park: The Pennsylvania State University Press, 2005), 51-112.

appreciation for the theme of the *imitatio Christi*.[69] This "following after" Christ is the pursuit of the kenotic pattern of self-giving love and its necessary embrace of lowliness and probable hostility. The story of Jesus, including the crucifixion, reveals not only the *kenosis* of the divine nature, but also the *kenosis* that should typify human lives. The human life of Jesus exhibits a self-emptying pattern that has its source in the abasement of God the Son, and then should be replicated in the lives of Jesus' followers. The hidden font of love, "however quiet in its concealment," is a "gushing spring" that flows into the disciple's visible works of love for the neighbor.[70] Because this self-giving love is the "highest,"[71] Kierkegaard rhapsodizes about the eternal joy of "redoubling" (although in quite imperfect ways) Christ's self-giving that culminates in the crucifixion.

This following after Christ the Prototype is not just an intentional emulation accomplished by the individual's will power. Neither is the life of love an instance of obedience to a heteronymous and burdensome commandment (although the command to love the neighbor does help stabilize the will and thereby nurtures love).[72] Following after the Prototype is an elicited response, not a purely external norm. Here, too, the beauty of the crucifixion plays a determinative role. Kierkegaard's assumption is that an individual tends to become like that which she loves. Consequently, if a person loves the love exhibited in Christ's ultimate self-giving, that enthusiasm for love will manifest itself in the individual's attitudes, passions, and behavior. This is evident in Kierkegaard's narrations of the story of the young boy who was shown a picture of the most loving person who had ever lived and who was then killed by those he was attempting to love. Eventually the boy finds the picture of Christ on the cross to be so enticing that he wants to become like the man in the picture; in fact, he

---

[69] See Barnett, *Kierkegaard, Pietism and Holiness*, 66-73.

[70] Kierkegaard, *Works of Love*, 9.

[71] See Michael Strawser, "Love Is the Highest," in *Kierkegaard's God and the Good Life*, 16-30.

[72] See Robert C. Roberts, "Kierkegaard and Ethical Theory," in *Ethics, Love, and Faith in Kierkegaard*, ed. Edward Mooney (Bloomington, IN: Indiana University Press, 2008), 72-92.

"want(s) to become the picture."[73] (In contexts like this Kierkegaard is quick to add that Jesus' work as the Redeemer of humanity from sin cannot be emulated; the follower of Christ must avoid messianic delusions.) The imitation of Christ is fueled by falling in love with the sublimity of Christ's unrestricted self-giving, most evident on the cross.

Even here the beauty of the cross is hidden, for the realization that following Jesus necessarily entails the possibility of persecution can trigger repulsion rather than attraction.[74] Nevertheless, even this initial trepidation can be transmuted into the joy of discipleship. The prospect of suffering love is so attractive that it can inspire a yearning to accept persecution and to be sacrificed as Christ was, as happened with the boy in Kierkegaard's story. For Kierkegaard this is not masochistic delight in suffering for its own sake. Rather, the willingness to accept suffering is a by-product of the self-forgetful joy of loving the neighbor in spite of the neighbor's hostility.

To conclude, Kierkegaard's many reflections on the cross suggest that humiliation and exaltation are not purely sequential in the life of Christ, and they are not purely sequential in the follower's cruciform life. The follower of Christ should not be motivated by the anticipation of future glory, as if exaltation chronologically follows a period of lowliness which is entirely left behind. If the individual's pious expectations were focused on a future glory devoid of self-emptying, then the beauty of self-giving love, experienced in the present, would be obscured. Exaltation would then be nothing but a selfish reward for an obedient life or a compensation for earthly misery. Against this view, Kierkegaard insists that the follower's exaltation and joy is not a contingent benefit or a reward. Rather, it is the natural fruit of the individual's delight in the sublimity of divine self-emptying, a delight that generates identification with Christ's love and a desire to emulate it. Consequently, eternal blessedness will be the perfection of the self-giving that should characterize temporal existence. Joy is the organic consequence of a life of love that entails suffering, a life inspired by the kenotic pattern revealed most vividly by Jesus on the

---

[73] Kierkegaard, *Without Authority*, 55.

[74] Kierkegaard, *Practice in Christianity*, 105-21.

cross. If offense is avoided, God's extreme self-giving for the sake of mutuality can awaken a delight in the beauty of love, for God has implanted a taste for radically other-regarding love in the human heart. The cross can elicit joy because individuals can develop an *eros* for *agape*.

5.

BUSYNESS, WORRY AND THE PROTOTYPICAL LOVE OF CHRIST: ANOTHER LOOK AT THE CHARACTER OF KIERKEGAARD'S ETHICS IN *WORKS OF LOVE*

G. P. Marcar[1]

Introduction

Amongst the most serious objections to Kierkegaard's ethics in *Works of Love* (1847) is that it does not seek to change temporal socio-economic or political conditions; on these matters, it is alleged, Kierkegaard's thought is apathetic. After first discussing Jamie Ferreira's widely accepted answer to this charge, this chapter will further problematise the issue. Rather than downplaying the implications of Kierkegaard's claims, I will set the vision of *Works of Love*'s ethics against the intertextual backdrop of Kierkegaard's thought on the individual's relatedness to God, and the nature of the love which God mandates towards others. The linchpin of both these strands of thought is the figure of Jesus Christ: the self-revelation of God and "the prototype" for humanity. The result of this framing, it will be argued, is to heighten the potentially objectionable nature of Kierkegaard's remarks.

The Accusation of Otherworldliness in *Works of Love*

The charge of otherworldliness against Kierkegaard's 1847 *Works of Love* (*WOL*) commonly centres upon a much-discussed passage at the

---

[1] The material in this chapter originates from G. P. Marcar, "Temporal Goods, Divine Love and the Poverty of Christ: or, how Kierkegaard's Ethic in *Works of Love* is Economically Apathetic," *Participatio*, Supplemental vol. 5: "Søren Kierkegaard as a Christian, Incarnational Theologian" (2019): 102-126. The author would like to sincerely thank *Participatio* for feedback on the original piece and for the opportunity to re-present the material.

beginning of *WOL*'s discourse "IIIB: Love is a Matter of Conscience." In this passage, Kierkegaard points towards the economically disadvantaged within society, epitomized by his figure of a "poor, wretched charwoman," and argues that what Christianity advises is for every person (including the charwoman) not to "worry" or busy themselves [*travlt*] about changing their socio-economic conditions so as to achieve a higher social status.[2] The change in referent which occurs within Christianity from the temporal to one's relationship to the eternal/God means that "in inwardness everything is changed," while externally all remains the same.[3] Indeed, Kierkegaard comments that although people have "foolishly busied [*travlt*] themselves in the name of Christianity" to show that men and women should be socially and economically equal, Christianity has never even "desired" such equality.[4] It is on the basis of these provocative comments that Kierkegaard has been read as an apathetic thinker, economically naïve at best, and a "disingenuous advocate" for the bourgeois class of his time at worst.[5]

---

[2] Søren Kierkegaard, *Works of Love*, trans. David F. Swenson and Lillian Marvin Swenson (Princeton, NJ: Princeton University Press, 1946), 110-11. Where the original Danish words and phrases from this text are cited, these can be found in Søren Kierkegaard, *Kjerlighedens Gjerninger: nogle christelige Overveielser i Talers Form* (C.A. Reitzel, 1862). See also *Søren Kierkegaards Skrifter* (*SKS*).

[3] Ibid., 112. Throughout *Works of Love*, Kierkegaard often speaks of "the eternal" in a way which implies its synonymity with God's love. Notably, in his opening "Prayer" to *Works of Love*, Kierkegaard addresses God as "Eternal Love." See Ibid., 4. For a more detailed examination of this point, see also Andrew Burgess, "Kierkegaard's Concept of Redoubling and Luther's *Simul Justus*," in *International Kierkegaard Commentary 16: Works of Love*, ed. Robert L. Perkins (Macon, GA: Mercer University Press, 1999), 39–55.

[4] Kierkegaard, *Works of Love*, 112–13.

[5] David R Law, "Cheap Grace and the Cost of Discipleship in Kierkegaard's *For Self-Examination*," in *International Kierkegaard Commentary 21: For Self-Examination and Judge for Yourself*, ed. Robert L. Perkins (Macon, GA: Mercer University Press, 2002), 111–42. For the classical formulation of this charge against Kierkegaard's ethic, see Theodor W. Adorno, "On Kierkegaard's Doctrine of Love," *Studies in Philosophy and Social Science* 8 (1939): 413–29.

Ferreira's Defence of Kierkegaard

Among the most persuasive attempts to rescue Kierkegaard from these readings is that of Jamie Ferreira. In her commentary on *WOL*, Ferreira argues that Kierkegaard's apparent dismissal of socio-economic conditions is not intended to promote an attitude of apathy, but to ensure that there can be no grounds for excluding anyone from the commandment to love your neighbor.[6] In support of this, Ferreira points towards the formal structure of IIA-IIC in *WOL*. Whereas IIB focuses on the object of Christian love—the "neighbor"—and maintains that no one can be excluded, IIC ("*Thou* shalt love") focuses upon the subject of love's duty and argues that no one can exclude themselves from the obligation.

Taken together, Ferreira argues that the three chapters which comprise the second deliberation of *WOL* (IIA, IIB and IIC) "provide a formal account of the unconditionality of the commandment."[7] Seen in this context, the temporal conditions which Kierkegaard instructs his reader to ignore are those which "blind us to our kinship" and thereby undermine the command to love one's neighbor.[8] Turning to the example of the charwoman in "IIIB: Love is a Matter of Conscience," Ferreira argues that Kierkegaard addresses this hypothetical figure in her particular circumstances, in order to illustrate that even the poorest person is equal to the richest in her capacity to love the neighbor. Ferreira thus paraphrases Kierkegaard's advice in IIIB: "do not think that changing such external distinctions can make it easier for you to fulfil your obligations of love...as if it would be easier to be a better Christian if one were also a 'Madame.'"[9] Kierkegaard's central point here, for Ferreira, is not to deny the importance of socio-economic conditions *per se*, but rather to affirm that all human beings, irrespective of their temporal situation, are equal in their capacity to

---

[6] M. Jamie Ferreira, *Love's Grateful Striving: A Commentary on Kierkegaard's Works of Love* (Oxford: Oxford University Press, 2001), 56.

[7] M. Jamie Ferreira, "Equality, Impartiality, and Moral Blindness in Kierkegaard's 'Works of Love'," *The Journal of Religious Ethics* 25.1 (1997): 74.

[8] Ibid., 76.

[9] Ferreira, *Love's Grateful Striving*, 96.

obey the commandment to love and follow their consciences "before God."

The contention of this paper is that Ferreira too easily dismisses the extent to which Kierkegaard's thought seems to advocate disregarding temporal matters in favour of focusing upon the eternal. As has been pointed out, one should not expect a mid-19th century thinker such as Kierkegaard to advocate a paternalistic social or economic program.[10] Nevertheless, Kierkegaard's steadfast rejection of worldly cares remains striking. It is not simply that Kierkegaard's comments risk legitimizing a conformist attitude towards the *status quo*.[11] As this paper will aim to elaborate further, seen through the lens of *Purity of Heart Is to Will One Thing* (*POH*)[12] and Kierkegaard's *Discourses*, Kierkegaard can be seen to advocate a dismissal of temporal goods altogether.

The Commandment to Love thy Neighbor in IIA, IIB and IIC of *Works of Love*

One point at which Ferreira's reading may be instructively challenged is in her reading of IIA-C in the first series of *WOL*. As outlined above, Ferreira regards these deliberations as structured to collectively give an account of Christian love's unconditionality. Within this framework, IIA posits the imperative-form of the command ("shalt"), IIB that its object (the "neighbor") is everyone, and IIC that no ethical subject ("thou") can exclude themselves from its remit. In what follows, I will argue that, particularly when viewed together with Kierkegaard's other writings, this is not where the pressure of the text lies. Rather, Kierkegaard's unrelenting emphasis in these discourses is on the divine imperative. While it is true that Kierkegaard reads the commandment as mandating that every human being love all others, the overriding theme

---

[10] Margaret Daphne Hampson, *Kierkegaard: Exposition and Critique* (Oxford: Oxford University Press, 2013), 212.

[11] Sylvia Walsh, "Other-Worldliness in Kierkegaard's Works of Love—A Response," *Philosophical Investigations* 22. 1 (1999): 83.

[12] Although cited in its separately published form here, *Purity of Heart Is to Will One Thing*, also titled "An Occasional Discourse," was written as the first part of *Upbuilding Discourses in Various Spirits* (1847).

of these discourses is that the individual is subject to a divine command, to which he must respond immediately with the whole of his being.

IIA and IIB: The Commandment

This point can be illuminated by looking to Kierkegaard's treatment of the Parable of the Good Samaritan (Luke 10) in *WOL*. This parable has often been discussed by commentators as if its primary message was the universality of the neighbor and his identity as anyone in need of help. Perhaps in greater faithfulness to the text, however, this is not how Kierkegaard reads the parable.

Kierkegaard first references the Good Samaritan in "IIA: *Thou Shalt Love Thy Neighbor.*" In answering the question of "who is my neighbor?," Kierkegaard writes that Christ directs his questioner's attention to the subject of mercy, rather than its object. "Christ does not talk about knowing one's neighbor, but about oneself being a neighbor."[13] The neighbor, for Kierkegaard, is one who recognizes that he has a duty to love. It is the active dutifulness of love, seen in Christ's closing words to his questioner in Luke 10 of "[g]o and do likewise," which for Kierkegaard provides the key to understanding not just this parable, but the whole of Christianity. Christ's answer, Kierkegaard writes, may be regarded as implicitly etched "by the side of every word" in the Bible.[14] Kierkegaard's message here is one to which he returns repeatedly in *WOL* and elsewhere: Christians must not be preoccupied with self-interested thoughts or concerns, but must instead adhere to God's will without delay.

Against the "double-mindedness" of thinking that Christianity advocates both commanded neighbor-love and natural love, Kierkegaard insists that true Christianity thinks only of the former.[15] The correct pattern of Christian praxis is to direct one's attention to God in prayer, after which "the first [person] you meet is your neighbor whom you *must* love."[16] The category of "neighbor" here is a function

---

[13] Kierkegaard, *Works of Love*, 19.
[14] Ibid., 38.
[15] Ibid., 37–38.
[16] Ibid., 43.

of the divine imperative; the true object of Christian love remains God.[17] For Kierkegaard, all earthly love and friendship is self-love, love for "the other I" which effectively amounts to "self-worship."[18] The object of love is therefore either one's self (earthly love) or God (Christianity). In neither is the object the human "other." Put another way, the central message of IIB is not that the object of divinely-commanded love is every human being (although Kierkegaard does affirm this), but that earthly love and friendship are dethroned by the divine imperative ("shalt").

IIC: The Individual Subject of the Commandment

The ethical subject, or human "thou," of IIC's title is the single individual, "to whom eternity unceasingly speaks" to give the imperative to love his neighbor.[19] In yet another echo of Christ's closing words in Luke 10 of "[g]o and do likewise," IIC begins by reaffirming the urgency of the imperative: "So then go out and practice it."[20] In order to do this, Kierkegaard encourages the ethical subject to close his eyes and "become merely an ear for hearing the word of the commandment."[21] When eternity is the object of one's attention in this way, all temporal demarcations become irrelevant. That which is loved about the other is the presence of the eternal itself, which Kierkegaard likens to a "watermark" in all human beings.[22] In attending only to the eternal and its command to love the eternal, the ethical subject therefore adopts an attitude of disregard towards temporal features.

Only by loving one's neighbor as oneself can one "accomplish the highest," which is to serve the will of God as an "instrument in the hand of Providence [*Redskab i Styrelsens Haand*]."[23] Kierkegaard's logic in IIA-IIC may therefore be said to follow the overall structure of Matthew 22:34-41, where the command to "love thy neighbor as

---

[17] Ibid., 48.
[18] Ibid., 45–48.
[19] Ibid., 74.
[20] Ibid., 51.
[21] Ibid., 56–57.
[22] Ibid., 73.
[23] Ibid., 71; see also Ibid., 226.

thyself" is preceded by the imperative to unreservedly love and obey God "with all thy heart and with all thy soul and with all thy mind."[24] Indeed, Kierkegaard notably orders the focuses of each first-series discourse in *WOL* according to the ordering of objects in Matthew 22:34–41: God (the "*shalt*" of IIA), others ("*neighbor*" in IIB), self (the "*thou*" of IIC). The reason for this, I submit, is that for Kierkegaard all Christian love results from, and is directed towards, serving the will of the eternal/God.[25]

It is with this context in mind, I argue, that one is best able to understand the contours of what follows in Kierkegaard's third discourse (IIIA and IIIB) of *WOL*.

Another look at IIIA and IIIB: Busyness, Distraction and Double-Mindedness

Kierkegaard begins "IIIA: Love is the Fulfilment of the Law" with the story of the "man who had two sons" in Matthew 21. One son promises to do his father's will, but does not, while the other does not make this promise and yet acts. Drawing again on Christ's answer to the question of "who is my neighbor?" in Luke 10, Kierkegaard seeks to elucidate how the Christian, akin to the dutiful son in Matthew 21, acts immediately in order to fulfil the imperative to love one's neighbor.[26] Rather than examining the parameters of who should be loved, Christ's answer in the form of an imperative ("go and do likewise") cuts short the conversation and demands an ethical response.[27] As Kierkegaard

---

[24] See Ibid., 17. This also aligns with Luke 10, where the same injunction to neighbor-love is stated, directly prior to the Parable of the Good Samaritan, in the form of a single commandment with two clauses: "You shall love the Lord your God with all your heart, and with all your soul, and with all your strength, and with all your mind; and your neighbor as yourself" (Luke 10:27).

[25] For an account of how this conviction continues to underpin Kierkegaard's ethic in *Works of Love*'s second series of discourses, see G. P. Marcar, "The Divine Relationship Ethics of Kierkegaard's Love-Sleuth in *Works of Love*." *Studies in Christian Ethics*, 32.3 (2019): 341-51.

[26] Kierkegaard, *Works of Love*, 79–80.

[27] Ibid., 79.

sees it, Christ is here concerned with neither the object nor the subject of Christian love, but rather with its form as an imperative from God.

In Kierkegaard's view, worldliness and busyness have become "inseparable ideas."[28] Whether or not human beings are busy depends not on how they do things, but upon the object of their attention. If their object is the "manifold" of temporal matters, then they will be "divided and distracted" in their efforts and therefore "busy."[29] If, however, a person's love is focused entirely on the eternal, "undividedly present in every utterance" and "perpetually active," this is not busyness.[30] The problem of busyness, distraction and double-mindedness is also the subject of Chapter 7 of *POH*, which was published in the same year as *WOL*. Here, Kierkegaard's aim is to focus on the most common form of double-mindedness which prevents the individual from pursuing the Good in truth: commitment to the Good which is only "to a certain degree."[31] Busyness, for Kierkegaard, lies within double-mindedness, just as "stillness dwells in the desert."[32] Kierkegaard gives a hypothetical with clear parallels to the biblical parable with which he begins IIIA:

> Suppose that there were two men: a doubleminded man, who believes he has gained faith in a loving Providence, because he had himself experienced having been helped, even though he had hardheartedly sent away a sufferer whom he could have helped; and another man whose life, by devoted love, was an instrument in the hand of Providence [*Redskab i*

---

[28] Ibid., 80.

[29] Ibid., 81.

[30] Ibid., 80–81. Kierkegaard also no doubt has the rest of Luke 10 in mind here. Following the parable of the Good Samaritan, Luke 10:38-42 describes how Christ and his disciples were hosted by a woman called Martha and her sister, Mary. Mary sits at Christ's feet and focuses upon his words, while Martha, by contrast, is said to have been busily distracted [*travlt*] by her hosting duties and "worried" [*Bekymring*] about "many things." After observing this double-mindedness, Christ goes on to state that "only one thing" is necessary and that "Mary has chosen the better part" (Luke 10:42).

[31] Søren Kierkegaard, *Purity of Heart Is to Will One Thing; Spiritual Preparation for the Office of Confession* (New York: Harper, 1956), 104.

[32] Ibid., 108.

Forsynets Haand], so that he helped many suffering ones, although the help he himself had wished continued to be denied him.[33]

Just as the brother in Matthew 21 who said "yes" to God did not keep his promise, so too the "double-minded" man in *POH*, Chapter 7 believed in loving divine providence and yet did not follow that divine will in relation to others. This contrasts with the brother who said "no" in Matthew 21 but nevertheless did God's will, and the abovementioned man whose personal belief (or lack thereof) is not mentioned by Kierkegaard, but who was in any case a single-minded "instrument in the hand" of divine providence. In both IIIA of *WOL* and *POH*, Kierkegaard wishes to contrast the mentality of "busyness" and "double-mindedness," in which a person may claim to obey God but does not, with a mentality of single-minded obedience to God's providential will.

Unlike either of the brothers in Matthew 21, Christ was not divided in answering his Father, and did not delay. The love of Christ, Kierkegaard writes, was "perpetually active," without a single moment when it was "merely a passive feeling."[34] Kierkegaard describes how Christ's life was therefore akin to a "single working day."[35] This presented a "terrible collision" with the purely human conception of love.[36] Christ was misunderstood by all who encountered him, including his closest disciples. Commenting upon Christ saying to Peter "get behind me Satan," Kierkegaard remarks that this occurred because Peter (in his misunderstanding) wanted Christ to subscribe to the human conception of love.[37]

Kierkegaard goes on to claim that God is not simply a "third party" or "middle term" to love, but its "sole object," such that "it is not the husband who is the wife's beloved, but it is God."[38] That

---

[33] Ibid., 111.

[34] Kierkegaard, *Works of Love*, 82.

[35] Ibid., 90.

[36] Ibid.

[37] Ibid.

[38] Ibid., 99.

Kierkegaard illustrates his point with among the most exclusive of human relationships (the bond between marriage partners) arguably highlights his intention to leave no room for ambiguity or dilution. Within Kierkegaard's framework, all human love has God as its focus and endpoint: "to be loved is to be helped to love God."[39] Ferreira interprets this as simply meaning that an individual's own judgements must be sublimated to those of God. "[W]hat is at stake in this idea is that God should remain the judge of what true love is."[40] This reading, however, does not go far enough. As noted above, a thematic thread runs through the preceding content of *WOL* which stresses that being a Christian lover means acting according to the imperative-form of the commandment to love one's neighbor: "Go and do likewise" (IIA, IIB, IIC, IIIA). The imperative flows from a prior attentiveness towards the eternal/God (IIB) and stands opposed to any distracted, busy, double-mindedness which would prevent the individual from becoming a wholly committed instrument of divine providence (IIC; *POH*). Once this background context is taken into account, it is clear that, as John Lippitt observes, in stating that God is the "sole object" of love, Kierkegaard "certainly *seems* to be saying something stronger" than Ferreira allows.[41]

"IIIB: Love is a Matter of Conscience" continues this emphasis. Christianity renders every human relationship a "matter of conscience" between the individual and God.[42] As noted earlier, Kierkegaard here states (with the example of the poor working woman) that Christianity advises every individual not to busy themselves [*travlt*] with temporal matters. Reference to busyness occurs again when Kierkegaard comments that despite the fact that people have "foolishly busied [*travlt*] themselves" to demonstrate gender equality,

---

[39] Ibid.

[40] Ferreira, *Love's Grateful Striving*, 71.

[41] John Lippitt, *Kierkegaard and the Problem of Self-Love* (Cambridge: Cambridge University Press, 2013), 67. For a critique which argues extensively for the prominence of this "anti-social" element in *Works of Love*, see for instance Peter George, "Something Anti-Social About *Works of Love*," in *Kierkegaard: The Self in Society*, ed. George Pattison and Steven Shakespeare (Houndmills, Basingstoke: Palgrave Macmillan, 1998), 70–81.

[42] Kierkegaard, *Works of Love*, 110.

such equality has never been Christianity's concern.[43] Later in the discourse, Kierkegaard further comments that "[t]he idea…that we should first busy ourselves [*travlt*] in finding the beloved…is very far from being Christian love."[44] This stance against love which involves people being "busy" is immediately reminiscent of IIIA.

The conceptual and thematic affinity of IIIB with IIIA and *POH* becomes even clearer towards the end of this discourse, when Kierkegaard states that conscience requires a "pure heart."[45] Such a heart is "bound" to God, whose demands consequently take absolute priority for the individual in all situations. Those in this relation of conscience are thus entirely "before God," such that the "confidence of eternity" stands between them and even their closest human relations.[46] The individual's normative reference point is thus changed from the realm of temporal goods and earthly connections, to that of eternity and one's commitment to God.[47]

Seen in this light, a much stronger stance against caring about social or economic conditions begins to emerge in Kierkegaard's ethic. In order to better inform our interpretation of Kierkegaard in this area, it will be instructive to turn to his detailed critiques of caring about worldliness and temporal conditions in his *Discourses*. The centrality of Kierkegaard's concern that God be pursued through a singularly focused, undivided will, as well as the interconnectedness of this concern with the motifs of busyness, distraction and comparison, is seen clearly in *Upbuilding Discourses in Various Spirits* (*UDVS*) (1847), *Devotional Discourses* (1849) and *Christian Discourses* (*CD*) (1849).

---

[43] Ibid., 112–13.

[44] Ibid., 114.

[45] Ibid., 119.

[46] Ibid., 124.

[47] In positing that an undistracted focus on the eternal/God entails a rejection of temporal goods, Kierkegaard is, of course, saying no more than many of the Church Fathers who preceded him. See perhaps especially Maximus the Confessor, "The Four Hundred Chapters on Love," in *Maximus Confessor: Selected Writings*, trans. George C. Berthold (New York: Paulist Press, 1985), 33–98.

Kierkegaard's *Discourses* and Other Writings

Feathered and Stemmed Teachers: The Birds and the Lilies

A common motif in Kierkegaard's *Discourses* is the pedagogical value of the birds and the lilies cited by Christ during his teaching in Matthew 6. Kierkegaard refers to the birds and the lilies as "teachers,"[48] capable of exhibiting to humanity how it should relate itself in undivided obedience to the will of God. The example of the birds and the lilies is an analogous and ultimately imperfect one, as Kierkegaard recognises. The ultimate and perfect exemplar for human attitudes towards themselves and others in relation to God (as will be explored below) is Christ himself, "the prototype."

"Before God"

Kierkegaard describes how the birds and the lilies exist wholly "before God." In order to achieve and remain in this state, human beings must avoid comparison, busyness and worry. The interconnectedness of these practices is made explicit in "To be Contented with Being a Human Being" in *UDVS*. In this discourse, Kierkegaard bemoans how during one's daily associations with others, "one forgets through the busy [*travle*] or the worried [*bekymrede*] inventiveness of comparison [*Sammenlignings*] what it is to be a human being."[49] Kierkegaard then sets out to illustrate the deleterious effects of comparison through two stories. In the first story, the "worried [*bekymrede*] lily," a lily residing amongst small flowers is seduced by a visiting bird, who over time makes the lily envious by telling it about the beauty of other lilies and the splendour of the "Crown Imperial."[50] As a result, the lily becomes unhappy with its place in the world, and

---

[48] Søren Kierkegaard, *Without Authority*, ed. and trans. Howard V. Hong and Edna H. Hong (Princeton, NJ: Princeton University Press, 1997), 10.

[49] Søren Kierkegaard, *Upbuilding Discourses in Various Spirits*, ed. and trans. Howard V. Hong and Edna H. Hong (Princeton, NJ: Princeton University Press, 1993), 165. Where the original Danish words and phrases are cited from this text and *Purity of Heart Is to Will One Thing*, these can be found in Søren Kierkegaard, *Opbyggelige taler i forskjellig aand* (Reitzels forlag, 1862). See also *SKS*.

[50] Kierkegaard, *Upbuilding Discourses in Various Spirits*, 167–69.

eventually asks the bird to transport it to the other lilies and plant it in this richer environment. After the bird uproots the lily and carries it into the air, however, the lily perishes.

From this unhappy ending, Kierkegaard exhorts that "[a]ll *worldly* worry has its basis in a person's unwillingness to be contented with being a human being, in his worried craving for distinction by way of comparison."[51] Kierkegaard's second story further illustrates this point. In "the bird's worry" (*Fuglens Bekymring*), a wild wood-dove is told by a tame-dove and its partner of how they are looked after by a farmer who keeps an abundance of grain inside a barn.[52] After comparing its situation unfavourably to the apparent certainty and security enjoyed by the tame-doves, the wood-dove becomes "so busy [*saa travlt*] gleaning and hoarding that it scarcely had time…to eat its fill."[53] Although the wood-dove has enough to survive, "it had acquired an *idea* of need in the future. It had lost its peace of mind—it had acquired *worry*."[54] Kierkegaard makes it clear that it is not any material lack *per se* which prevents the creature from contentedly living "before God," but the mind-set which compares oneself with others, busily attempts to change one's situation, and worries about future prosperity.

As a result of its worrying and busyness, the wood-dove became physically and mentally diminished: "Its feathers lost their iridescence; its flight lost its buoyancy. Its day was passed in a fruitless attempt to accumulate abundance…. It was no longer joyful."[55] Driven by its envy of the wealthy doves, the wood-dove eventually contrives to sneak into the barn where the grain is kept. When, however, the farmer sees the bird, he places it in a box and kills it.[56] The wood-dove's original error, for Kierkegaard, was being discontented with what it was. To be contented as a human being is to live in recognition of one's dependency upon God, realizing that (irrespective of economic or

---

[51] Ibid., 171.
[52] Ibid., 174–76.
[53] Ibid., 175.
[54] Ibid.
[55] Ibid.
[56] Ibid., 176.

social status) one can ultimately "no more support himself than create himself."[57] Only with this understanding, Kierkegaard claims, can anyone be truly content as a human being.

This normative anthropology occurs again in Kierkegaard's "The Care of Lowliness" in *CD*. Unlike the carefree birds of Matthew 6, the "lowly Christian" is consciously aware of his socio-economic status in relation to others. Unlike the pagan, however, Kierkegaard writes that the Christian does not define himself according to his comparative status or desire to ascend the socio-economic ladder and be "something" in relation to others.[58] Instead, the Christian is wholly contented with being "himself before God."[59] In this way, Kierkegaard makes clear that the person should not care about their social or economic standing before others, as it simply has no bearing upon their status "before God."

Service and Obedience to the Divine Will

Existing "before God" without comparison, busyness or worry, the birds and the lilies are able to unconditionally seek God's kingdom, in absolute obedience to their Creator. The bird does not demand to have anything for itself, or to be anything by itself. This, according to Kierkegaard, is its "perfection."[60] Commenting on the injunctions in Matthew 6:33 to not worry and "seek first" God's kingdom, Kierkegaard similarly describes how the bird does not "seek" anything for itself during even the longest of migrations.[61] All of the bird's actions are done as imperatives from God. Its will being extensions of God's will, the bird and the lily accept their temporal circumstances as they are, even if these appear disadvantageous to the organism. The kingdom of God must be unconditionally sought from where one is, as to try and begin elsewhere is *prima facie* not to seek God's kingdom

---

[57] Ibid., 177.

[58] Søren Kierkegaard, *Christian Discourses: The Crisis and a Crisis in the Life of an Actress*, ed. and trans. Howard V. Hong and Edna H. Hong (Princeton, NJ: Princeton University Press, 1997), 40–41.

[59] Ibid.

[60] Kierkegaard, *Upbuilding Discourses in Various Spirits*, 205.

[61] Ibid., 208–9.

"first."[62] Applied to human beings in their various social and economic circumstances, this would seem to imply that one should not aspire to a higher socio-economic status, as such an aspiration is contrary to unconditionally seeking God's will.

In the second of his *Devotional Discourses* on the birds and the lilies (1849), Kierkegaard focuses on the statement that "no one can serve two masters" (Matthew 6:24). As the creator and sustainer of every person's existence, God is "infinitely closer" to a person than anyone else could be.[63] Consequently, indifference towards God is impossible. One either loves God, or hates Him. Due to the relation being one of creature to Creator, love takes the form of unconditional obedience. The implication of this for one's attitude towards temporal goods is dramatic and uncompromising. Either God is served, or mammon. To believe that one can have "a little mammon" to oneself (for instance, a "single penny") is to be decisively not serving God.[64]

Humanity's Difference

The bird and the lily, as with all of nature for Kierkegaard, exist in a state of "unconditional obedience" to God.[65] There is no double-mindedness in the bird; God's will simply *is* its will,[66] and its obedience is therefore never only "to a certain degree." In this way, the birds and the lilies in Matthew 6 analogously exemplify how human beings ought to exist wholly "before God" in absolute obedience to His will. However, as alluded to above, the bird and the lily remain imperfect teachers for the human pupil.

In contrast to non-human animals (which only exist as part of a collective or "crowd"), each human being is a distinct individual.[67] Moreover, unlike the bird and the lily, who possess only one will

---

[62] Ibid., 211.

[63] Kierkegaard, *Without Authority*, 23.

[64] Kierkegaard, *Upbuilding Discourses in Various Spirits*, 207.

[65] Kierkegaard, *Without Authority*, 25–26.

[66] Ibid., 26.

[67] Kierkegaard, *Upbuilding Discourses in Various Spirits*, 190.

(God's) and are unalterably "bound in necessity,"[68] the human person has an autonomous will which must be sacrificed, freedom with which to make this determination,[69] and consciousness of what it lacks or will need in the future.[70] In addition, humanity's most profound difference is its capacity to worship God. Human beings are capable of this because, as created in the image of God, they harbour an internal, invisible glory which the bird and the lily lack.[71] In becoming as nothing in absolute dependence on God, human beings inversely "image" their Creator and thereby "resemble" Him.[72] This is paradigmatically exemplified for Kierkegaard by Jesus Christ, "the prototype" who, as the fullest instantiation of what it is to be a human being, could teach humanity in a way that the birds and the lilies (which he pointed to out of humility) could not.

In this sense, the Christian is not simply "before God" in the same sense as the bird and the lily, but also "before his prototype" who is at once fully God and fully human. "As a *human being* he was created in *God's image [Billede]*, but as a *Christian* he has God as the prototype *[Forbillede]*."[73] Although a person may therefore start with the example set by the bird and the lily so as to ascertain what it means to be "before God" and undividedly obey His will, this cannot be where the lesson stops. "The lowly Christian, who before God is himself, *exists* as a Christian *before his prototype*."[74] As seen earlier,

---

[68] Ibid., 205.

[69] Ibid., 207.

[70] Ibid., 195–96.

[71] Ibid., 192.

[72] Ibid., 192-93. See also Kierkegaard's 1844 discourse, "One Who Prays Aright Struggles in Prayer and Is Victorious—in That God Is Victorious": "God can imprint himself in [a person] only when he himself has become nothing. When the ocean is exerting all its power, that is precisely the time when it cannot reflect the image of heaven, and even the slightest motion blurs the image; but when it becomes still and deep, then the image of heaven sinks into its nothingness." In Søren Kierkegaard, *Eighteen Upbuilding Discourses*, ed. and trans. Howard V. Hong and Edna H. Hong (Princeton, NJ: Princeton University Press, 1990), 399.

[73] Kierkegaard, *Christian Discourses*, 41 (emphasis original).

[74] Ibid., 42 (emphasis original).

Kierkegaard in IIIA of *WOL* presents Christ as the exemplar *par excellence* of a love which was "perpetually active" in service to the divine imperative, causing a "terrible collision" with the world's understanding. Only by looking at the example of Christ can one appreciate the full picture of how the Christian, for Kierkegaard, should relate to the temporal world around him.

Christ's Prototypical Lowliness in Human Obedience to God

In *UDVS*, Kierkegaard describes how, through enduring the "heaviest suffering" of any human being, Christ "learned obedience" to God.[75] This is aptly demonstrated for Kierkegaard in Christ praying to the Father in the garden of Gethsemane that the cup be taken from him, but not "if it be your will." The first part of obedience is the discernment of God's will; the second part is the fulfilment of that will.[76] In *Practice in Christianity* (*PC*), Anti-Climacus parses this matter in terms of Christ's "task" (*opgave*) of obedience to God. Christ manifested this task externally through his lowliness, which lasted the duration of his entire life and culminated in his death on the cross.[77] Christ *qua* human being understood this and regarded his entire life as a test in obedience, with God as the examiner. Indeed, Anti-Climacus suggests that Christ's exaltation after death can be viewed as a result of him passing this test "at every moment" of his life. It is at this point that he is the "prototype" whose life guides others in passing the same test.[78] Passing the test of obedience to God, as shown in the lifespan of Christ, involves abasement and lowliness.

In *Judge for Yourselves!* Kierkegaard posits Christ as the sole example of one who served only one master. As a result of this, Christ could not be tolerated by humanity which, to varying degrees, always

---

[75] Kierkegaard, *Upbuilding Discourses in Various Spirits*, 254–55.

[76] Ibid., 255.

[77] Søren Kierkegaard, *Practice in Christianity*, ed. and trans. Howard V. Hong and Edna H. Hong (Princeton, NJ: Princeton University Press, 1991), 182. See also Kierkegaard, *For Self-Examination; And, Judge for Yourselves; And, Three Discourses 1851*, trans. Walter Lowrie (Princeton, NJ: Princeton University Press, 1944), 80–81.

[78] Kierkegaard, *Practice in Christianity*, 183–84.

serves more than one master. Christ's single-mindedness is shown in the entire "pattern" of his life, in which he had no family connections, belonged to no country, took no property, and married no spouse.[79] Christ embraces poverty and lowliness, living "without a nest, without a hole...whereon to lay His head."[80] As such, Christ is "an alien in the world," whose entire existence is deliberately orientated towards serving only one master.[81] This necessitated a complete rejection of all temporal goods and worldly status. To be a disciple of Christ is to relate to him through his connection with God.[82] The world insists on compromise; Christianity demands an unambiguous and "absolute" choice of either/or in its injunction that one "cannot serve two masters."

In *CD*, Kierkegaard cites two reasons why it is more difficult for an eminent person (in the worldly sense) to be or become a Christian, while it is conversely easier for the lowly. Firstly, although the lowliness which is constitutive of being a Christian is primarily spiritual and internal in nature, biblical scriptures show a clear normative preference for being literally (i.e. physically and externally) lowly.[83] A faithful following of these scriptures should take this emphasis into account. Secondly (and more pertinently for

---

[79] Kierkegaard, *For Self-Examination; And, Judge for Yourselves; And, Three Discourses*, 172–75. The constitutive absence of personal connections in Christ's prototypical life for Kierkegaard should also arguably be taken into account in the contemporary debate on the place of "special relationships" in Kierkegaard's ethic. For a sample of contributions to this debate, see Ferreira, *Love's Grateful Striving*, 43–65; C. Stephen Evans, *Kierkegaard's Ethic of Love: Divine Commands and Moral Obligations* (Oxford: Oxford University Press, 2004), 203–23; Joseph Carlsmith, "Essentially Preferential: A Critique of Kierkegaard's Works of Love," *Gnosis* 12.1 (2012); John Lippitt, "Kierkegaard and the Problem of Special Relationships: Ferreira, Krishek and the 'God Filter'," *International Journal for Philosophy of Religion* 72.3 (2012): 177–97; Sharon Krishek, "In Defence of a Faith-like Model of Love: A Reply to John Lippitt's "Kierkegaard and the Problem of Special Relationships: Ferreira, Krishek, and the 'God Filter'," *International Journal for Philosophy of Religion* 75.2 (2014): 155–66.

[80] Kierkegaard, *For Self-Examination; And, Judge for Yourselves; And, Three Discourses*, 178.

[81] Ibid., 180.

[82] Ibid., 181.

[83] Kierkegaard, *Christian Discourses*, 54.

Kierkegaard), "the prototype" for Christian living was literally lowly.[84] This, for the Christian, entails that being a lowly person has the potential (actualised in the life of Christ) to mean "infinitely much."[85] Kierkegaard thus writes that in being lowly, and yet "forgetting" their socio-economic state before others, the Christian "looks more or less like the prototype."[86]

The Offensive Love of God in Christ

In *Works of Love*'s first discourse, Kierkegaard makes clear that all Christian love has the love of God as its source: "[a]s the peaceful lake is grounded deep in the hidden spring which no eye can see, so a man's love is grounded even deeper in the love of God."[87] In order to fully appreciate the Christo-centric character of Kierkegaard's ethic, however, one must begin even further back at *Works of Love*'s opening prayer, in which Kierkegaard states that love is known through God's prior initiative of love towards humanity God "didst hold nothing back but didst give everything in love" and "made manifest what love is" in being humanity's redeemer, giving himself to "save us all."[88] Kierkegaard proceeds to call on the Holy Spirit, or "Spirit of Love," to "remind the believer to love as he is loved, and his neighbor as himself."[89] The juxtaposition of biblical verses here is highly instructive. The first clause ("love as he is loved") alludes to John 13:34 or John 15:9-12, where Christ—prior to or after telling his disciples that he is the sole "way" to God the Father and the Holy Spirit will remind them of his teaching (John 14)—newly commands that his

---

[84] Ibid.

[85] Ibid., 42.

[86] Ibid., 43. Fruitful comparisons might here be made with late medieval writers Johannes Tauler and Thomas à Kempis, amongst others. See Johannes Tauler, *The Following of Christ*, trans. J. R. Morell (London: T. Fisher Unwin, 1910); Thomas à Kempis, *The Imitation of Christ*, trans. William C. Creasy (Macon, GA: Mercer University Press, 2007); Anonymous, *Theologia Germanica*, trans. Susanna Winkworth (Grand Rapids, MI: Christian Classics Ethereal Library, 1907).

[87] Kierkegaard, *Works of Love*, 8.

[88] Ibid., 4.

[89] Ibid., For Ferreira's commentary on this point, see Ferreira, *Love's Grateful Striving*, 18.

disciples "love one another as I have loved you." In placing this imperative as the antecedent to the commandment that one should love one's neighbor as oneself (Matthew 22:37; Luke 10:27), Kierkegaard's prayer appears to treat the first commandment or imperative in Matthew 22 and Luke 10—"love the Lord your God with all your heart"—as substitutable with Christ's instruction that his disciples should love as he, the self-revelation of God, has *already* acted towards them.

This, I suggest, provides a new angle on the current discussion. By beginning *Works of Love* with his prayerful and Christo-centric affirmation of divine love, Kierkegaard places all discussion about love in the context of God's prior soteriological initiative towards humanity in becoming incarnate as "humanity's redeemer": Jesus Christ. To apply this lens to our current discussion, while Kierkegaard's *Discourses* and *WOL* may jointly detail what it means to love God as a creature through doxological obedience to His will and becoming "an instrument in the hand of Providence," one's interpretation of this divine will must be conditioned by considering the form of God's antecedent outreach of love towards the believer in Christ; "love as he [*already has been*] loved." The nature and implications of this outreach is not discussed explicitly by Kierkegaard under his own name, but by his pseudonyms, Climacus and Anti-Climacus.

"The wonder" of God's Love in Philosophical Fragments *and* The Sickness Unto Death

In Chapter 2 of *Philosophical Fragments* (*PF*), Johannes Climacus embarks on a "poetic venture" which tells of "a king who loved a maiden." This is intended to explore how and why "the Teacher" or "the god" might choose to reveal Himself to the learner. Climacus begins with an unequivocal affirmation that God's motivation is love, and winning the learner's love is His end.[90] Love for Climacus entails a desire for absolute equality with the beloved. Consequently, God's self-revelation to the learner in the form of a humble "servant" is

---

[90] Søren Kierkegaard, *Philosophical Fragments; Johannes Climacus*, ed. and trans. Howard V. Hong and Edna H. Hong (Princeton, NJ: Princeton University Press, 1985), 25.

not a guise, but his "true form."⁹¹ For Climacus, that God in love seeks absolute equality with the learner is simply too incredible for human comprehension. He explains:

> it is indeed less terrifying to fall upon one's face while the mountains tremble at the god's voice than to sit with him as his equal...for if the god gave no indication, how could it occur to a man that the blessed god could need him? This would indeed be...so bad a thought that it could not arise in him, even though, when the god has confided it to him, he adoringly says: This thought did not arise in my heart...for do we not...stand here before the *wonder* [*Vidunderet*].⁹²

Climacus' acknowledgment here that "the wonder" of God's loving initiative towards the learner "did not arise in [a human] heart" references 1 Corinthians 2:9, the full text of which reads "[w]hat no eye has seen, nor ear heard, nor the heart of man imagined, what God has prepared for those who love him."⁹³ The "paradox" becomes "absolute," Climacus goes on to claim, in two respects: Firstly, that "absolute equality" is sought with the learner, and secondly that this learner is resultantly revealed to be in a state of untruth (i.e. sin).⁹⁴ The first aspect (that absolute equality is sought with the learner) is the crux of Climacus' "poetic venture."⁹⁵ As C. Stephen Evans notes in his commentary on *PF*, the Incarnation as presented by Climacus' parable of the king and the maiden "represents the epitome of pure, selfless love" which is nowhere encountered in human experience and therefore

---

⁹¹ Ibid., 32.

⁹² Ibid., 34–36.

⁹³ See also "Strengthening in the Inner Being" (1843), where Kierkegaard affirms that "God's love...is more blessed than anything which arose in the human heart" Kierkegaard, *Eighteen Upbuilding Discourses*, 97.

⁹⁴ Kierkegaard, *Philosophical Fragments*, 47.

⁹⁵ Further support for this view can be found in a sermon on 1 Corinthians 2:9, delivered by Kierkegaard at Trinity Church in Copenhagen just 4 months before *Philosophical Fragments* was published. Commenting on the line "what no eye hath seen," Kierkegaard challenges his reader to "visualize" a king, clad as a lowly man and living amongst the people. This, Kierkegaard says, makes the human imagination "quail." See Søren Kierkegaard, *Johannes Climacus (or De Omnibus Dubitandum Est) and A Sermon*, trans. T. H. Croxall (Stanford: Stanford University Press, 1958), 167.

presents a decisive and threatening challenge to human self-understanding.⁹⁶

Through his parable of the "poor day laborer and the mightiest emperor" in *Sickness Unto Death* (*SUD*), Anti-Climacus similarly locates the offensiveness of Christianity in God's selfless outreach towards humanity. One day, the emperor suddenly requests the day-laborer, "in whose heart" (Anti-Climacus remarks in a clear reference to 1 Corinthians 2:9), "it had never arisen" that the emperor even knew he existed.⁹⁷ The emperor reaches out to make the laborer an in-law. Such an invitation is almost impossible for him to believe. "A little favor—that would make sense to the laborer…But this, this plan for him to become a son-in-law, well, that was far too much."⁹⁸ Just as Climacus ends his parable of the king and the maiden by professing that God's initiative to be "the wonder" which did not originate in any human heart, so too Anti-Climacus concludes that the divine action his story portrays is "too high for me, I cannot grasp it."⁹⁹

While Climacus does not explore the reason for this incomprehension and awe, Anti-Climacus proceeds to offer a brief account. "The *summa summarum* of all human wisdom," Anti-Climacus writes, is encapsulated by the saying that "too much and too little spoil everything."¹⁰⁰ The principle which underlies this saying, "*ne quid nimis*"¹⁰¹—nothing in excess—was inscribed, along with "know thyself," at the Delphic Oracle of Ancient Greece. The Christian narrative of God's communicative love in the Incarnation decisively contravenes this human wisdom in its apparent excessiveness; it is simply "too high" for the self-orientated understanding of human beings. "The uncharitableness of the natural man cannot allow him the

---

[96] C. Stephen Evans, *Passionate Reason: Making Sense of Kierkegaard's Philosophical Fragments* (Bloomington: Indiana University Press, 1992), 107.

[97] Søren Kierkegaard, *The Sickness unto Death: A Christian Psychological Exposition for Upbuilding and Awakening*, ed. and trans. Howard V. Hong and Edna H. Hong (Princeton, NJ: Princeton University Press, 1980), 84.

[98] Ibid., 84–85.

[99] Ibid., 85.

[100] Ibid., 86.

[101] Ibid.

extraordinary that God has intended for him; so he is offended."[102] In this way, Anti-Climacus' account in *SUD* can be seen to complement and expand upon that of Climacus in *PF*. Both ground their stories with a clear nod to 1 Corinthians 2:9 and its declaration that no human heart has ever "conceived" that which "God has prepared for those who love him."

Christ's servant form, Climacus writes, "means only that he was a lowly human being," indistinguishable from others.[103] Unlike all other human beings, however, Christ in his servant form expresses that an absolute indifference (akin to the lilies and "birds of the air" of Matthew 6) to the distribution of earthly goods, "as one who owns nothing and wishes to own nothing."[104] Instead, the entirety of Christ's focus is on seeking the love [*Kjærlighed*] of his disciples [*Disciplens*].[105] Provided that they remain "absorbed in the service of the spirit," Climacus affirms that this way of existing within the world is possible for every human being, whereupon they will be "even more glorious" than the lily.[106]

It might here be asked why Christ's lowliness and disregard for temporal goods was constitutive of total selflessness. The answer to this may be found through a brief detour to *CD*, where Kierkegaard posits that all temporal goods are intrinsically selfish or "begrudging" [*misundelig*]. While an individual acquires, possesses or maintains such goods, his mind is not wholly attentive to the other.[107] By contrast, in assuming a state of absolute lowliness and poverty, Christ was able to constantly and entirely focus on others.[108] As the Prototype for all humanity, nothing in Christ's life was accidental. His way of living, which was "indeed *the way*,"[109] therefore reveals the

---

[102] Ibid.
[103] Kierkegaard, *Philosophical Fragments*, 56.
[104] Ibid.
[105] Ibid., 56–57.
[106] Ibid., 57.
[107] Kierkegaard, *Christian Discourses*, 121.
[108] Ibid., 123.
[109] Ibid., 114 (emphasis original).

"essential truth" that "in order to make others rich one must oneself be poor."[110] The consequences of this way of living within the world are further explored by Anti-Climacus in *PC*.

Christ's Reckless Love, Poverty and Lowliness in Practice in Christianity

Anti-Climacus begins the first part of *PC* by inquiring into why Christ's contemporaries unanimously opposed him. This would not have been the case, Anti-Climacus argues, if he had conformed to the world's conception of compassion.[111] Proceeding from the "fixed point" of oneself and the belief that "everyone wants to cling to his own," human compassion is anchored in selfishness; as such, it is only ever "to a certain degree," and never "reckless."[112] This contrasts absolutely with the divine love revealed in Christ. Being "unconditionally" concerned with all others and without any self-regard, Christ's love manifested as "unlimited *recklessness*" to humanity.[113] This alone, Anti-Climacus comments, would have been "sufficient for [Christ] to come to grief in the world."[114]

Anti-Climacus goes on to further describe how a constant outcome of Christ's self-giving *modus operandi* was others' failure to understand him. This is exemplified by the Pharisees' presentation of Christ with a coin, accompanied by the question of whether taxes

---

[110] Ibid., 122. See also Climacus in *Concluding Unscientific Postscript* (1848). Unlike temporal goods such as money and knowledge (which can be acquired in different ways and yet have the same form), Climacus writes that the absolute good of happiness in the eternal *"can be defined only by the mode in which it is acquired,"* which is by selflessly and absolutely "venturing everything." Søren Kierkegaard, *Concluding Unscientific Postscript to Philosophical Fragments*, ed and trans. Howard Hong and Edna H. Hong (Princeton, NJ: Princeton University Press, 1992), 427 (emphasis original).

[111] Kierkegaard, *Practice in Christianity*, 56–57.

[112] Ibid., 59.

[113] Ibid., 58; A similar point is made by Kierkegaard in *UDVS*. Human wisdom, he there affirms, states that "everyone is closest to himself." From this standpoint, "Christ's life was foolish, since…it seemed as if he were closest to everyone else but the furthest from himself." Kierkegaard, *Upbuilding Discourses in Various Spirits*, 232.

[114] Kierkegaard, *Practice in Christianity*, 58.

should be paid to Caesar (Matthew 22:15-22). Anti-Climacus writes that through his answer ("Render unto Caesar the things that are Caesar's, and unto God the things that are God's"), Christ expresses "infinite indifference" towards the very premise of the question, as to do otherwise would detract from giving obedience to God, and selfless love to humanity.[115] In the lowly life of the prototype, these orientations towards God and humanity are shown to be co-extensive parts of the same whole which, out of relational selflessness, entails "infinite indifference" towards temporal matters.

Conclusion

While Ferreira rightly identifies Kierkegaard's focus in *WOL* as the ethical subject of love, she downplays the significance of Kierkegaard's insistence that God is love's "sole object." As outlined above, behind Kierkegaard's claim as to what Christianity advises in IIIB of *WOL* are motifs of comparison, busyness and double-mindedness which are also present in preceding discourses IIA-C and IIIA. To will only one thing, for Kierkegaard, is to have absolute attentiveness, commitment and love towards the Good (*POH*)/God (*WOL* and *Discourses*). The individual's commitment will either adhere to this absolute standard, or be only "to a certain degree." This insistence on *sola Dei*, I submit, may be an instructive hermeneutical lens through which to view Kierkegaard's advice to the charwoman not to "busy herself" with trying to achieve a higher socio-economic status.

For Kierkegaard, not only does social and economic lowliness not exclude one from the obligation to practice Christian love, but it is normatively conducive to this end. An attitude of disregard towards temporal matters is not an accidental quality of faithful Christians; rather, it is essential to having an undivided will in service to, and "before," God. The paradigmatic expression of this is Christ, "the prototype," in whom a dismissal and rejection of temporal goods is made normative. In his human nature, Christ is the definitive prototype for how human beings should unreservedly conform themselves to the divine will. As God, Christ also reveals that this divine will seeks

---

[115] Ibid., 169–70.

absolute equality with all of humanity in selfless love. In light of this Christological framework and normative theological anthropology, Kierkegaard's advice to the charwoman in IIIB of *Works of Love* might thus be paraphrased: "do not engage in busy double-mindedness, comparing yourself with others and self-centeredly striving for temporal status. Instead, imitate the prototype, whose undivided will was always perpetually active in selfless service to God and love for others." Kierkegaard's ethical vision of the individual "before God" here is, in fact, *more* problematic than is often asserted.

Part II

Faith, Sin, and Offense

6.

KIERKEGAARD:
FATHER OF EXISTENTIALISM OR CRITIC OF EXISTENTIALISM?

C. Stephen Evans

Kierkegaard is frequently described as the father of existentialism. But is this correct? If we mean simply that Kierkegaard had a profound influence on certain twentieth century thinkers—such as Heidegger, Jaspers, Unamuno, Sartre, Camus, and Marcel—it is certainly correct. However, such a claim does not tell us very much and can in fact be very misleading. Hegel had a profound influence on Marx, as everyone recognizes, but it would be somewhat misleading to describe Hegel as the father of Marxism. Normally, to describe someone as the "father" of a particular movement is to claim that there are basic similarities between that individual and the main tenets of the movement in question.

So let us rephrase the question. Does Kierkegaard share basic similarities with the twentieth century existentialists? Here is where the question becomes difficult. To begin, there is a problem identifying the existentialists. Heidegger, for example, rejected the label, as did Gabriel Marcel. Even Camus often writes about "the existentialists," implying that he is not one himself. And even if we could agree on who qualifies as an existentialist, we would still have the problem of determining what are the main views of the movement. It is not easy to find a set of beliefs or convictions that thinkers as different as Sartre, Heidegger, Jaspers, Camus, and Marcel all hold. Perhaps we could say that all of them share a passionate concern for the meaning of human existence, but this could be said about many philosophers that no one would call existentialist, including Socrates, Augustine, and Pascal. Perhaps they all could be said to emphasize the importance of choice in the formation of the self, but, once again, this would appear to be something held in common with a great many thinkers from the past.

Faced with these difficulties, I think our best strategy is to seek to understand existentialism with reference to an "ideal type." When most people think of existentialism, I think the figure who comes most prominently to mind is the Jean Paul Sartre of the 40's and 50's, the Sartre who wrote *Being and Nothingness* as well as the famous lecture essay on "Existentialism" as a form of humanism. So I am going to take Sartre to be the prototypical existentialist, and I will count other thinkers as existentialist to the degree that they resemble Sartre.

Measured by this criterion, my thesis will be that Kierkegaard is better thought of as a radical critic of existentialism than the father of existentialism. Despite the influence of Kierkegaard on Sartre, the differences between the two thinkers are large and fundamental. I shall try to show that Kierkegaard, writing 100 years before Sartre, anticipated Sartre's basic viewpoint, and subjected it to devastating criticism. Thinking of Kierkegaard as the father of existentialism has had a generally baneful effect on our understanding of Kierkegaard himself, because it has resulted in a tendency to read Kierkegaard through Sartrean eyes, emphasizing commonalities between the two figures while making it harder to see the fundamental differences.

Sartre and the Idea of Radical Choice

What is Sartrean existentialism? The key idea to grasp is, I believe, the notion that Alasdair MacIntyre has termed "radical choice." The idea is that our most basic values, including moral values, are *chosen* by human beings. Sartre begins his essay on "Existentialism" by saying that there are two kinds of existentialism, the atheistic kind, among which he names Heidegger as well as himself, and the Christians, among whom he includes Marcel and Jaspers. Oddly, however, after making this admission, Sartre goes on to define existentialism in such a way that only atheistic existentialism is consistent. Existentialism, he says, is the denial that there is any common human nature. If there were a God, Sartre tells us, then God's purposes in creating humans would define our nature and give us an ideal to live for. Without God, there is no basis for saying what human beings are or should be. Many atheists, however, according to Sartre, have irrationally continued to believe that there is human nature even without a God. Sartre rejects this kind of atheism, and says he wants to recognize the full implications of a world without God:

> Atheistic existentialism, which I represent, is more coherent. It states that if God does not exist, there is at least one being in whom existence precedes essence, a being who exists before he can be defined by any concept, and that this being is man, or as Heidegger says, human reality.... Thus, there is no human nature, since there is no God to conceive it.[1]

Since there is no human nature, there is no objective good for human beings. Sartre says that when we make a choice, we are defining the good, not just for ourselves, for all humans, but there are no prior criteria to help us choose. If we appeal to instincts, it is up to us to determine the meaning of our instincts. If we ask for advice from others, we decide whom to ask and whether to accept the advice.

When facing the criticism that such radical choices are ultimately arbitrary, since if values are created by my choices, I cannot appeal to those values to justify the choices, Sartre's reply is revealing: "My answer to this is that I'm quite vexed that that's the way it is; but if I've discarded God the Father, there has to be someone to invent values."[2] So the question is whether Kierkegaard shares this Sartrean view of values as the product of radical choice. To answer it, I want to begin by looking at Kierkegaard's basic view of the self.

Two Views of the Self

Broadly speaking, there are two views of selfhood that can be found in the western intellectual tradition. One view sees persons as substances, entities within the natural order of things. Such a view goes back at least as far as Aristotle, who famously defined the human self as a

---

[1] Jean-Paul Sartre, "Existentialism," in *Existentialism and Human Emotions* (New York: Citadel Press, 1985), 15.

[2] Ibid., 48-49.

rational animal. This kind of view continued to prevail during the middle ages, and can still be clearly seen in Descartes' conception of the human self as a "thinking thing."

However, many contemporary discussions of selfhood and personhood describe selfhood as a special status that accrues to something by virtue of some achievement. For example, some contemporary ethicists have argued that even a newborn child is not a person because it lacks the capacities to do the right things. Clearly, Sartre's view of the self falls solidly in this camp.

Kierkegaard has, I believe, a foot in both of these camps. His Christian convictions allow him to think of human persons as creatures, part of the natural order made by God. However, God has made humans with a special character; and holds them responsible for becoming what he intended them to be. Thus, to be a self is to be assigned a task.

Johannes Climacus, the pseudonymous author of *Concluding Unscientific Postscript*, expresses this thought in a whimsical and ironical manner: "Well, of course, every human being is something of a subject. But now to become what one is as a matter of course—who would waste his time on that?"[3] The human task is to become a self in truth, a task that *seems* insignificant, because it amounts to becoming what one already is. A genuine understanding of the nature of the self reveals that this task is no triviality, however, because "what one already is" includes potentialities that must be actualized to fully become oneself. The human self is "an existing self," in that pregnant sense of existence that Kierkegaard made famous. Climacus describes human existence in language very similar to that used by Anti-Climacus for the self in *The Sickness Unto Death*: "But what is existence? It is that child who is begotten by the infinite and the finite, the eternal and the temporal, and is therefore continually striving."[4] Climacus compares the process of existing as a self to driving a

---

[3] Søren Kierkegaard, *Concluding Unscientific Postscript to Philosophical Fragments*, ed. & trans. Howard V. Hong and Edna H. Hong (Princeton: Princeton University Press, 1992), 130.

[4] Ibid., 92.

carriage or wagon pulled by two very unequal horses, one "like Pegasus" and the other "an old nag":

> And this is what existing is like if one is to be conscious of it. Eternity is infinitely quick like that winged steed, temporality is an old nag, and the existing person is the driver, that is, if existing is not to be what people usually call existing, because then the existing person is not a driver but a drunken peasant who lies in the wagon and sleeps and lets the horses shift for themselves. Of course, he also drives, he is also a driver, and likewise there perhaps are many who —also exist.[5]

There is a sense in which we humans cannot help but exist. To use language popularized much later by Sartre and Heidegger, we are "condemned to be free," "thrown into existence." However, most of us simply drift through life; we let the horses run where they wish. Kierkegaard wants to challenge his readers to become selves in truth.

Is Kierkegaard a Proponent of "Radical Choice"?

But what does it mean to become a self in truth? Is there some kind of ideal for selfhood that is normative? What would this even mean? If there is such an ideal, how could someone committed to a particular view of the self defend such an ideal against rival accounts? These are difficult questions indeed, and raising them places us right in the middle of what we might call Kierkegaard's implicit epistemology.

Kierkegaard is well-known for his view of the three stages or spheres of existence—life viewed aesthetically, ethically, and religiously. I believe there is no doubt that Kierkegaard thinks of these spheres of existence as ranked; the ethical is superior to the aesthetic overall, just as the religious is superior to the ethical. But what makes one stage superior to another?

One answer, which we might call the "existentialist" answer, is that no stage is objectively superior to another, but that what makes one "better" is simply the choice or affirmation of the self. According to

---
[5] Ibid., 311-12.

this view, Kierkegaard's ranking of the stages is simply his personal choice, and it leaves open the possibility that for others different choices would imply a different ranking or perhaps no ranking at all. On this view a person's most basic choices are indeed Sartrean "radical choices." No reasons for such choices can be given, because the choice is essentially a choice about what is going to count as a good reason for a person. Since Kierkegaard is often called "the father of existentialism," it is not surprising that such a Sartrean view is often read back into Kierkegaard.

One influential source of this Sartrean reading of Kierkegaard is Alasdair MacIntyre's provocative book, *After Virtue*. According to MacIntyre, the Enlightenment set itself the project of giving a rational foundation for ethics to replace tradition or religion. Kierkegaard, says MacIntyre, was the first to see that this project could not succeed, and MacIntyre claims that Kierkegaard's *Either/Or* embodies this insight. What Kierkegaard essentially tried to do, on MacIntyre's reading, is to substitute a radical act of the will for reason as the foundation of ethics:

> Kierkegaard and Kant agree in their conception of morality, but Kierkegaard inherits that conception together with an understanding that the project of giving a rational vindication of morality has failed. Kant's failure provided Kierkegaard with his starting-point: the act of choice had to be called in to do the work that reason could not do.[6]

Either/Or confronts the reader with a choice between the aesthetic life, represented in Part I by the papers of "A," and the ethical life, represented in the papers of "B." But the reader is not told who is right and must choose for himself or herself, with no external "result" to confirm the rightness of the choice. MacIntyre says that Kierkegaard thinks this choice must be a radical, "criterionless" choice:

> Suppose that someone confronts the choice between them [the ethical and the aesthetic lives] having as yet embraced neither. He can be offered no *reason* for

---

[6] Alasdair MacIntyre, *After Virtue: Second Edition* (Notre Dame: University of Notre Dame Press, 1984), 47. See also the fine reply to MacIntyre, *Kierkegaard After MacIntyre*, ed. John J. Davenport and Antony Rudd (Chicago: Open Court Publishing Co., 2001).

preferring one to the other. For if a given reason offers support for the ethical way of life—to live in that way will serve the demands of duty or to live in that way will be to accept moral perfection as a goal and so give a certain kind of meaning to one's action—the person who has not yet embraced either the ethical or the aesthetic still has to choose whether or not to treat this reason as having any force. If it already has force for him, he has already chosen the ethical; which *ex hypothesi* he has not. And so it is also with reasons supportive of the aesthetic.[7]

This argument is far from decisive. Consider the following parallel argument. Suppose that in a political theory class I present my students with arguments for and against a libertarian view of the state, without tipping my hand as to which view I personally favor. Let us assume that prior to the class the students are not familiar with libertarian views of the state and have no settled commitments either way. Would we say in such a case that the students "can be offered no reason for preferring one position to the other?" Would we say that a student who is considering an argument for libertarianism "still has to choose whether or not to treat this reason as having any force," and if he or she does see it as having force, the student has already chosen libertarianism, contrary to the hypothesis that the student is as yet uncommitted? Clearly, it is possible for a student in this situation to find a reason compelling. There must be something wrong with this argument that the student must perform an act of radical choice in order to decide the issue, and the same flaw infects MacIntyre's argument concerning Kierkegaard.

It is not difficult to detect the flaw. The problem arises from the assumption that an individual must choose to regard a reason as having force in order for the reason to have any force for the individual. This is simply not the way reasons work. In the normal case, if someone gives me a reason for supporting or opposing a policy, the reason will or will not strike me as having force of some degree or other, and whether this is so is not under my voluntary control.

---

[7] MacIntyre, *After Virtue*, 40.

The argument between the aesthetic and the ethical is an argument where both sides give reasons that they believe could be appealing to the other. Both the aesthete and the ethicist are pictured as concrete individuals with desires and needs. The aesthete assumes that human beings want to satisfy their desires and avoid boredom, and tries to show that the ethical life constricts and undermines the individual's quest for a satisfying existence. The ethicist tries to show that the ethical life is superior to the aesthetic life, even when judged by aesthetic criteria, because a human life without ethical commitments turns out to be meaningless and unsatisfying. No appeal to radical, criterionless choice is made by either party.

Subjectivity and Kierkegaard's Rejection of Classical Foundationalism

However, does the fact that Kierkegaard gives us no "result" show that MacIntyre must be right? Does the fact that both the aesthete and the ethicist have arguments they think should be appealing to the other show that neither view is objectively superior to the other? It might appear that this is so, since Kierkegaard gives us no scorecard on which to rank the views. So far as we know, neither party to the argument is convinced. The ethicist does not succumb to temptation and have an affair; the aesthete does not repent of his scandalous ways and choose the path of marriage and respectability.

Modern western philosophy has been dominated by a certain epistemological picture that is today termed "classical foundationalism." There are two important elements of this type of foundationalism. First, the classical foundationalist holds that genuine knowledge must be based on truths that are known with a high degree of certainty. Second, the classical foundationalist believes that the method we must follow to achieve such certainty requires objectivity. Descartes himself sets the tone in his *Meditations*. The standard for certainty is set very high, so that even the possibility of error becomes a ground for doubt. And Descartes thinks that the only way to obtain such certainty is to become entirely objective, setting aside all emotions and other "subjective" attitudes, which are seen as sources of bias and distortion.

From the standpoint of classical foundationalism, the argument between Kierkegaard's aesthete and ethicist looks undecidable. However, Kierkegaard's own perspective is profoundly different. For although Kierkegaard rarely discusses epistemological issues in a formal way, his whole outlook is a challenge to this classical foundationalist picture. Both the elements I have identified in the picture are rejected. On the one hand, the kind of absolute certainty sought by modern, western philosophy is unattainable for finite human existers. Human persons are historically situated beings, and they are incapable of thinking "*sub specie æternitatis*," as Spinoza thought we should aspire to do.

On Kierkegaard's view, to have knowledge that is absolutely certain would be to have knowledge that is complete and final; it would be to have "the System," which indeed Hegel claimed to possess. Johannes Climacus surely speaks for Kierkegaard in renouncing any claims to possess a system of existence. Climacus says that a "logical system is possible" but that "a system of existence is impossible" for an existing human person."[8] He does not thereby deny that there is such a thing as the final, objective truth about reality, since "existence itself is a system—for God."[9] The problem is that we humans are not God, and thus we are not capable of seeing the world from God's point of view.

From this Kierkegaardian perspective, uncertainty is simply part of the human condition, and the aspirations of the classical foundationalist are aspirations to transcend that condition. It follows from this that the fact that neither the ethicist nor the aesthete can produce a logical proof or demonstration that makes his or her viewpoint objectively certain is not a reason to despair. We human beings find uncertainty painful, and we would like to escape it. The history of western philosophy is, as John Dewey has said, the history of

---

[8] Kierkegaard, *Concluding Unscientific Postscript,* 109. The Hongs translate this literally, but awkwardly in English, as "a logical system can be given, but a system of existence cannot be given." I have here removed Kierkegaard's original italics.

[9] Ibid., 118.

"the quest for certainty."[10] However, in reality, most of us, most of the time, find ways of resolving this uncertainty. Despite our finitude, we develop convictions and act on the basis of commitments.

How do we do this? Here is Kierkegaard's break with the other main plank of classical foundationalist epistemology. The foundationalist typically sees human emotions as distorting filters and biases; the epistemological task is to put these aside somehow and become purely "rational" and objective. However, Kierkegaard sees what he variously calls "subjectivity" and "inwardness" as lying at the heart of human existence. Without desires, hopes, fears, and loves human life would be impossible because human choice and action would be impossible.

Despite our finitude, Kierkegaard does not embrace skepticism, at least with respect to what he calls "essential human knowledge," the knowledge a human person must have to be fully human and live a truly human life. It is true that we cannot stand at some impossible place of pure neutrality and objectivity and grasp the truth as a matter of pure logic. Anyone who tries to occupy what Thomas Nagel has called "the view from nowhere" will fail to grasp what human life is all about.[11] Rather, the path to truth requires us to embrace our subjectivity. The evil of cruelty cannot be recognized apart from our emotional repugnance to cruelty, just as the goodness of love cannot be perceived apart from our emotional embrace of its splendor.

However, there are emotions and there are emotions. Our task is not to divest ourselves of subjectivity, but to allow our subjectivity to be formed and developed in the right way. To explain this requires an exploration of the famous Kierkegaardian claim that "truth is subjectivity," and I will now try to say something about this important theme.

---

[10] See John Dewey, *The Quest for Certainty* (New York: Capricorn Books, 1929).

[11] Thomas Nagel, *The View From Nowhere* (New York: Oxford University Press, 1986).

"Truth is Subjectivity"

The claim by Johannes Climacus in *Concluding Unscientific Postscript* that "truth is subjectivity" is one of the most well-known and yet misunderstood Kierkegaardian claims. Climacus himself says that this claim is a "Socratic" one, and thus it is perhaps right that it should be voiced by a pseudonym rather than Kierkegaard himself. At the very least, Kierkegaard the Christian writer will want to balance this Socratic claim with the apparently contradictory claim that "subjectivity is untruth," reflecting Kierkegaard's commitment to the Christian doctrine of human sinfulness. However, the contradiction between the two claims is only apparent, and there is little doubt that Kierkegaard himself is firmly committed to this "Socratic" thesis.

But what does it mean to say that truth is subjectivity? We can begin by saying what it does not mean. It is not an endorsement of epistemological subjectivism or some form of relativism. The relevant section of *Concluding Unscientific Postscript* is difficult to interpret because Climacus brings together two kinds of issues that are not usually seen as connected: epistemology and soteriology, or what theologians call a theory of salvation. He begins with epistemology by examining two classical philosophical definitions of truth. However, his real concern is not with the adequacy of a philosophical theory of truth, but with the question of what it means for a human being to possess the truth. To grasp the significance of this, we must not think of truth in the way characteristic of contemporary philosophy, focusing on the properties of propositions, but in the way ancient thinkers conceived of truth. For Socrates and Plato, at least as Kierkegaard understood them, having the truth meant having the key to human life, possessing that which makes it possible to live life as it was intended to be lived. We might think, even more pertinently for Kierkegaard, of Jesus' promise to his followers that "You shall know the truth, and the truth shall make you free."[12] Here the possession of truth is the philosophical expression of what is termed in theology "salvation" for Christians, "enlightenment" for Buddhists.

---

[12] John 8:32.

So we should not be too surprised when Johannes Climacus suddenly switches from a discussion of philosophical theories of truth to the issue that really concerns him: How does a human being acquire the truth that makes life worthwhile? How can a human person live "true-ly?" He poses a stark alternative between "objective" and "subjective" answers to this question:

> *When the question about truth is asked objectively, truth is reflected upon objectively as an object to which the knower relates himself. What is reflected upon is not the relation but that what he relates himself to is the truth, the true. If only that to which he relates himself is the truth, the true, then the subject is in the truth. When the question about truth is asked subjectively, the individual's relation is reflected upon subjectively. If only the how of this relation is in truth, the individual is in truth, even if he in this way were to relate himself to untruth.*[13]

Climacus attaches a footnote to this passage in which he makes an important qualification by noting that he is no longer trying to give a general philosophical definition of truth but only intends to discuss "the truth that is essentially related to existence."

In this passage Climacus does not deny the existence of objective, propositional truth, but rather presupposes there is such a thing. What he wants to know is whether a person who knows what is objectively true is thereby personally "in the truth," and whether a person whose beliefs are objectively false can nevertheless have a life that can be described as true. The answer is given through a famous thought-experiment in which he compares a "Christian" of sorts with a passionate pagan:

> If someone who lives in the midst of Christianity enters, with knowledge of the true idea of God, the house of God, the house of the true God, and prays, but prays in untruth, and if someone lives in an idolatrous land but prays with all the passion of infinity, although his eyes are resting upon the image of an idol—where then, is there more truth? The one prays in truth to God

---

[13] Kierkegaard, *Concluding Unscientific Postscript,* 199. Italics original.

> although he is worshiping an idol; the other prays in untruth to the true God and is therefore in truth worshiping an idol.[14]

Climacus finds no need to argue this point; he thinks his answer is "obvious for anyone who is not totally botched by science and scholarship."[15]

Perhaps things are not so obvious as this, but the view Climacus defends here is certainly reasonable. For if we are trying to determine what makes a human person's life "true," it seems very plausible that objectively true intellectual beliefs are neither sufficient nor necessary. Such beliefs are not sufficient, because in order for a person to live truly, it is not enough to affirm the right propositions. The person must allow his or her beliefs to transform his or her life. Climacus uses religious examples to make his point, but we could use a non-religious example also. Suppose, for example, that it is true that global warming is occurring as a result of human activity. Perhaps I believe this is so and even believe that humans ought to cut their use of fossil fuels and do other things to reduce greenhouse gases. Surely, however, it is not enough for me to have the right belief about this; what is crucial is that this belief in some way shapes my actions and leads me to change my behavior in appropriate ways.

It is just as clear that true objective beliefs are not necessary, either. Assume for the moment that the truth about human life is that the best kind of life is one devoted to compassion and loving service to others. Imagine an individual who has come to believe, perhaps by reading Nietzsche or Ayn Rand, that compassion is in fact a vice, and that truly ethical people care only about themselves. Despite this objectively wrong belief, it might be possible for this individual to respond with genuine compassion and love when confronted by actual human suffering. Whatever the ultimate ethical and religious truth may be, human persons may be better—or worse—than their theories. The Kierkegaardian view is that it is subjectivity, the inward emotions and

---

[14] Ibid., 201.
[15] Ibid.

passions that give shape to human lives and motivate human actions, that makes the difference.

We can see, therefore, that the claim that "truth is subjectivity," far from supporting a Sartrean conception of radical choice, actually presupposes that there is an objective ideal for humans to strive for. To be sure, Kierkegaard does not view the ideal self as a "one size fits all" pattern. Although there are universal elements to the ideal, and a universal structure to human existence, God has created all humans as unique individuals, and his intentions are for them to affirm and even celebrate that uniqueness. Despite this individuality, however, there is still something like an objective standard for every person, defined by God's intentions. If Kierkegaard is right to think that there is something like an ideal of selfhood that each of us should strive for, then it makes sense to describe our lives as representations of that ideal that can be true or false.

This point suggests another problem, however. Even if it makes sense to talk of human lives as true or false, why think of objective, propositional truth and subjectivity as if they were mutually exclusive options? Perhaps it is right that a person can believe true things and yet live falsely, and thus it is not enough to have the right beliefs. And perhaps a person who has the wrong beliefs can still live truthfully in some ways. But is it not better to have true beliefs *and* to appropriate those beliefs in the right way? Can't true beliefs sometimes shape a life in the right way? And don't false beliefs sometimes hamper a person from living in a truthful manner? Would it not be better for Kierkegaard's pagan to have the "inner passion of infinity" *and* to have true beliefs about God? In my own earlier example, it is possible for the Nietzschean who thinks compassion is a vice to live compassionately, but it might be harder for him to do this, perhaps even impossible. So it seems better for him to have both true beliefs about the value of compassion and the appropriate emotional response to those beliefs.

I think that Kierkegaard recognizes the force in this line of thinking and would concede the point. Notice that in the example of the nominal Christian and the pagan, Climacus only claims that the pagan has *more* truth in his life than the hypocritical Christian, not that the pagan's situation is ideal. Kierkegaard does not want to defend a sloppy relativism that holds that "it does not matter what you believe as long as you are sincere." The point is not that everything is fine so long as one is passionate about one's beliefs, so that a sincere and dedicated Nazi would become an exemplar of human life, or that the perpetrators of the 9/11 attacks were justified because of their passionate commitment to their cause. Of course the truth of our beliefs does matter, and Climacus recognizes this: "Exactly equally important as the truth, and if one of the two must be preferred still more important, is the manner in which the truth is received: it would help only a little if someone got millions to receive the truth, if these receivers precisely by their manner of reception were transformed into untruth."[16]

The words here are carefully chosen. Subjectivity is "exactly equally important" as objective, propositional truth, and is to be preferred only if one is forced to choose between them. But when, one might ask, would such a choice be forced on us? The answer, I think, is that the choice is forced on us when we are told that objective truth requires the complete suppression of subjectivity, the adoption of the "view from nowhere" in which I put aside emotions and passions and resolve to believe only what can be demonstrated on the basis of objective reason.

We can now understand why this discussion of living "truly" began with a discussion of philosophical theories of truth. From a Kierkegaardian standpoint, the person who chooses pure objectivity loses the truth both in life and in belief; the person who chooses subjectivity has a chance at truth in both arenas. The quest for certainty ends up in skepticism, for humans are finite, historically situated beings who can see nothing if they adopt "the view from nowhere." Kierkegaard consistently sees the universal doubt that supposedly stands at the foundation of modern philosophy to be impossible, and that is a good thing, since if it could be achieved it could never be overcome. He argues that it is impossible for doubt to "overcome itself," but that doubt can only be stopped by personal resolve.[17] To see

---

[16] Kierkegaard, *Concluding Unscientific Postscript*, 247.

[17] See, for example, *Concluding Unscientific Postscript*, 335-336, especially the footnote that begins on 335.

we must stand somewhere and trust that our perspective, finite and limited as it is, is one that enables us to see something.

Kierkegaard's polemic is directed against a philosophical tradition that would claim we must first settle our intellectual questions and then turn our attention to how to put our beliefs into practice. Kierkegaard believes that in one sense our questions are never "settled," since we do not have "the System." Doubts can always be raised, and questions can always be asked. If we demand intellectual certainty before we begin to live our convictions we will never live at all.

Nor will we make much progress on the intellectual questions themselves. With respect to what he calls "essential truth," the truth about living, progress in answering our intellectual questions goes hand in hand with progress in becoming better people. This is hardly a new idea. The idea that knowing the truth requires the knower to strive to become a better person was common in the ancient world. Even Aristotle says that it is probably hopeless for someone who has been brought up poorly, and thus has a bad character, to study ethics.[18] Kierkegaard accepts the ancient principle that "only like knows like," and this implies that one must be good to know the Good.

Thus, the answer to the charge that our beliefs matter is to agree that they do, but to argue that we cannot hope to settle questions of belief in a way that is prior to and independent of our struggle to become selves of a certain sort. Subjectivity is not only essential if we are to put our beliefs into practice, but plays an essential role in the acquiring of those beliefs.

This helps us see why Kierkegaard, though he rejects the possibility that ethical and religious truths can be demonstrated through some objective, logical method, does not see this as a failure that requires some "radical choice" or arbitrary act of will. He is no Sartrean existentialist. The reasons an ethicist offers to an aesthete for becoming ethical may or may not move the aesthete. If the reasons do move the aesthete, that will be because they have made contact with the desires

---

[18] See Aristotle, *Nicomachean Ethics,* Book 1, Chapter 3 (1095b 3-8).

and hopes and fears of an actual individual. Arguments do not have to be convincing to "all sane, rational people" to be good arguments, and arguments that do move people do so by making contact with actual individuals, replete with subjectivity.

Kierkegaard does not assume, as some "postmodern" thinkers are prone to do, that the failure of classical foundationalism leads to the collapse of the ideal of truth. This kind of postmodernist is in reality much more indebted to the modern philosophical tradition than he realizes. Both the modern and postmodern philosophers are committed to the following premise: "If there is an objective truth, then there must be a method which guarantees us access to that truth." Modern philosophers, from Descartes through Husserl, accepted the premise and concluded that there must be such a method, even if they disagreed about what the method is. The skeptical postmodernist doubts we have such a method and concludes that we must give up on objective truth.

Kierkegaard, however, rejects the premise both kinds of thinkers share. For reality is a system for God, and there is thus a way things truly are, regardless of whether I can attain the right view of things. The fact that we have no "method" that gives the foundational certainties sought by the modern philosopher is no reason to give up on objective truth. He thus thinks it is possible for the ethical life to be superior to the aesthetic life, and the religious life to be superior to the ethical life, regardless of whether it is possible to demonstrate this to a particular aesthete or ethicist. There is no escape from subjectivity and no logical techniques will free us from the possibility of mistakes. He has faith that humans can discover what they need to know to live truly, but the process God has designed to make this possible is one that goes through subjectivity:

> Truly, no more than God lets a species of fish to come into existence in a particular lake unless the plant that is its nourishment is also growing there, no more will God allow the truly concerned person to be ignorant of what he must believe.... The need brings the *nourishment* along with it; what is sought is in the seeking that seeks it; faith is in the concern over not having faith; love is in the self-concern over not loving.... The need brings the nourishment along with,

not *by itself,* as if the need produced the nourishment, but by virtue of a divine determination that joins the two, the need and the nourishment.[19]

Kierkegaard's Critique of Sartre

Perhaps it is not too surprising then that we find in Kierkegaard's writings a prophetic description of Sartre's view of the self, along with a powerful critique. In *The Sickness Unto Death*, Anti-Climacus, Kierkegaard's Christian pseudonym, describes a form of despair in which the self attempts to invent itself, relying on the "infinite form" of the self, which is the self's power to distance itself from itself through consciousness.

> But with the help of the infinite form, the negative self, he wants first of all to take upon himself the transformation of all this in order to fashion out of it a self such as he wants, produced with the help of the infinite form of the negative self...he himself wants to compose his self by means of being the infinite form.[20]

The passage in question reads as if Kierkegaard had been reading Sartre's *Being and Nothingness*, which is a phenomenological exploration of just this form of negativity. Anti-Climacus struggles to find a term to describe this kind of philosophy: "If a generic name for this despair is wanted, it could be called stoicism, but understood as not referring only to that sect."[21] Today we have a better term for what Anti-Climacus is trying to label; we call it existentialism.

The criticism that Anti-Climacus goes on to make of this philosophy is telling. The problem with radical choice is that it cannot be the basis of values that make any kind of claim on us, for we are aware that the values we have chosen are grounded in a choice that could be undone at any time. Thus, on this view, "the negative form of the self exercises a loosening power as well as a binding power; at any

---

[19] Søren Kierkegaard, *Christian Discourses*, ed. & trans. Howard V. Hong and Edna H. Hong (Princeton: Princeton University Press, 1997), 244-45.

[20] Søren Kierkegaard, *The Sickness Unto Death*, ed. & trans. Howard V. Hong and Edna H. Hong (Princeton: Princeton University Press, 1980), 68.

[21] Ibid., 68.

time it can quite arbitrarily start all over again, and no matter how long one idea is pursued, the entire action is within a hypothesis."[22] Thus, the self that has created itself turns out to be empty: "this absolute ruler is a king without a country, actually ruling over nothing; his position, his sovereignty, is subordinate to the dialectic that rebellion is legitimate at any moment."[23]

I conclude that Kierkegaard is better thought of as a prophetic critic of existentialism than as the father of the movement. If Jean Paul Sartre is the exemplar of existentialism, then Kierkegaard is no existentialist.

---

[22] Ibid., 69.
[23] Ibid.

7.

THE THEOLOGICAL SELF IN KIERKEGAARD'S *SICKNESS UNTO DEATH*

Philip G. Ziegler

"For truth, which is what the gospel of justification of the ungodly is about,
shatters not a few of what were to us till now self-evident beliefs.
But it does this only to generate new self-evident beliefs:
ones which can stand before God."[1]

Introduction

Approaches to Kierkegaard in contemporary theology vary widely. And among those who take Kierkegaard primarily to be an "expositor of Christian concepts," there is specific debate concerning whether and just how he might stand in formative relation to the traditions and trajectories of Lutheran theology.[2] It seems incontrovertible that Kierkegaard's searching reflections upon the conception of the human person as *coram deo*—i.e., before God—represents a deep investment in a distinctively Lutheran theological motif. This essay explores the

---

[1] Eberhard Jüngel, *Justification: The Heart of the Christian Faith* (London: T&T Clark, 2001), xxxvi.

[2] See Lee C. Barrett, "Kierkegaard as Theologian: A History of Countervailing Interpretations," in *The Oxford Handbook of Kierkegaard*, ed. J. Lippitt and G. Pattison (Oxford: Oxford University Press, 2013), 541-543 and more extensively on Kierkegaard's own relation to Luther also Ernest B. Koenker, "Søren Kierkegaard on Luther," in *Interpreters of Luther: Essays in Honor of Wilhelm Pauck*, ed. J. Pelikan (Philadelphia: Fortress Press, 1968), 231-252, and Lee C. Barrett, "Kierkegaard's Appropriation and Critique of Luther and Lutheranism," in *A Companion to Kierkegaard* (Oxford: Blackwell, 2015), 180-192, especially in relation to the themes of justification and conscience, 182-185. Notably, discussion of the concept of *coram deo* itself does not feature in either Koenker's or Barrett's valuable accounts.

place and function of the *coram deo* motif in the Dane's theological programme seeking thereby to discern and account for its significance. Focusing on the text of *Sickness Unto Death* in particular, I will argue that the *coram deo* motif serves to secure the fact that the human self is at once constituted and governed by its relationship to God such that true human subjectivity—one of Kierkegaard's central preoccupations—is shown to have as its decisive condition of possibility the transcendent reality of God's sovereign claim and mercy. More than this, Kierkegaard's use of the *coram deo* motif republishes key features of the essential logic of Luther's theological anthropology, even as it sharpens the explication of human sinfulness and so also radicalizes the appreciation of divine grace as the sole possibility of genuine human selfhood.

What is commonly referred to as Luther's own "relational" anthropology has at its heart the claim that standing "before God" is fundamentally constitutive of human reality as such.[3] As Hans-Martin Barth observes, in light of his "experience of transcendence in the encounter with the word" Luther "saw his life with an immediacy that can scarcely be exaggerated as existence 'before God,' *coram deo*."[4] That humans *qua* creatures "cannot subsist for a moment by their own strength" but rather rest entirely upon God's creative sustaining is essential to this claim; but so too, and most distinctively, is the idea that human beings are constituted in and by their confrontation with the *iustitia dei* and so ultimately are *per definitionem* those tried by divine righteousness and justified by faith.[5] Indeed, the logic of justification supplies, for Luther, the logic of creation as such, in as much as *qua*

---

[3] For recent summary discussion of Luther's anthropology, see Notiger Slenczka, "Luther's Anthropology," in *The Oxford Handbook to Martin Luther's Theology*, ed. R. Kolb, et al, (Oxford: Oxford University Press, 2014), 212-232 and Oswald Bayer, *Martin Luther's Theology: A Contemporary Interpretation*, trans. T. H. Trapp (Minneapolis: Fortress, 2008), 154-176.

[4] Hans-Martin Barth, *The Theology of Martin Luther: A Critical Assessment* (Minneapolis: Fortress Press, 2013), 491.

[5] The citation is drawn from Luther's *Bondage of the Will*, *Luther's Works*, vol. 33, ed. P. S. Watson (Philadelphia: Fortress Press, 1972), 103.

creature, "human existence is 'justified through faith' existence."[6] As Gerhard Ebeling emphasizes, the phrase *coram deo* announces that reality itself "is only understood for what it is if the word of God, through which it has its being and which is what is truly reality in it, is heard" because human reality is simply and fundamentally "existence in the sight of God, in the presence of God, under the eyes of God, in the judgement of God, and in the world of God."[7]

"Before God" is, of course, a spatial rather than temporal trope. Minimally, it carries the meaning "with reference to God." But such rendering is far too formal to deliver adequately the force of Luther's idea of the existence determining Word of God, i.e., of the divine address that effectively constitutes human reality. To be *coram deo* is to find oneself in a determinative and inescapable encounter with the God of the gospel mediated concretely by God's word, which means *via* both law and gospel. As we shall see, Kierkegaard's own talk of the human self "before God" is substantive in just this way, reiterating as it does the biblical idiom which speaks of the human being set "before the countenance of the Lord."[8] In unfolding this case that Kierkegaard is here best understood with close reference to Luther, I am pushing in a quite different direction than other readings of this theme in *Sickness unto Death*. On the one hand, the reading I offer does not concern itself

---

[6] Bayer, *Martin Luther's Theology*, 156. Famously, Luther offers this definition in thesis 32 of his *Disputatio de homine*: "The human being is human in that s/he is justified by faith," see "The Disputation on Man (1536)," in *Luther's Works*, vol. 34, ed. L. W. Spitz (Philadelphia: Fortress Press, 1960), 137-40. See also William C. Weinrich, "*Homo Theologicus*: Aspects of a Lutheran Doctrine of Man," in *Personal Identity in Theological Perspective*, ed. R. Links et al. (Grand Rapids: Eerdmans, 2006), 29-44.

[7] Gerhard Ebeling, *Luther: An Introduction to His Thought*, trans. R. A. Wilson (London: Collins, 1972), 198-99.

[8] The Vulgate makes use of the actual phrase *coram deo* regularly in this sense of "in the sight of God," not least in passages where judgments and solemn declarations of truthfulness are made, e.g., Gen 6:11; Ps 56:13; 2 Cor 2:17, 4:2, 7:13, 8:21, 12:19; Gal 1:20; 1 Tim 5:4, 5:21; 2 Tim 4:1. Luther's own usage (*vor Gott*) typically means decisively "in the sight of God"—see, e.g., Martin Luther, "The Bondage of the Will," *LW* 33, 239-240; and in comments on Psalm 73:16 (*LW* 10, 418) and Psalm 95:2 (*LW* 11, 252). In Danish language Bibles, *coram deo* is typically rendered by the phrase "*for Guds Åsyn*."

directly with the "social function" of the idea of *coram deo* which others have discerned.[9] On the other, my reading also pulls away from those that restrict their interest either to the role of the idea in the outworking of Kierkegaard's own poetic autobiography, or else consider "before God" a kind of rational "postulate," i.e., a strictly formal and "regulative" concept whose meaning is purely "heuristic" and not at all "ostensive," as Kant himself would put it.[10] For a dynamic, realist account of the concept of *coram deo* allows us to understand the structure and content of *Sickness unto Death* as an elaboration of Kierkegaard's core conviction, that:

> Paganism required: Know yourself. Christianity declares: No, that is provisional—know yourself—and then look at yourself in the mirror of the Word in order to know yourself properly. No true self-knowledge without God-knowledge or [without standing] before God. To stand before the mirror means to stand before God.[11]

The Despairing Self "Transparent to its Ground"— The Sinful Self "Before God"

The argument of *Sickness unto Death* unfolds in two parts. In the first, Kierkegaard sets out a wide-ranging discussion of the manifold ways in which human beings fail at—and so *despair* of—being "a self."

---

[9] Seung-Goo Lee, "A Social Function of *Coram Deo* in the Thought of Kierkegaard," *Journal of Reformed Theology* 1 (2007), 153-177, and in quite a different mode also John D. Caputo, "Hauntological Hermeneutics and the Interpretation of Christian Faith: On Being Dead Equal Before God," in *Hermeneutics at the Crossroads*, ed. K. Vanhoozer (Bloomington, IN: Indiana University Press, 2006), 95-109.

[10] For the former, see Joackim Garff, *Søren Kierkegaard: A Biography*, trans. B. H. Kirmmse (Princeton: Princeton University Press, 2005), 542-45; for the latter, George Pattison, "'Before God' as a Regulative Concept," in *Kierkegaard Studies Yearbook*, ed. N. J. Cappelørn et al. (Berlin: Walter de Gruyter, 1997), 70-84. The remark from Kant comes from the *Critique of Pure Reason*, ed. and trans. P. Guyer and A. W. Wood (Cambridge: Cambridge University Press, 1997), 606.

[11] Søren Kierkegaard, *Søren Kierkegaard's Journal and Papers*, ed, and trans. H. V. Hong and E. H. Hong (Bloomington, IN: Indiana University Press, 1967-78), vol. 4, 40 (X.4 A4120).

Famously, he defines the self in reflexive and agential terms, suggesting that a human being is established as a three-fold synthesizing of the finite, the infinite, and the relation between them. If all were as it should be, one would say that "in relating itself to itself and in willing to be itself, the self rests transparently in the power that established it."[12] As it is, the self perpetuates, suffers, and so becomes a *mis-relation*, namely, "the misrelation in the relation of a synthesis that relates itself to itself."[13] Such misrelating is despair. It has as its dual condition of possibility, the constitution of the human self in its proper and "original state from the hand of God," and the reality of the human self as spirit, i.e., as a free relating that can forfeit its proper and original state by choosing the possibility of relating to itself otherwise from the very moment it is "released from [God's] hand, as it were."[14] As Kierkegaard represents it, this "fall" is ceaselessly enacted in the present precisely because it is constantly reproduced by the active misrelating of the self to itself and its eternal ground. Never just sick, but always also self-sickening, the self spirals through all-manner of variations of despair: suspended in the dialectic of infinitude and finitude, possibility and necessity, the self enacts its constitutive freedom and consciousness in ways that consistently fail at its task and forfeit its destiny of "becoming itself." The majority of section one of the work schematically analyses the many "forms of this sickness" with alarming acuity *en route* to the final, maximal, "demonic despair" of absolute nihilistic defiance in which a self "in hatred towards existence, it wills to be itself, wills to be itself in accordance with its misery."[15]

As the invocation of "God" in this brief discussion signals, even before the argument becomes explicitly hamartiological in section two, Kierkegaard's anthropology is already theological in character. All despair is properly "despair of the eternal and over oneself."[16] That a

---

[12] Søren Kierkegaard, *Sickness unto Death: A Christian Psychological Exposition for Upbuilding and Awakening*, ed. and trans. H. V. Hong and E. H. Hong (Princeton: Princeton University Press, 1980), 14.

[13] *SUD*, 15.

[14] *SUD*, 16.

[15] *SUD*, 42, 73.

[16] *SUD*, 60.

human being is in despairing mis-relation to itself is something that can only be discerned with reference to the original and final reality of a *proper* relating won in and through relation to God.[17] In fact, Kierkegaard avers here that the reality of the self cannot be conceived correctly in anything other than a theological register, as the concept of the human as *spirit* only really exists here. Below and outwith this register—i.e., without the self being "conscious of itself as spirit or conscious of itself before God as spirit"—all despair will be suffered in ignorance; indeed, Kierkegaard suggests this is the most prevalent form of despair in the world.[18] Never just the self, but the self *and* "the God relationship"—indeed, the self *in* the God-relationship—is what is fundamentally at issue. This is made more patent when Kierkegaard declares that "the opposite to being in despair is to have faith": the definition of faith is that of genuine selfhood, namely, that "in relating itself to itself and in willing to be itself, the self rests transparently in the power that established it."[19] This means that the discussion of despair concerns the pathology of unbelief. In view of this, it would be difficult to sustain the view that Part One of *Sickness Unto Death* represents a pure and independent phenomenology of the despairing self; rather, it substantively anticipates the more extensively theological discussion which follows in Part Two.[20] Here we discern an evident parallel with Luther's *Disputatio de homine*, where the Reformer asserts the severe limitations of the philosophical approach to the question of humanity on the basis that there is "no hope" that one "can himself know what he is until he sees himself in his origin which is God."[21]

---

[17] *SUD*, 16, 30.

[18] *SUD*, 46, 45.

[19] *SUD*, 49.

[20] For supple and detailed discussion of the interpretative issues involved, see Arne Grøn, "The Relation Between Part One and Part Two of *The Sickness unto Death*," in *Kierkegaard Studies Yearbook*, ed. N. J. Cappelørn et al. (Berlin: Walter de Gruyter, 1997), 35-50.

[21] Luther, *Disputatio de homine*, thesis 17, cf. theses 11-18, *LW* 34, 137-38.

This character of Kierkegaard's anthropology becomes all the more robust in Part Two of the work with the explicit introduction of the decisive concept of *coram deo* in the definition of sin:

> Sin is: *before God, or with the conception of God, in despair not to will to be oneself, or in despair to will to be oneself.* Thus sin is intensified weakness or intensified defiance: sin is the intensification of despair. The emphasis is on *before God*, or with the conception of God; it is the conception of God that makes sin dialectically, and religiously what lawyers call "aggravated" despair.[22]

As Dietrich Bonhoeffer suggested in his own 1930 inaugural lecture,

> The person who understands himself from the perspective of his possibilities understands himself within his own self-reflection. In revelation, however, the human being is torn out of this reflection and receives the answer to his question only from and before God [*nur von und vor Gott*]. Here we find the fundamental difference between philosophical and theological anthropology.[23]

Kierkegaard's concern in the second part of *Sickness unto Death* is precisely to display this very difference, as he undertakes an ever-more-explicitly *theological* anthropological reflection; indeed, he explicitly styles his new subject here the *"theological self"* which is simply, as he explains, "the self directly before God."[24] I suggest that in doing so he specifically echoes Luther's own use of the parallel Latin phrase *"homo theologicus"* in his 1536 *disputatio de homine*.[25] Further, like Luther, for Kierkegaard the theological self is the human being understood firmly with reference to its career as created, fallen, and set under the

---

[22] *SUD*, 77.

[23] Dietrich Bonhoeffer, *Barcelona, Berlin, New York: 1928-1930. Dietrich Bonhoeffer Works*, ed. C. J. Green, trans. D. W. Stott (Minneapolis: Fortress Press, 2008), vol. 10, 403. Setting out the logic of this claim is the core ambition of Bonhoeffer's early dissertation, *Act and Being*.

[24] *SUD*, 79.

[25] Thesis 28 speaks of Aristotle as one "who knows nothing of theological man," *LW* 34, 139. The meaning of the "theological self" is spelt out explicitly in theses 20-23, 32, and 35.

divine promise of reconciliation and redemption. Theological anthropology organised by the concept of existence *coram deo* is not merely or primarily keyed to the doctrine of creation as such, but rather to the reality of sin, judgment and redemption, and so to soteriology.

The phraseology of the opening remark of Part Two intimates close continuity with the preceding discussion of despair: talk of "intensification" and "aggravation" suggest that the effect of the introduction of the *coram deo* is to effect a *quantitative* adjustment. But Kierkegaard's fuller exposition deploys concepts designed to express the *qualitative* difference at stake with the advent of God most fully into the discussion. The "theological self" is "no longer merely the human self" and the discussion must, now "dialectically take a new direction"[26] because the introduction of the reality of the self *coram deo* amplifies the significance of the situation of the self "*infinitely*"[27] by placing it in the register of *eternity*[28]; *this* qualification of human existence makes the self a matter of "extraordinary" importance.[29] To place the self before God is to eliminate at a stroke the importance of every partial and measured assessment of human reality as "more or less" or "in part" in which nothing decisive is (or ought to be) taken too far.[30] Kierkegaard here suggests that this natural, all-too-human—indeed "pagan"—style of moderate reasoning domesticates and so betrays the radicality of the human situation, a radicality that only dialectical theological reflection can honour. As in other Kierkegaard texts, the ideas of "paradox" and "offense" operate here to announce the humiliation of reason before the reality of the Christian God whose coming profoundly qualifies our human reality in judgment and grace. As he puts it memorably: "Here Christianity steps in [and] makes the sign of the cross before speculation."[31]

---

[26] *SUD*, 79.

[27] *SUD*, 80, 100.

[28] *SUD*, 105.

[29] *SUD*, 83, 86.

[30] Kierkegaard refers to the golden mean—*ne quid nimis*—here as a shorthand for all of this, *Sickness unto Death*, 86.

[31] *SUD*, 120.

This is all to acknowledge that the introduction of the *coram deo* into the discussion affects both the content but also decisively the form of reflection itself. Both the "what" and the "how" of our thinking and discourse are implicated in the situation of the despairing self *coram deo*, which is to say, in sin. This insight is concentrated in Kierkegaard's claim that the advent of the concept of sin brings with it "the category of individuality" and of "the single individual."[32] In fact, when pressed, the idea of sin *coram deo* properly reduces to acknowledgement of the reality of *the actual sinner*: Sin "cannot be thought speculatively" because the reality of God and of human existence before God disallow such abstraction and instead demand "earnestness" from a discourse that "immerses itself in actuality."[33] This pressure derives from the fact that, as Kierkegaard puts it, such "abstractions simply do not exist for God; for God in Christ there live only single individuals (sinners)…God does not avail himself of an abridgement."[34] Although the *coram deo* arrives late discursively and conceptually, its arrival—when taken seriously—presses the whole business of human self-reflection into the existential situation of a genuine confrontation with God: indeed, merely to think and talk *about* the human *coram deo* is not yet to have suffered and acknowledged the reality of actually having being placed *coram deo*.

It is worth noting that Kierkegaard's exposition of the self in sin *coram deo* also develops along the lines of the traditional Lutheran law and gospel pattern. In the first instance, the encounter with God takes the form of law in the sense that God comes to provide the "criterion"[35] that qualifies and "infinitely magnifies" the desperate human situation. In Ebeling's concise phrasing: "The *coram*-relationship reveals that the fundamental situation of man is that of a person on trial."[36] With the image of the human "before God" Kierkegaard directly evokes the biblical picture of the person confronted with the holiness of God, placed before the divine judgment

---

[32] *SUD*, 119.
[33] *SUD*, 119-20.
[34] *SUD*, 121.
[35] *SUD*, 79, 81, 114.
[36] Ebeling, *Luther*, 197.

seat, or addressed by the divine commandment and claim. This is in keeping with the idea that it is exclusively in and through the encounter with God that the reality of sin is disclosed and known as such. In traditional Lutheran doctrine, it is the primary work of the law to aggravate and illumine sin, and so to drive the sinner to despair of his or her own efforts at putting life to rights. The exposure of the self *coram deo* is a compressed depiction of precisely this encounter with the law: "Christianity proceeds to establish sin so firmly as a position that the human understanding can never comprehend it."[37]

But the theological self is finally forged by both law *and gospel*. As Kierkegaard considers, the self is never only *coram deo* but always *coram Christi*, which means it is confronted with the reality of sin because confronted with the reality of *forgiveness* of sins.[38] Now Kierkegaard's specific interest here is not in elaboration of the evangelical promise. It is in expounding the modalities of human sin, including those ways in which sin despairs of the gospel itself, i.e., refuses to entrust itself to the "infinite love of [God's] merciful grace" enacted in the incarnation[39] and so—in the language of the thesis of the work—refuses to "rest transparently in the power that established it." As Kierkegaard observes in the very last sentence of the work, this refusal is precisely the refusal of *faith*.[40] If the gospel is received as gospel, "the person who does not take offence *worships in* faith."[41] But what we have, in effect, is a reflection on how the word of the gospel can and does itself become "law," as it were: confronted by the reality of God come low for us to save in Jesus Christ, the self can and does yet take offense and, despairing, declines worship and refuses to believe. Precisely because here the encounter with God is concretized fully and finally in the paradox of the incarnation—because the sinner is before God *in Christi*—this represents for Kierkegaard "the highest intensification of sin."[42]

---

[37] *SUD*, 100.
[38] *SUD*, 113.
[39] *SUD*, 126.
[40] *SUD*, 131.
[41] *SUD*, 129.
[42] *SUD*, 131.

It is a matter of note that in all of this *Sickness unto Death* closely parallels the discussion of sin which features in the argument advanced earlier in *Philosophical Fragments*.[43] In that text, Kierkegaard had contrasted what might be involved in coming to know the truth in the situation of ignorance—detailed in the text by reference to Socrates and the Platonic idea of knowing as recollection—with what would be involved in coming to know the truth in the situation of sin, i.e., where one exists in *untruth*. The learner in the latter case is one who exists in "polemical" contradiction of the truth and lacks the very condition of possibility for coming to truth; indeed, such a person cannot even form the question about the truth. Such a person, Kierkegaard says there, "has forfeited and is forfeiting the condition" for coming to the truth.[44] The one who is able to teach the truth in this situation is no less than a saviour, i.e., the one whose coming sets one in a relation to the truth in which the truth itself affords the very conditions for its reception, and so, as Kierkegaard says, effectively delivers a person from "not existing" to "existing."[45] In spinning out his account of the manifold refusal to "be a self" in despair before God, Kierkegaard is expositing the subjectivity—and so inescapable existential self-involvement—that corresponds to this very scenario of decisive revelatory encounter of the divine with the human being *in sin*. In both texts, the human can and must be *placed into the truth* by the effective advent of God which places our despair into the truth and so renders it sin, even as it overreaches it in judgment and forgiveness. This is what Kierkegaard means when he asserts in *Sickness unto Death* that "sin is a position": sin can only be acknowledged on the basis of "a revelation of God"[46] because the reality of being "*before God* is the definitely positive element in it."[47] This important claim, and more fully the close interrelation of the arguments of these two different works—one concerned with the subjectivity of the human being before

---

[43] Søren Kierkegaard, *Philosophical Fragments*, ed. and trans. H.V. Hong and E. H. Hong (Princeton: Princeton University Press, 1985).

[44] Kierkegaard, *Philosophical Fragments*, 14-15.

[45] Kierkegaard, *Philosophical Fragments*, 22.

[46] *SUD*, 96.

[47] *SUD*, 100.

God and the other with the sheer historical positivity of the eternal moment of saving revelation—makes it difficult to accede the thought that "before God" is, as Pattison suggests, a strictly regulative concept with only the logical and discursive force of an "*as if.*" Instead, it displays the logic of a theology of the Word, in which the divine address effectively delivers its hearers into the truth of its own declaration and judgment (law) and grace (gospel). "That sin is a position," Kierkegaard observes in this vein, "can be made clear from only one side," namely from the side of the God before whom the human stands.[48]

Conclusions

Kierkegaard explores the idea of the human self in its despair in order to disclose that the human is a creature in revolt against itself *and its God*, in short, that the human being exists in sin. The presentation is highly schematic, offering as he says an "algebraic" definition of sin capable of expressing the essential logic of any and all its horrid actuations.[49] The concept of *coram deo* proves to be the decisive factor in this algebra: it individuates, infinitely intensifies and qualifies human existence against its sole, ultimately relevant criterion, namely the *absurd*, *offensive* and *paradoxical* reality of the saving advent of God for us in Jesus Christ.[50] But finally, it is in virtue of the reality of the *gracious* regard of God that the self may in faith *rest*—as Kierkegaard has it—transparently in God as its ground. In view of the reality of the incarnation of God in Christ, a truly human life—and so a Christian life of faith—is not beyond our reach. As Bonhoeffer once observed, Christian existence simply means "that one both may and must live as a human being before God."[51] He explains,

> Since it is unable to place itself into the truth, [the self] "is" only in the instance of God's decision for it, which

---

[48] *SUD*, 99.

[49] *SUD*, 82.

[50] *SUD*, 83.

[51] Dietrich Bonhoeffer, *Ethik*, *DBW 6*, trans. I. Tödt, et al. (München: Chr. Kaiser Verlag, 1992), 404, my translation.

must also be understood, of course in some way as its decision for God. In other words, existence "is" in its "being in reference to God"...Only that existence which stands in the truth—that is that stands in the decision—understands itself and does so in such a way that it knows itself placed into the truth by Christ in judgment and in grace.[52]

This existence "in reference to God" is precisely that "theological self" to which the reality and event of human existence *coram deo* gives rise in Kierkegaard's account.[53] In all this, Kierkegaard has clearly discerned the significance of the core Lutheran conviction that "in the *coram Deo* relationship we see ourselves as we really are—created, forgiven sinners because God sees us."[54]

Kierkegaard's hamartiologically focused account of the reality of the *theological self* can teach a number of fundamental lessons that are readily forgotten or side-lined in much contemporary theological anthropology. Let me name but two.

The first is the important place that the doctrine of sin has in the elaboration of any theological anthropology. Sylvia Walsh has persuasively argued that Kierkegaard lavishes attention upon the "negative qualifications" of the Christian life, including sin, precisely as a reflective and discursive strategy for making great the full force of the divine claim and the radicality of divine grace.[55] Beyond this, as *Sickness unto Death* itself makes patent, the reality of sin is self-obfuscating: intrinsic to the dynamic of sin is its capacity to render those trapped within it ignorant of their situation. Attending to this

---

[52] Dietrich Bonhoeffer, *Act and Being*, in *Dietrich Bonhoeffer Works*, ed. W. Whitson Floyd, trans. H. M Rumscheidt (Minneapolis: Fortress Press, 1996), vol. 2, 96. The language of being "placed into the truth" of course suggests the influence of Kierkegaard's own idiom in *Philosophical Fragments*.

[53] *SUD*, 79.

[54] Mary E. Lowe, "Sin from a Queer Lutheran Perspective," in *Transformative Lutheran Theologies: Feminist, Womanist, and Mujerista Perspectives*, ed. M. J. Steufert (Minneapolis: Fortress, 2010), 82.

[55] Sylvia Walsh, *Living Christianly: Kierkegaard's Dialectic of Christian Existence* (University Park, PA: Pennsylvania State University Press, 2005), 13-14, et passim.

peculiar feature of hamartiology requires that theologians be recalled to acknowledge their own self-involvement in the reality of which they speak, and all the more, that they admit the permeability of the boundary between theological reflection and kerygmatic witness. Concentration upon the question of sin in theological anthropology beneficially reminds theology of its place firmly within that soteriological setting which the word of God bespeaks and indeed establishes as the context of all Christian theological reflection.

The second lesson concerns the cardinal place of faith in the constitution of true human reality. Especially in a time marked by strong interest in the recovery and reassertion of the concept of virtue in the elaboration of theological anthropology and ethics, Kierkegaard here reiterates in his own distinctive way the essential Protestant claim that *to be a truly human being* is to be justified by faith. As he says, himself:

> Very often, however, it is overlooked that the opposite of sin is by no means virtue. In part, this is a pagan view, which is satisfied with a merely human criterion and simply does not know what sin is, that all sin is before God. No, *the opposite of sin is faith*, as it says in Romans 14:23: "whatever does not proceed from faith is sin." And this is one of the most decisive definitions for all Christianity—that the opposite of sin is not virtue but faith.[56]

While Kierkegaard himself has much to say about the crucial role of discipleship, the imitation of Christ as an exemplar, and the centrality and rigorous practice of the "works of love" within the Christian life, these emphases are misunderstood when taken up as a straightforward insistence upon the life of virtue or as a derogation of faith as the hallmark of Christian existence. It is true that Kierkegaard contends that great "confusion has entered the sphere of religion since the time when 'thou shalt' was abolished as the sole regulative aspect of man's relationship with God," but he immediately suggests that the most fundamental divine imperative is in fact *"thou shalt believe."*[57] Faith

---

[56] *SUD*, 82.
[57] *SUD*, 113.

names that posture of receptivity and utter dependence which marks a human life that relates itself to the truth of God *truly*. As he puts it sharply in his notebooks, a Christian life is one determined by "infinite humiliation and grace, *and then* a striving born of gratitude."[58] The properly *theological self* is thus constituted first and foremost by suffering this "infinite humiliation" before the judgment of God, and the reality of "grace" before the gospel of God: trust in the saving power of this encounter affords that gratitude from which all Christian witness, service, and moral striving arise and by which they are sustained. Or, as he says programmatically here, "the antithesis of sin/faith is the Christian one that Christianly reshapes all ethical concepts."[59] In this, again, we have a clear echo of Luther's own account of the relation of faith and works set out programmatically in *The Freedom of a Christian* (1520) and elsewhere.[60]

Overall, it seems that there is a good deal of interpretative traction to be gained when *Sickness unto Death* is read as a kind of a kaleidoscopic conceptual elaboration of sinful human existence under divine judgment and grace which accords with the anthropological claims advanced in Luther's *disputatio de homine*. Here, as elsewhere, Kierkegaard's extraordinary examinations of Christian subjectivity rest, if not on the "robustly metaphysical and ontological version of faith put forward by the Neo-Thomists," then certainly upon a robustly relational and realist version of the same Christian faith as advanced by Luther.[61] Kierkegaard's theological account of the human person *coram deo* displays the contours of a dynamic Reformation view of human existence—indeed, of the *theological self*—which moves from the fundamental acknowledgement that, as Karl Barth put it, "What I am, I am in relation to God," because, in view of the gospel "human ontology is not a settled condition, a 'nature' of any kind, but a response to the

---

[58] Kierkegaard, *Journals and Papers,* vol. 1:993, 434. Emphasis added.

[59] *SUD*, 83.

[60] Martin Luther, "The Freedom of a Christian," in *Luther's Works,* ed. and trans. J. Pelikan, H. C. Oswald, and H. T. Lehmann (Philadelphia: Fortress Press, 1957), vol. 31, 333-377.

[61] The remark is taken from Pattison, "'Before God' as a Regulative Idea," 72.

imposing presence of God, who summons me to live beyond myself."[62] In short, in and through all its despairing reflexivity, the justifying truth of the self is finally a function of God's saving regard with faith as its fitting human corollary. In Luther's idiom, to be justified by faith is what makes a human being human. In Kierkegaard's own idiom, the primary anthropological claim is just this: "according to your faith, be it unto you, or, as you believe, so you are, *to believe is to be*."[63]

---

[62] Karl Barth, *The Epistle to the Ephesians*, ed. R. D. Nelson and trans. R. M. Wright (Grand Rapids: Baker Academic, 2017), 89. The last remark comes from Christopher Asprey, *Eschatological Presence in Karl Barth's Göttingen Dogmatics* (Oxford: Oxford University Press, 2010), 24.

[63] *SUD*, 93.

8.

COMMUNION AND THE REMISSION OF SIN:

A KIERKEGAARDIAN ACCOUNT

Joshua Cockayne

Introduction

The sacrament of Holy Communion (or, the Eucharist), is of central importance to almost every Christian tradition; it is a practice which unites churches both geographically and historically. However, just what the nature of this practice is has raised countless theological schisms and debates in the history of the Church. Yet, despite widespread theological disagreement on both the nature and the practice of Communion, as Eleonore Stump notes, typically there is agreement amongst theologians in holding that "Christ's passion and death work their effect of saving human beings through faith from the human proclivity to sin...the means by which this process is effected can (and ideally should) include the Eucharist."[1] Just how the Eucharist plays a role in overcoming the problem of sin and allowing for reconciliation with Christ is where things become less clear. This is the issue to which this paper seeks to provide a response.

In this paper, I argue that Søren Kierkegaard's extensive work on Communion (which largely consists of a number of sermon like discourses written for the occasion of a Communion service) can provide an account of what Terence Cuneo describes as "remission of sin."[2] I begin by outlining the problem of the remission of sin in the Eucharist as it outlined in Cuneo's work and explore his own response

---

[1] Eleonore Stump, "Atonement and Eucharist," in *Locating Atonement: Explorations in Constructive Dogmatics,* ed. Oliver Crisp and Fred Sanders (Grand Rapids, MI: Zondervan, 2015), 221.

[2] Terence Cuneo, *Ritualized Faith* (Oxford: Oxford University Press, 2016), 188.

to the problem. Then, by drawing a parallel between Kierkegaard's discussion of the Communion in the *Discourses at Communion on Fridays* and his account of sin in *The Sickness Unto Death*, I suggest an alternative solution to this problem. According to this solution, the remission of sin is achieved by means of a person's encounter with Christ at the Communion table. This encounter allows an individual to become conscious of her sin in a way which she could not achieve by herself, and thus, by focusing on Christ, a person can be released from the bonds of sin and draw near to him.

Communion and the Remission of Sins: The Problem

As Cuneo describes the problem of the remission of sin in the Eucharist,

> it is difficult to see what the connection could be between the activities of participating in the Eucharist …on the one hand, and the state of enjoying remission of sin on the other…. If these activities do effect the remission of sin, they appear to do so (at least in part) at a sub-doxastic level. How they accomplish this, however, is something that is not easy to understand.[3]

Before considering Cuneo's solution to this problem, let us get clear on just what the problem is. To do so, it will be important to clarify the terms involved more specifically.

First, to see how there could be remission of sin, it will be important to give an account of sin. As Cuneo defines it, sin is "a state of deep disorder, which has moral, legal, aesthetic, and therapeutic dimensions, some of these dimensions being such that they needn't imply that an agent who suffers from them is morally guilty in virtue of suffering from them."[4] In developing the Kierkegaardian account of sin, I will refine this definition further, but for now, let us assume this definition as correct.

---

[3] Ibid., 186-187.
[4] Ibid., 189.

Second, following Cuneo, we can make a distinction between "forgiveness" and "remission."[5] To be forgiven for some wrongdoing is often taken to involve no longer holding that wrongdoing against a person.[6] In contrast to forgiveness, Cuneo claims that remission "is best rendered as something along the lines of *being released or liberated from the grip of sin.*"[7] A helpful way of mapping out this difference between remission and forgiveness, as I intend to use it, can be seen by focusing on Stump's distinction between the "problem of past sin" and "the problem of future sin."[8] If David, an alcoholic, kills his friend Susan's daughter in a car accident, Stump imagines, Susan can *forgive* David, thereby focusing on David's past actions. However, there still remains the ongoing effects of David's alcoholism to be addressed.[9] That is, David needs to receive remission for his alcoholism to come into right relationship with Susan. The same is true for our sin, Stump thinks; whilst God can *forgive* our past sin, what remains after being forgiven is the ongoing grip of the sin disease from which we need to receive *remission*.

Although this is not a distinction on which Kierkegaard draws (at least not explicitly), as we will see, Kierkegaard is interested in discussing both the forgiveness of sin and the remission of sin in the context of Communion. Before outlining my own Kierkegaardian account, however, I will first consider Cuneo's response to this problem, which will provide a helpful contrast with the account I go on to develop.

---

[5] Ibid., 188-89.

[6] See, for instance, Richard Swinburne's account of forgiveness which holds that forgiveness is the removal of someone's objective guilt by means of the victim of wrongdoing no longer holding the act of wrongdoing against them. Richard Swinburne, "The Christian Scheme of Salvation," in *Oxford Readings in Philosophical Theology*, ed. Michael Rea (Oxford: Oxford University Press, 2009), vol. 1, 299.

[7] Cuneo (2016), 189.

[8] Eleanore Stump, "Atonement According to Aquinas," in *Oxford Readings in Philosophical Theology*, ed. Michael Rea (Oxford: Oxford University Press, 2009), vol. 1, 270.

[9] Ibid., 278.

Cuneo suggests that eating and drinking the elements in the Eucharist might play a similar role to that played by the eating of food in cases of anorexia.[10] As he notes, drawing from Harriet Brown's discussion of having a child with anorexia, "rational persuasion, therapy and…pharmaceuticals tend not to help, at least not on their own," but rather, "the road to recovery lies in getting them to eat."[11] As Cuneo describes it, recovery from anorexia is not primarily a cognitive process, but rather, the power of eating as medicine acts in a sub-doxastic way.[12] The result is that the individual comes to see food and the world in a different way. It is not that she is persuaded to come out of her eating disorder, but rather, her eating causes her to see the world differently. Cuneo argues that something very similar happens in the remission from the grip of the sin disorder by partaking in the Eucharist. He writes,

> important elements that contribute to the loosening of the grip of the disorder do not consist in the presentation or acceptance of propositions about God or God's activity or experiences that aim to evoke beliefs about God or God's activity…instead…there are important elements that contribute to the loosening of the grip of the sin-disorder that operate—at least in large measure—at a sub-doxastic level, below the level of understanding or belief.[13]

By participating in the Eucharist, Cuneo thinks that an individual in the grip of the sin disorder can come to see her own sin in a new light. Thus, the elements of bread and wine undergo a change in "function" when they are consecrated by the priest, namely, the function of bringing about communion with God.[14] As he goes on to describe it, the

---

[10] Cuneo (2016), 194.

[11] Ibid. See Harriet Brown, *Brave Girl Eating* (New York: Harper Collins, 2010).

[12] Cuneo (2016), 195.

[13] Ibid.

[14] Ibid., 198.

elements somehow provide "a point of contact...with God" and thereby play a functional role in the loosening of sin disorder.[15]

In the remainder of this paper, I develop an alternative account of remission of sins, drawn from Kierkegaard's works, according to which the remission of sin is not achieved by the acts of eating, but rather through an encounter with the presence of the living Christ.

Sin Remission in Kierkegaard's *Communion Discourses*

It might be surprising to some, given his disdain for the established Church, that Kierkegaard has anything resembling a theology of the Eucharist.[16] Yet, whilst Kierkegaard's writing is often anti-ecclesial, it is not anti-praxis. And central to Kierkegaard's understanding of Christian practice is the sacrament of Communion. In his journals, for instance, he affirms that Communion is the "true center" of the Church.[17] Indeed, we know that Kierkegaard gave prominence to this

---

[15] Ibid., 202. Whereas it is the sub-doxastic act of eating which provides the solution to the problem of sin remission for Cuneo, for Stump, it is the engagement in the narrative of liturgy which plays this role. Stump maintains that the Church's practice of the Eucharist consists in retelling the story of Christ's passion and death in such a way that it brings home to the participant certain features of their sin and God's forgiveness; Stump (2015), 218-224. As Stump describes, the participant in the Eucharist "will have in mind her own need for help in consequence of things in herself that she herself finds hateful. But she will also have brought home to her that, however alienated she may be from herself, God is not alienated from her." The result of this kind of personal engagement, Stump suggests, is that the Eucharist allows the participant to "be strengthened for perseverance, in virtue of growing in love of God and in experience of God's continued love and presence to her." Stump (2015), 223-224.

[16] Throughout his writings, Kierkegaard shows a distrust and disdain for organised religion. As Pattison summarises, "[i]n his later writings on the Church, Kierkegaard puts the very idea of a Church as such up for question to the extent that what he effectively asks is, simply: Does Christianity actually need a Church?" George Pattison, *Kierkegaard and the Theology of the Nineteenth Century* (Cambridge: Cambridge University Press, 2012), 203.

[17] *JP*, 5: 5089.

practice throughout his life.[18] Along with three discourses which Kierkegaard prepared to deliver at a Friday Communion service in Copenhagen, he also produced another ten discourses intended for, or written in the style of, a Friday Communion sermon. As Sylvia Walsh notes, these *Communion Discourses* formed an important genre of writing in Kierkegaard's oeuvre, and Kierkegaard wished to give an important role to them in his authorship.[19] It is here, in the *Communion Discourses*, that we can find something resembling the issue which Cuneo is attempting to address. I will begin by drawing on relevant passages from Kierkegaard's thirteen *Communion Discourses*, before attempting to make connections with other areas of his writings which can help us to construct a Kierkegaardian account of sin remission.

The Purpose of Communion

First, it will be helpful to begin by considering what Kierkegaard takes to be the overall purpose of Communion. Or, more specifically, what the end goal of the Christian life is, for which Communion plays a role in helping to achieve. Throughout the discourses, he emphasises that the role of Communion is to draw us near to God through Christ. For instance, in a discourse found in *Practice in Christianity*, reflecting on a verse from John's gospel (John

---

[18] In the 19th Century Danish Lutheran Church, into which Kierkegaard was confirmed, the Sunday service focused around the preaching of the Word, with an optional Communion attached to the service, for those who wished to receive it. The Friday service, in contrast to this, focused around the practice of Communion, with preaching attached to the sacrament. We know that Kierkegaard was a regular attendee at Friday Communion, but hardly ever attended church on a Sunday; Niels Jørgen Cappelørn, "Søren Kierkegaard at Friday Communion in the Church of Our Lady," *International Kierkegaard Commentary: Without Authority* (Princeton: Princeton University Press, 2007), 258-264.

[19] Sylvia Walsh, "Introduction," from *Discourses at the Communion on Fridays*, trans. and ed. by Sylvia Walsh (Bloomington: Indiana University Press, 2001), 15-17. In the preface to a collection of these discourses, found in *Without Authority*, Kierkegaard writes that the authorship, "that began with *Either/Or* and advanced step by step seeks here its decisive place of rest, at the foot of the altar" (WA, 165). Furthermore, in reflecting on the purpose and structure of his authorship in *The Point of View,* Kierkegaard lists the *Communion Discourses* as having a crucial role alongside his other texts (PV, 5-6).

12:32), Anti-Climacus writes, "This was your [Christ's] task, which you have completed and which you will complete until the end of time, for just as you yourself have said it, so will do it: lifted up from earth, you will draw all to yourself."[20]

Whilst there might be an eschatological component to Anti-Climacus' remarks here (especially given the use of *"until the end of time"*), more often than not, rather than focusing on future union with God, Kierkegaard focuses his attention on the immediate purpose of Communion, namely, renewing an individual's communion with Christ. Of course, the two are not incompatible, but Kierkegaard's focus in the discourses, as is often the case, is on the practical and the immediate, rather than on the intangible and far off. We can find examples of reference to communion with Christ in almost all of the thirteen discourses. For instance, he writes, "Father in heaven! We know well that you are the one who enables both willing and completing and that longing, when it draws us to renew communion with our Savior and Atoner, is also from you."[21] Elsewhere, he propounds a similar idea, in writing that, "we also thank you in this way, as those who are now gathered here today, by going up to your altar in order to renew communion with you."[22] As Kierkegaard presents it in many places, then, there is a specific purpose to Communion, namely, God's drawing all people to himself through the renewal of an individual's communion with Christ.

The Problem of Sin

If the aim of Communion is to draw us into communion with Christ, then the problem which prevents this from occurring is the person's sin. As I will suggest, we can find something resembling Cuneo's distinction between forgiveness and remission. That is, in Kierkegaard's discussion of Communion we can see that we need to be forgiven from our past sin, but we also need God's assistance in recovering from the ongoing effects of sinfulness. As I will suggest in

---

[20] *DACF*, 120, *PC*, 151.

[21] *DACF*, 37; *CD*, 251.

[22] *DACF*, 63; *CD*, 276.

the concluding section, noticing this can help us develop a Kierkegaardian account of the remission of sin through Communion.

First, let us consider Kierkegaard's focus on God's forgiving human sin in the context of the Communion sacrament. In a number of places, Kierkegaard describes sin as requiring God's judgement and Christ as providing satisfaction, thereby making forgiveness possible. However, as Murray Rae highlights, for Kierkegaard, "Christ is not the judge in some punitive sense; rather, the infinite and unconditional nature of his love reveals the poverty of our own love. It is love then that provides the most severe judgement."[23] In reflecting on this distinction between love's judgement and punitive judgment, Kierkegaard writes that "love's judgement is the severest judgement…. The word of judgement does not say: '[The one] to whom little is forgiven sinned much, so his sins were therefore too great and too many to be forgiven.' No, judgement says: 'he loves little.'"[24] As Rae notes, Kierkegaard's concern here, is "essentially relational" and indicates "the re-establishment of right relationship" with God.[25] Nevertheless, as we can see, sin results in a kind of alienation from God due to the guilt of past action and a person's failure to love.

Yet, this focus on guilt and the need for forgiveness is not the only aspect of sin which Kierkegaard brings to light in the discourses. Arguably, the focus on remission (at least as Cuneo describes the difference) is far more prominent. Kierkegaard focuses, for instance, on the problem of unconfessed or unconscious sin which weighs heavily on a believer. To take one of many examples, he writes that "nothing else rests as heavy upon a person as sin's heavy secret; there is only one thing that is heavier: to have to go to confession. Oh, no other secret is as frightful as the secret of sin; there is only one thing that is even more frightful: confession."[26] Elsewhere, he describes unconfessed sin as

---

[23] Murray Rae, *Kierkegaard and Theology* (Edinburgh: T&T Clark, 2010), 103.

[24] *DACF*, 129-30; *WA*, 171-172.

[25] Rae (2010), 104.

[26] *DACF*, 110; *WA*, 139.

having a "deep...eternal concern."[27] Thus, a part of what keeps human beings from communion with Christ is that their unconfessed sin weighs heavily on their hearts, and this results in their unwillingness to seek forgiveness—we might properly describe this heaviness of heart as a lack of sin remission. The problem is not that God has not forgiven the individual, but rather, unacknowledged sin somehow prevents a person drawing near to Christ.

However, even after acknowledging their sin, Kierkegaard thinks that individuals have difficulty in receiving forgiveness from Christ. Again, this might be described as a part of the problem of remission. For instance, Kierkegaard writes, "just as it is a difficult matter in praying rightly to be able to come to the Amen...likewise it is also a difficult matter rightly to receive the forgiveness of sins at the altar."[28] Continuing on from the discussion of the judgment of love, Kierkegaard highlights the self-inflicted nature of judgment once one realises that God offers forgiveness for sin. He writes, "When love judges you, and the judgement is—oh horror!—the judgement is 'Your sins are forgiven you!'...there is something within you that makes you feel that they are not forgiven you."[29] Thus, although Kierkegaard does think that Christ must act as satisfaction to provide forgiveness for sin, there is also the ongoing problem of self-inflicted sin, even after being forgiven. The judgement of love, he writes, "thinks not of his many sins, oh no, it is willing to forget them all, it has forgotten them all."[30] The problem that remains, then, is that "it is self-inflicted...for the charge is not his sins, no, the charge is: it is forgiven him, everything is forgiven him."[31]

We can see that what keeps human beings from communion with Christ is not God's judgement and lack of forgiveness, but rather, it is the revelation and acceptance of this loving forgiveness on the part of the individual, that is, the ongoing problem of the sin dis-order. Or,

---

[27] *DACF*, 51; *CD*, 264.
[28] *DACF*, 128; *WA*, 169.
[29] *DACF*, 131; *WA*, 173.
[30] Ibid.
[31] Ibid.

in Cuneo's terminology, the individual needs to receive remission from sin.

As we will see, the Kierkegaardian account of sin remission has a number of layers. Ultimately, for Kierkegaard, it is through becoming contemporary with Christ at the altar that an individual is cured of his sin. First, Christ must provide satisfaction for this sin in order to atone for a person's wrongdoing to allow for forgiveness. However, such forgiveness is not sufficient for remission of a person's sin. For remission to occur, a person must also come to terms with her own sin and realize the extent of the problem; there must be a consciousness of sin. Moreover, this person must accept forgiveness and be healed from the psychological torment of self-inflicted guilt. As we will see, although human striving plays some role in Kierkegaard's account, the reconciliation that is achieved is the work of God in all three of these stages.

The Solution to the Problem of Sin: Forgiveness from Sin

While, as we have seen, (at least in the way Cuneo describes the distinction) forgiveness and remission refer to different aspects of how God overcomes the problem of sin, it will be helpful for our purposes to first consider Kierkegaard's discussion of forgiveness in the context of Communion.

As Rae notes, in general, "Kierkegaard is concerned above all with how one responds to the declaration of forgiveness and grace rather than with the mechanics of how atonement is accomplished," yet within the *Communion Discourses*, Rae writes, "we gain some indication of how Kierkegaard conceives the atonement doctrinally."[32] As Olli-Pekka Vainio puts it, Kierkegaard's atonement theology seems to be an articulation of an "amazingly classical" substitution view.[33]

We can see this, for instance, when Kierkegaard writes, "Christ put himself entirely in your place. He was God and became a human

---

[32] Rae (2010), 101-102.

[33] Olli-Pekka Vainio, "Kierkegaard's Eucharistic Spirituality," *Theology Today* 67, no. 1 (2010): 19.

being—in this way he put himself in your place."[34] Later in the same discourse, he continues, "[f]or what is the 'Atoner' but a substitute who puts himself entirely in your place and in mine; and what is the consolation of the atonement but this, that the substitute, making satisfaction, puts himself entirely in your and in my place!"[35] Elsewhere, he describes this satisfaction in terms of Christ's hiding sin from judgement with his *"holy body."*[36] So, Kierkegaard clearly holds that a part of the problem of sin is that human beings need Christ to pay satisfaction for their sin to avoid judgement. What is more, this satisfaction can only be the work of God. Kierkegaard writes, "In relation to the atonement you cannot be a co-worker of Christ, not in the remotest way. You are wholly in debt, he is wholly the satisfaction."[37]

It is important to note that whilst Christ's atonement provides the means of our being forgiven from sin, one of the important roles of Communion in providing remission from the ongoing effects of sin is to *remind* us of Christ's sacrificial atonement. Indeed, he writes that while at the pulpit the life of Christ is proclaimed, "at the altar it is his death."[38] While Christ's death cannot be repeated, what is repeated is that, "he died also for you, you who in his body and blood receive the pledge that he has died also for you, at the altar, where he gives you *himself* as a hiding place."[39]

The Solution to the Problem of Sin: Remission and Sin-Consciousness

Let us now consider how Kierkegaard describes the role of Communion in the remission of sin.

An important part of our restoration from the ongoing effects of sin, for Kierkegaard, is that we become more conscious of our sin. For this reason, Kierkegaard often stresses that before even

---

[34] *DACF*, 93; *WA*, 116.
[35] *DACF*, 99; *WA*, 123.
[36] *DACF*, 141; *WA*, 185.
[37] *DACF*, 86; *CD*, 299.
[38] *DACF*, 142; *WA*, 186.
[39] *DACF*, 142; *WA* 186-87.

approaching the Communion table, a person must be properly prepared. We know that Friday communion services which Kierkegaard attended were preceded by a confession in which the priest would absolve the sins of the people.[40] This confession ritual also included a confession discourse delivered by the priest. So, while the *Communion Discourses* are *not* confession discourses, their focus is often on the consciousness and confession of sin.[41]

The role of confession in preparation for Communion, as Kierkegaard describes it, is to bring to mind the sins that prevent us from enjoying communion with Christ.[42] Kierkegaard thinks that this consciousness of sin plays an important role in a person's reconciliation with God through Christ. For instance, he states, "it is no doubt a restful position when you kneel at the foot of the altar, but God grant that this indeed may truly be only a faint intimation of your soul's finding rest in God through the consciousness of the forgiveness of sins."[43] As Lee Barrett has argued, there is a tension at work in Kierkegaard's writings on Communion here: there is both an emphasis on the need for human striving (he writes of the *requirement* of sin-consciousness, for instance) but at the same time, even in receiving consciousness of sin, it is only God who is at work; the remission of sin is a gift of grace.[44]

One of the ways that God provides the person with a consciousness of sin is through the work of the Holy Spirit in speaking through a person's conscience. Kierkegaard describes this voice as a kind of inner preacher which convicts individuals of sin.[45] So, even

---

[40] Cappelørn (2006), 265-272.

[41] Kierkegaard writes his own discourse on the occasion of confession (see *UDVS*, 3-154). Given its length, it is very unlikely he ever intended this discourse to actually be used in such a context.

[42] *DACF*, 37; *CD*, 251.

[43] *DACF*, 54; *CD*, 267.

[44] Lee C. Barrett, "Christ's Efficacious Love and Human Responsibility: The Lutheran Dialectic of 'Discourses at the Communion on Fridays,'" *International Kierkegaard Commentary*, vol. 17, *Christian Discourses and the Crisis and a Crisis in the Life of an Actress* (Princeton: Princeton University Press, 2007).

[45] *DACF*, 139; *WA*, 183.

though he speaks of the requirement of confession and sin-consciousness, Kierkegaard is keen to stress that in Communion, it is not that we do something to achieve reconciliation with Christ. In fact, he strongly emphasises the opposite: "At the altar you are able to do nothing at all, not even this, to hold fast the thought of your unworthiness, and in this to make yourself receptive to the blessing."[46]

The Solution to the Problem of Sin: Remission from Psychological Bondage

Lastly, as well as providing a context for a person to become conscious of both their sin and also the forgiveness of this sin, Kierkegaard also describes Communion as playing a role in overcoming some of the psychological effects of sin. It is in discussing the psychological burden of sin that he is closest to providing an account of something like sin remission.

As well as providing satisfaction for sin, Kierkegaard writes that Christ "came to the world in order to free us from the chains in which we were bound or in which we had bound ourselves, and in order to rescue the redeemed."[47] This freeing from the bonds of self-inflicted punishment, is described in many places as a kind of "rest" for the soul.[48] However, this rest for the soul must be connected with forgiveness and penitence; "only the penitent properly understands what it is to pray for rest for the soul, rest in the only thought in which there is rest for a penitent that there is forgiveness."[49] Here, Christ's humanity plays an important role in this freeing from the bonds of sin. Later in the same discourse, he notes, "He is indeed not only your spiritual advisor but also your savior; he understands not only all your sorrow better than you yourself understand it, oh, but he wants precisely to take the burden from you and give you rest for your soul."[50] On Kierkegaard's account, then, coming to the altar at Communion allows a person to be made aware of Christ's atoning work

---

[46] *DACF*, 87; *CD*, 300.
[47] *DACF*, 120; *PC*, 151.
[48] *DACF*, 52; *CD*, 265.
[49] *DACF*, 52; *CD*, 265.
[50] *DACF*, 53; *CD*, 266.

in providing forgiveness, but also, it provides a strengthening of the will to remove an individual from the self-inflicted bonds of sin in their life.

Kierkegaard also has a clear answer to how this is made possible, namely, by a concrete encounter with the living person of Christ. As George Pattison argues, Kierkegaard clearly espouses a Lutheran view of Christ's being truly present in the Eucharist, in which the emphasis is not on the body of Christ, but rather on the living presence of Christ.[51] For instance, in the discourse on Luke 22:15, he writes that Christ "is not a dead person but one who is living."[52] The Communion table is particularly associated with Christ's living presence; in *Practice in Christianity,* Anti-Climacus, opens his Communion discourse with the prayer: "God grant that at this sacred moment you may feel yourself entirely drawn to him, sense his presence, he who is present there."[53] Notably, as Kierkegaard puts it elsewhere, Christ's presence is something which the individual experiences by means of hearing Christ's voice.[54] Whereas preaching intends to "instruct or impress" the listener, the Communion discourse, "wants to give you pause for a moment on the way to the altar."[55] The reason for this, Kierkegaard continues, is that, "[a]t the altar…it is *his* voice that you must hear…. At the altar…no matter how many are gathered there, yes even if everyone is gathered at the altar, there is no crowd at the altar. He himself is personally present, and he knows those who are his own."[56]

It is through this encounter with the living presence of Christ, then, that a person is able to find rest for their soul and receive remission for their sin. Note again, that this release from the bondage of sin at the Communion table is not a work of human striving, but rather, it is a work of Christ. This is made apparent in Kierkegaard's contrast

---

[51] Pattison (2012), 158.
[52] *DACF*, 48; *CD*, 261.
[53] *DACF*, 124; *PC*, 156.
[54] *DACF*, 58; *CD*, 270.
[55] *DACF*, 58; *CD*, 270.
[56] *DACF*, 58-59; *CD*, 270-271.

between the act of human forgetting and the act of focusing on the person of Christ; by focusing on the person of Christ, Kierkegaard thinks, a person is able to somehow *forget* her sin.[57] Lastly, not only does participation in Communion bring with it a release from self-inflicted condemnation, but it also strengthens the believer's will for the future. Kierkegaard writes, "we pray for those who are gathered here that they may go up to the Lord's table today with heartfelt longing and that when they leave there, they may go away with increased longing for him our Savior and Atoner."[58]

Thus, as I have presented it, Kierkegaard's account of the remission of sin in Communion is achieved by becoming aware of Christ's work in providing satisfaction for sin, by the work of the Holy Spirit in bringing a person to consciousness of their sin and through an encounter with the living Christ at the Communion table which allows a person to be released from the self-inflicted bondage of sin and for their will to be strengthened. So, while it is clear that Communion is a means of sin remission, what is not clear from the *Communion Discourses* alone, is just how this encounter with Christ brings about sin remission. Whilst this may not be Kierkegaard's aim in these discourses, by looking elsewhere in his writings, we can construct a more detailed account of sin remission which can help to construct a Kierkegaardian account.

Sin, Sin-Consciousness, and Communion in *The Sickness Unto Death*

We have seen the role that the Eucharist plays in the remission of sin and renewal of communion between an individual and Christ. However, while David Law is surely right to note that in the *Communion Discourses*, Kierkegaard does not provide a full

---

[57] *DACF*, 120-21; *PC*, 152-53.
[58] *DACF*, 37; *CD*, 251.

Eucharistic theology,[59] by looking elsewhere in Kierkegaard's writings we can provide a more detailed account of the remission of sin in the Eucharist. In particular, one aspect of Kierkegaard's account which can be supplemented by looking elsewhere is an account of the nature of the problem of sin and how encountering Christ can overcome this problem.

One of the most detailed accounts of sin in Kierkegaard's writings is found in *The Sickness Unto Death* in which the pseudonymous author, Anti-Climacus, presents a psychological view of the widespread sickness of human sin, and the possibility of its remedy through the work of Christ.

To give a brief summary of the account of sin in *Sickness*: the human sickness, according to Anti-Climacus, is that of despair, a disease of the will which prevents a person from willing to exist as a self in the appropriate way. Because despair is a disease of the will, the more self-conscious one is, the more aware one is of one's own despair. It is this disease of the will which prevents human beings from relating properly to God, the source of their selfhood. This sickness requires a medicine, which begins with a person's self-awareness, but this is not something which human beings can arrive at by themselves; they need the antidote of faith, a gift of grace from God, to reveal the extent of despair and to realign the will. This provides the Christian with a kind of *superiority* over other human beings who are in despair, that is, the Christian has an awareness of her despair.[60] Now, although the beginning of faith brings with it an awareness of one's despair, faith is an ongoing task which seeks to repair the human will and to unite the human self with God, in order that she might eventually "rest transparently in God."[61] Sin, then, is to despair before God. As it is presented in *Sickness,* whilst the Christian is given a kind of superiority because of her awareness of despair, she is yet to receive full healing

---

[59] David Law, "Kierkegaard's Understanding of the Eucharist in Christian Discourses, Part Four," *International Kierkegaard Commentary*, vol. 17, *Christian Discourses and the Crisis and a Crisis in the Life of an Actress* (Princeton: Princeton University Press, 2007), 275.

[60] *SUD*, 15.

[61] *SUD*, 30.

from her sickness. Indeed, over the course of one's life, sin and despair must be rooted out and repaired by the ongoing work of Christ. As Anti-Climacus puts it, "to be cured of this sickness is the Christian's blessedness."[62]

As we can see already, many of the themes presented in *Sickness* reflect those themes which Kierkegaard focuses on in the *Communion Discourses*. By giving a more detailed overview of these themes, I will show that we can come to a more detailed understanding of sin remission in the practice of Communion.

The Purpose of the Christian Life

First, just as in the *Communion Discourses*, we see that in *Sickness,* Anti-Climacus holds that there is an ultimate goal or purpose for the Christian life. This is described throughout by Anti-Climacus as to "rest transparently in God," or to rest "transparently in the power that established it."[63] It is interesting, as we have seen, that this theme of *rest* is one that Kierkegaard describes throughout the *Communion Discourses* in contrast to the restlessness and weariness of sinfulness. In *Sickness*, this state of resting in God is presented as the resolution to the problem of despair, the sickness which all humanity is stricken by. Whereas despair is a willful mis-relation to oneself, what God provides by faith is a willed communion with him which brings with it a state of restfulness. Thus, as Anti-Climacus tells us, the truth of Christianity is that we are "invited to live on the most intimate terms with God."[64]

The Problem of Sin

What is it that prevents a human being from resting transparently in God and living on the most intimate terms with him? For Anti-Climacus, the answer to this question is found in focusing on the nature of the human self. He describes the self as (i) "relating itself to itself," (ii) existing as a "synthesis of the infinite and the finite, of the temporal and the eternal, of freedom and necessity," and, (iii) "in

---

[62] *SUD*, 15.
[63] *SUD*, 30 and 14.
[64] *SUD*, 85.

relating itself to itself relates itself to another."[65] This account of the self is notoriously obscure and hard to understand, and we need not worry overly about its intricate details here. The important point to note is that this account of the self presents human beings as in the process of willing their own existence to various degrees of success. These success criteria are relational. Thus, a person can will to be properly related to herself, that is, she can exist in a state of self-conscious freedom in relationship to herself, or she can exist in a state of bad faith, by denying her own freedom. Moreover, for Anti-Climacus, the human self does not exist only in relation to itself, but also to God, its creator. Another way of failing to relate as a self, then, is by failing to relate properly to God. Finally, Anti-Climacus also describes the human self as existing as a relation of various competing components—she is both infinite and finite, temporal and eternal, free and necessary—by willing to relate only as a finite being, or only as a temporal being, we fail to relate properly as a self on this account.

It is in reference to this account of the self that Anti-Climacus explains the pervasive problem of human sinfulness, understood as a kind of despair. Despair, as he characterizes it, is a failure of the will to exist as a self in the way described above. This despair can occur in a variety of forms. For instance, despair can occur through ignorance and a lack of self-consciousness,[66] through a kind of weakness of the will,[67] or through a kind of defiance.[68] Building on this account of despair, Anti-Climacus holds that sin is simply a kind of despair "before God."[69] Sin is not defined as a disobedience to some external force, but rather, the account is very similar to what Cuneo describes as the *sin dis-order.*[70] Anti-Climacus rejects defining sin in terms of action types; it is entirely possible to be "quite in order" having refrained from murder, adultery, stealing, etc., and still fail to relate properly to God.[71]

---

[65] *SUD*, 13-14.
[66] *SUD*, 42.
[67] *SUD*, 67.
[68] *SUD*, 68.
[69] *SUD*, 77.
[70] Cuneo (2016), 189.
[71] *SUD*, 81.

What is lacking from the sinful person is not right action, but, rather, a proper relation to God and to oneself.

We can see the connection between some of the psychological effects of sin, which Kierkegaard discusses in the *Communion Discourses* outlined in more precise terms in *Sickness*. For instance, Anti-Climacus talks of "[t]he sin of despairing over one's sin" as well as "[t]he sin of despairing of the forgiveness of sins (offense)."[72] Both of these forms of despair, he thinks, are ways of continuing to be defiant or weak before God in willing to be a self, even after becoming conscious of one's sin. On the *despair over one's sin*, for example, Anti-Climacus writes that, such a person "may not say: I can never forgive myself (as if he had previously forgiven himself sins—a blasphemy). No, he says that God can never forgive him for it. Alas, this is just a subterfuge. His sorrow, his cares, his despair are selfish."[73] To take another example, on the sin of despairing of the forgiveness of one's sins, Anti-Climacus maintains that, "Ordinarily defiance is: in despair to will to be oneself. Here this is weakness, in despair to will to be oneself—a sinner—in such a way that there is no forgiveness."[74]

The similarity between these kinds of despair and the discussion of self-inflicted or unconfessed sin in the *Communion Discourses* is striking. Here we also have a more explicit explanation of the nature of this sin. As Rae summarises Anti-Climacus' position,

> Sin may be conceived…as a mis-relation between the finite and the infinite, the temporal and the eternal, freedom and necessity…. Those guilty of such mis-relation exist in despair. This does not mean that they will appear to be miserable; such people may indeed be, and often are, very comfortable and happy. Their despair, consists, rather in their misplaced and thus false hope. They have staked their existence on something that will not endure. [Anti-Climacus] is in no doubt that we are all to be numbered in this group. We all fall short. We have all plunged ourselves into the bondage of sin, and stand in need, therefore of

---

[72] *SUD*, 109, 113.

[73] *SUD*, 112.

[74] *SUD*, 113.

forgiveness and re-creation. We are all afflicted with "the sickness unto death."[75]

Thus, we can see that although the Christian's *superiority* is that they are brought to the realisation of their wilful despair by a revelation from God, a Christian does not reach the *blessedness* of being free from despair immediately. But rather, there is an ongoing problem of sin which individuals need remission from; a person must become more self-aware and somehow realign their will to eventually will only the good, thereby, coming to rest entirely in God.

The Solution to the Problem of Sin: Forgiveness and Remission in *The Sickness Unto Death*

So how does one move from a position of despair to begin the process of becoming free from despair? The structure of this solution closely fits with the account given in the *Communion Discourses*—Christ deals with the problem of sin through the cross, a person must become aware of her sin (the Christian's *superiority*), and the life of faith is the life spent repairing the damage done by sin through the remission of sin (leading to the Christian's eventual state of *blessedness*).

First, let's look at what Anti-Climacus writes on the atonement and the mechanism by which Christ deals with the enormity of human sin. Anti-Climacus describes the atonement as a "paradox" which stresses the impossibility of eliminating the widespread problem of sin but also the fact that Christ wants "wants to eliminate sin as completely as if it were drowned in the sea."[76] While Kierkegaard is uncharacteristically detailed in the *Communion Discourses* about the doctrine of atonement, we see here, in *Sickness*, that Anti-Climacus describes the doctrine as paradoxical, that is, beyond the limits of human speculation. Yet, the two positions are at least consistent—in both places, Kierkegaard emphasises that human sin is a problem which is pervasive and much larger than humans have comprehended, and also, that Christ eradicates human sin in some way, even if this is beyond our comprehension (at least as he describes it here).

---

[75] Rae (2010), 93-94.
[76] *SUD*, 100.

We have also seen that the consciousness of sin is a vital stage in the process of reconciliation with God in both the *Communion Discourses* and *Sickness*. What's more, it is only God who can bring a human being to this place of realization. According to Anti-Climacus, "there must be a revelation from God to teach man what sin is and how deeply it is rooted."[77] For this reason, he writes, "salvation is, humanly speaking, utterly impossible; but for God everything is possible!"[78]

Moreover, whilst the moment of salvation provides an awareness of sinfulness, the task of sin-consciousness must continue throughout a person's life for them to be released from the sickness of sin. Anti-Climacus explicitly links the consciousness of sin with a person's experience of Christ. He writes that, "The greater conception of God, the more self...the greater conception of Christ, the more self...the more self there is, the more intense sin is."[79] The sins of despairing over sin or despairing of the forgiveness of one's sins, for instance, are sins of which we must become aware in order to be cured of them. How does Anti-Climacus envisage this awareness taking place? His answer is that one must be before Christ in some way. Moreover, it is clear that this process is an ongoing process and that the moment of salvation does not entirely eradicate the sin disease from a person, despite the fact that her sin is forgiven.

Thus, as we can see, Anti-Climacus' account provides a more detailed framework for understanding just what the problem of sin is by describing it in terms of misrelation of the will and lack of self-consciousness. What is needed to be fully repaired from sin is the gradual and lifelong reorientation of the will to relate properly to oneself and to God. Whilst it is less clear is what this amounts to, at least practically, here the earlier account from the *Communion Discourses* is helpful. As we have seen, it is through the encounter with Christ at the Communion Table that a person becomes aware of her sin and by focusing on Christ, she can receive the strengthening of her will and can worship God in faith. As Anti-Climacus describes it, "Faith is:

---

[77] *SUD*, 96.
[78] *SUD*, 39.
[79] *SUD*, 114.

that the self in being itself and in willing to be itself rests transparently in God."[80]

A Kierkegaardian Account of Communion and the Remission of Sin

Let us return to Cuneo's question. What is the connection between "the activities of participating in the Eucharist…on the one hand, and the state of enjoying remission of sin on the other?"[81] As we have seen, Cuneo claims that the elements themselves provide a kind of sub-doxastic medicine for our disease, which slowly train us to see the world differently in light of God's forgiveness. Kierkegaard's account is vastly different to this in a number of ways. For Kierkegaard, the elements seem to be of very little significance in explaining how it is that we are repaired from the damage of sin. Instead, it is primarily by our encounter with the living Christ at the Communion table that we are made aware of sin, reminded of Christ's sacrifice and receive Christ's help in strengthening and repairing our will.

By drawing comparisons between the discussions of sin and sin-consciousness in *The Sickness Unto Death* and *Discourses at Communion on Fridays* I have outlined a different Kierkegaardian response to this problem. In both texts, Kierkegaard focuses primarily on the presence of Christ as providing something like remission for human sin. As we have seen, the sin which prevents a person being united to God in this life is not removed by God's forgiving us. But rather, there remains an ongoing sickness which is best characterized as a sickness of the will, by which human beings fail to will to be united to God because of their lack of self-awareness and sin-consciousness, or because of a weakness of the will in which they are too psychologically fragmented by sin to will union with God. The important feature of recovering from sickness is self-awareness. In becoming aware of just who one is and how one is related (or misrelated) to Christ, one is more able to receive Christ's grace, and thereby repair the will. Not only does Communion bring about an

---

[80] *SUD*, 82.
[81] Cuneo (2016), 186-87.

awareness of one's willed distance from God, but it also strengthens the will in such a way that one draws closer to Christ. Whilst there is no doubt much more to be said on this issue, by drawing together these seemingly distinct areas of Kierkegaard's writings, I have shown that we can begin to explain how the ordinary actions involved in the Eucharist can release human beings from the grip of sin. Thus, unlike Cuneo's account, the bread and wine do not play a therapeutic role in the restoration of right relationship with God. For Kierkegaard, only the living presence of Christ could play such a role.

9.

KIERKEGAARD ON SIN, AMBIGUITY, AND GOSPEL RADICALITY: TOWARDS A RESPONSE TO GEORGE PATTISON

Aaron P. Edwards

For the last two centuries there have been many Kierkegaards in this world. Some of these are, of course, Kierkegaard's own creation. But many are also due to his long, ever-expanding list of academic interpreters. Kierkegaard's complex authorship certainly gives rise to this hermeneutical multiplicity, despite his wry protestations that scholars would distract themselves for many years trying to interpret him. However, it can become all too easy to settle for an ambivalence as to what Kierkegaard's convictions actually were, particularly those theological convictions which were most fundamental.

Perhaps the most prominent theological interpreter of Kierkegaard's authorship in recent decades has been George Pattison, whose work has often taken the stance of blurring the lines between Kierkegaard's theological, philosophical, and literary intentions. This article is not an attempt to respond to George Pattison's work *in se* but it will engage with him on a particular point that seems crucial to what Kierkegaard really stood for theologically. This relates to Kierkegaard's conviction about the Gospel, and its implications for sin, redemption, and the wider homiletical tone of Kierkegaard's theology. I will argue, contrary to Pattison, that Kierkegaard's theology of sin and redemption is indeed radical. One might even be tempted to call it "unnuanced," however odd that might sound of one of the most complex and reflective thinkers of the modern era. To see Kierkegaard in this way, however, would be to misunderstand the inherent nuance of polemical simplicity that characterised much of his directly theological work.

Notwithstanding the ongoing interaction between the direct and indirect aspects of his authorship (including the mystique of the pseudonymous characters), it is the second authorship—in light of his journals and his subsequent reflections—which yields the possibility of a confident reading of Kierkegaard's "view." It will be affirmed, in distinction to Pattison's immanentist hermeneutic, that for Kierkegaard, both sin and Gospel are radically transformative. Sin is not an inconvenience, but a pure corruption of the human self; and its effects cannot be undone without the radical redemption of a Gospel which is apocalyptically invasive rather than naturally immanent. Some reflection will also be offered in the conclusion regarding the notion of reflective nuance in light of Kierkegaard's more radically emphatic theological expressions, a point which will first be introduced by discussing the "problem" of hermeneutical ambiguity when interpreting Kierkegaard's kerygmatic thought.

Between Ambiguity and Extremity

One key feature of George Pattison's reading of Kierkegaard's project is that Kierkegaard's view of sin and the implications of the Gospel—accentuated most overtly in his so-called "later period"—is a significant departure either from his distinctively Christian position, and from evangelical orthodoxy as a whole. Pattison asserts that Kierkegaard's position "darkened" with the attack literature,[1] and by this seems to imply that this darkening provides us with a trajectoried hermeneutic for the inherent untrustworthiness of Kierkegaard's radical kerygmatic emphases in general. There is no question that there is a *kind* of darkening in certain moments in Kierkegaard's attack period, especially vis-à-vis his echoes of Schopenhauer, who begins to creep into the journals more frequently in the 1850s. In one journal entry from 1854—where he is actually critiquing Luther—Kierkegaard cites Schopenhauer before going on to state that "the world is immersed in evil."[2] However, it might be a little too convenient to tar the late

---

[1] See George Pattison, *Kierkegaard and the Theology of the Nineteenth Century: The Paradox and the "Point of Contact"* (Cambridge: Cambridge University Press, 2012), 125.

[2] Søren Kierkegaard, *Søren Kierkegaard's Journals and Papers*, Vols. 1–6, ed. and trans. Howard V. Hong and Edna H. Hong (Bloomington and London: Indiana University Press, 1967–78), vol. 3, no. 3044, 376.

Kierkegaard with the brush of Schopenhauerian pessimism as though this colored any of his other (to some eyes) "extreme" views about the seriousness of humanity's sinful state *coram deo*.

For one thing, Kierkegaard himself regularly showed a sense of frustrated self-awareness at the idea that he was somehow a "mad" Christian.[3] Indeed, he often contrasts this with the problem of the perpetual middle way:

> In the world of mediocrity in which we live it is assumed—and this is one of the ways used to safeguard mediocrity—that only crackpot boldness, etc. should be deplored as offensive, as inspired by Satan, and that the middle way, however, is secure against any such charge. Christ and Christianity are of another mind: mediocrity itself is the offense, the most dangerous kind of demon possession, farthest removed from the possibility of being cured.[4]

This journal entry was written on 5th July 1855, in the year of his death, and just two days before his infamous "Medical Diagnosis" in *The Moment*, whereby he compared the Danish Church to a disease-ridden hospital deceptively poisoning its patients to death.[5] One can sense Kierkegaard's frustration at how impossible it was for those within the Christendom system to see the system's inherent madness precisely in its mediocre failure to embody its central Christian message. Such an approach, though, is not exclusive to the attack period. Five years earlier, we see a critique along similar lines regarding devotion to Christ:

> In respect to God, the how is what. He who does not involve himself with God in the mode of absolute devotion does not become involved with God. In relationship to God one cannot involve himself to a certain degree, for God is precisely the contradiction to

---

[3] Kierkegaard, *Journals and Papers,* 6:6257, 57.

[4] Kierkegaard, *Journals and Papers,* 4:4494, 320.

[5] See Søren Kierkegaard, *Attack Upon "Christendom," 1854-1855*, trans. Walter Lowrie (Oxford: Oxford University Press, 1944), 139-41.

all that which is to a certain degree.[6]

For Kierkegaard, to speak of and relate to *this* God cannot be done on "mediocre" or "ambiguous" terms; it can only be one-sided and all-encompassing.

Such "unambiguous" expressions cannot be conveniently excised from the authorship as though they were a mere unfortunate aberration, the crazed ramblings of an unhinged penitent winding himself up before the impending doom of death row.[7] Where Roger Poole warns against "blunt" readings of Kierkegaard which interpret his religious consistency with all too much certainty,[8] it is perhaps even more important to counteract those "incisive" readings of Kierkegaard which actually serve to blunten his homiletical Gospel emphasis. It was, after all, Kierkegaard's radical commitment *to* the Gospel's radical existential implications that undergirded the great doctrinal experiment that was his authorship.

Pattison offers an account of Kierkegaard's journey in and through the fog of ambiguity in such a way that his final convictions (theological or otherwise) merely reflect one of the many oscillating moments in a dominantly ambiguous existence: "'Kierkegaard' is not to be identified with one or other unambiguous gesture, poetic or political,

---

[6] Kierkegaard, *Journals and Papers*, 2:1405, 123. Indeed, Kierkegaard's critique of holiness "to a certain extent" goes hand in hand with his theology of suffering as the mark of devotion which was so overtly missing in Christendom: "One who in truth has become involved with God is instantaneously recognizable by his limp." Kierkegaard, *Journals and Papers*, 2:1405, 123. For Kierkegaard, the Danish Church, in its comfortable assimilation and social religious guise, existed very much *without* a limp. This context dominated his expression of the Gospel throughout the second authorship.

[7] What is more, we might ask, why ought Kierkegaard's "central period" be privileged as his most trustworthy or reasonable? Although he certainly thought much about death, it cannot be the case that he had succumbed to some kind of death-row morosity in his later theological stances, as though he *knew* that he was, in fact, *in* his "latter period" at the time rather than an ongoingly "present" period.

[8] Roger Poole, "The Unknown Kierkegaard: Twentieth Century Receptions," in Alastair Hannay and Gordon Marino, eds., *The Cambridge Companion to Kierkegaard* (Cambridge: Cambridge University Press, 1998), 48-75.

but is rather found in the complex movements he traced in the contested and ambiguous elliptical space."[9] This is why, for Pattison, Kierkegaard's "unambiguity" is seen as a "quest," that which teems with mystery and without necessary conclusiveness.[10] Although he is right to stress the importance of the ambiguous elliptical space, it might be more appropriate to call Kierkegaard a "post-ambiguitarian." This is where we might retain the nuance in his more acerbic expressions of thought. To be post-ambiguous is not to reject ambiguity entirely but to see that even though one recognizes the role of ambiguity, it does not dictate one's outlook, nor—more importantly—one's quest.

What, though, is the problem at the heart of the Kierkegaardian quest—and how much of a "problem" is it? That is, how much does humanity truly *need* the revelation of the Gospel, and *why* do we need it?

Between Religiousness and Reformation

Kierkegaard's view of the Gospel is undoubtedly shaped by his Reformational inheritance, which was key to his pervasive (albeit varied) impact upon twentieth century Protestant theology.[11] Central to this inheritance is a necessarily "low" view of natural humanity prior to divine revelatory encounter. It is this foundation that underlies his view of what is accomplished in the work of redemption, as will be seen. However, Pattison counters this: "Kierkegaard's actual position is considerably more nuanced than this rather standard account of what is going on in his theology…his position involves both a theology of redemption and a theology of creation."[12] It is certainly the case that Kierkegaard did not *merely* hold a view of total depravity which

---

[9] George Pattison, *Kierkegaard and the Quest for Unambiguous Life: Between Romanticism and Modernism* (Oxford: Oxford University Press, 2013), 28.

[10] On this, note a somewhat jarring contrast with Kierkegaard's negative reference to "the knight errant" who embarks upon a quest in inconclusive doubt of what may befall him. Kierkegaard, *Gospel of Sufferings*, trans. A. S. Aldworth and W. S. Ferries (Cambridge: James Clarke & Co., 2015), 92.

[11] See Jon Stewart, ed., *Kierkegaard's Influence on Theology, Tome I: German Protestant Theology* (Farnham: Ashgate, 2012).

[12] Pattison, *Kierkegaard and the Theology of the Nineteenth Century*, 81.

ignored the ongoing redemptive work of God, but neither can his position on the necessity of the divine rescue of fallen humanity be masked by God's subsequent sanctifying work. We see this radical position most overtly in the distinction between the two "types" of Religiousness.

At the apex of Kierkegaard's three stages of existence (aesthetic; ethical; religious) is the distinction between Religiousness A and B. Where Religiousness A tends to refer to the natural religiosity of the human spirit, Religiousness B is the recipient of radical divine revelation.[13] At the heart of the endeavour to interpret Kierkegaard theologically is to work out what to do with this distinction and how it might apply more widely across his soteriological thought. It appears that a clear dialectical taxonomy exists between the two. Religiousness A and B are precisely and necessarily a binary distinction. Within this, the radicality of Religiousness B cannot be a mere "option" of equal weighting, but can *only* and *always* be "the ideal" and "essence" of true Christianity—and indeed, true religion. This does not mean that there is no interaction or movement between the two, but merely that at *all* points, the great taxonomical headline remains in place: that faith comes by hearing, that revelation from without is *required* in order to rescue and liberate us into true freedom.

To hold to a theology more inclined to Religiousness A, as Pattison does—with all the implications of human possibility therein—is not the primary issue here. The more pertinent question is why he would choose Kierkegaard (of all people) for this task, when doing so inevitably invokes so much pushback from Religiousness B *against* the notion of divine immanence? After all, there are plenty of more suitable suitors within the history of theology for that particular marriage of divinity and contingency. Kierkegaard—though perhaps far more interesting to read than a Schleiermacher or a Tillich—is far too committed to the radicality of the Gospel to allow for any notion of individual freedom that might compete with the radical impact of

---

[13] See Søren Kierkegaard, *Concluding Unscientific Postscript to "Philosophical Fragments,"* Vol. 1, ed. and trans. Howard V. Hong and Edna H. Hong (Princeton: Princeton University Press, 1992), 555-585.

Christ's unique revelation *upon* the individual.[14] Indeed, it was this Christological fixation, coupled with the time/eternity dialectic, that was—unsurprisingly—the very thing that so captivated those dialectical revolutionaries of the *Zwischen den Zeiten* journal in 1920s Weimar Germany.

Perhaps one could even say that the Barth/Brunner debate over natural theology (including Barth's radical "Nein!" to Brunner's entire "eristic" project) centred precisely around the same kind of problem of the impasse between Religiousness A and B.[15] The idea of an *Anknüpfungspunkt* in humanity, to which Barth was so hostile, was an issue of dialectical taxonomy. For Barth, one cannot somehow have and eat one's revelational cake. In Pattison's reading, however, Religiousness A offers a "privileged position" vis-à-vis faith, that might somehow avoid what he calls "the 'crater' left by the exploding shells of revelation à la Barth."[16] This notion of A as "privileged" is another way in which Pattison is attempting to add "nuance" to what might otherwise appear an uncouth rendering of human religiosity. However, it seems to summon the image of a "first class" compartment in the reception of divine revelation as though it comes "closer" to it than others. This seems oddly out of sync with Kierkegaard's ear for identifying and satirising hypocrisy.

In many respects, Barth's *Römerbrief*—that famous "bombshell"—was Barth's own Diet of Worms with nineteenth century theology (or, Religiousness A). And like Luther, whom Barth would go

---

[14] See Kierkegaard, *For Self-Examination* and *Judge for Yourself!*, ed. and trans. Howard V. Hong and Edna H. Hong (Princeton: Princeton University Press, 1990), 145-209; Kierkegaard, *Practice in Christianity*, ed. and trans. Howard V. Hong and Edna H. Hong (Princeton: Princeton University Press, 1991), 124-144.

[15] See Kierkegaard's influence on Brunner in Cynthia Bennett Brown, *Believing Thinking, Bounded Theology: The Theological Methodology of Emil Brunner* (Cambridge: James Clarke & Co., 2015), 141-81.

[16] George Pattison, "Kierkegaard, Freedom, Love" (paper presented at the UK Søren Kierkegaard Society, University of Glasgow, 7th May 2016), 6.

on to love and hate in appropriately tumultuous measure,[17] he wanted to stress the *one thing needful*: that God is in heaven and you are on earth.[18] It was that and precisely that, as ludicrously crude as it sounds to the so-called "privileged" ears of Religiousness A, that required Barth's radical break—a break he made with the help of Kierkegaard.[19] It was this same kind of radical expression that Kierkegaard articulated in the time-eternity disjunction,[20] the double-paradox of the Atonement,[21] and the infinite qualitative distinction.[22]

There is, in Pattison's case against the radical Kierkegaard, an apparent ease with which the doctrinal substance of the Gospel which Kierkegaard so vigorously proclaimed is simplistically categorized under rubrics like "the Augustinian-Lutheran view" or "the Reformation doctrine."[23] One does not, of course, want to exude naïveté or ignorance by bypassing the hermeneutical reality that singular figures or traditions have always held doctrinal truth claims which exhibit contextual particularity. Yet this is a different thing to the obvious implication of a condescending use of a phrase like "the Augustinian-Lutheran view," which suggests not just particularity, but idiosyncrasy. This would even seem to be the very kind of bourgeois

---

[17] See Rustin E. Brian, *Covering Up Luther: How Barth's Christology Challenged the* Deus Absconditus *That Haunts Modernity* (Eugene: Cascade, 2013).

[18] Karl Barth, *The Epistle to the Romans*, Sixth Edition, trans. E. C. Hoskyns (London: Oxford University Press, 1968), 310-311.

[19] Barth, *Epistle to the Romans*, 10, 99.

[20] Søren Kierkegaard, *The Concept of Anxiety*, ed. and trans. Reidar Thomte in collaboration with Albert B. Anderson (Princeton: Princeton University Press, 1980), 87-9.

[21] "The paradox is the implicit consequence of the doctrine of the Atonement. First of all, Christianity proceeds to establish sin so firmly as a position that the human understanding can never comprehend it; and then it is this same Christian teaching that again undertakes to eliminate this position in such a way that the human understanding can never comprehend it." Søren Kierkegaard, *The Sickness Unto Death*, ed. and trans. Howard V. Hong and Edna H. Hong (Princeton: Princeton University Press, 1980), 100.

[22] Kierkegaard, *Practice in Christianity*, 28-9.

[23] See Pattison, *Kierkegaard and the Theology of the Nineteenth Century*, 8, 93, 158, 160; *Kierkegaard and the Quest for Unambiguous Life*, 216.

strategy Kierkegaard might have mocked in his day, to deflect attention from the substance of the doctrine itself by calling it "the X view" as a sly ruse to deny its potential existential implications.

For all the wealth of caveats surrounding Luther's legacy, it is abundantly clear that he had that unique ability to see through the mire and to take a courageous stand for that which was being quietly but violently neglected in his time.[24] Although arguably Kierkegaard's "stand" actually seems virtually the opposite of Luther's, by accentuating striving rather than mere grace, he always maintained that his emphasis is precisely what Luther himself would have preached in nineteenth century Copenhagen.[25] Thomas Carlyle, in his famous 1840 lectures on the "heroic" motif in human history, called Luther the great "Prophet Idol-breaker; a bringer-back of men to reality."[26] It can become all too easy, with a half-millenium of hindsight, to assert that the intensity of Luther's experience negates the possibility that his imperatives can speak meaningfully beyond his time.[27] But this would surely be to miss the entire point of the Reformation: "The Reformation

---

[24] "His greatest intellectual gift was his ability to simplify, to cut to the heart of an issue—but this also made it difficult for him to compromise or see nuance." Lyndal Roper, *Martin Luther: Renegade and Prophet* (London: Vintage, 2017), 422. However, this does seem to underplay Luther's dialectical nuance, particularly in his varied homiletical expression, alert to various diversities of congregation and context. See Robert Kolb, *Martin Luther and the Enduring Word of God: The Wittenberg School and Its Scripture-Centred Proclamation* (Grand Rapids: Baker, 2016), 174-208.

[25] Kierkegaard, *For Self-Examination*, 24. For a revised view of Kierkegaard's reading of Luther vis-à-vis their respective kerygmatic emphases, see David L. Coe, "Kierkegaard's Forking for Extracts from Extracts of Luther's Sermons: Reviewing Kierkegaard's Laud and Lance of Luther," in *Kierkegaard Studies Yearbook* 1 (2011): 3-18.

[26] Thomas Carlyle, *On Great Men* (London: Penguin, 1996), 58. The heroic motif also evokes the potential idolatry inherent in Religiousness A, and the problem at the heart of theological immanence whereby the eternal is infused with the temporal indiscriminately, whereby God's revelatory activity is minimized under a false ideality.

[27] The opposite case is made by Ryrie, who argues that Luther's "shattering spiritual experiences" continue to speak today not for their theological import but for their resonance within the culture of modern individualism they helped create. Alec Ryrie, *Protestants: The Radicals Who Made the Modern World* (London: William Collins, 2017), 19-20.

age, amid grievous destruction, swept away the clutter, pursued simplicity of vision, and directed the gaze of the worshipper towards that which truly mattered."[28] Indeed, Luther's reformation was of a most *existential* kind. At heart it was primarily only about himself, and only secondarily (or, accidentally) did it happen to affect the rest of world history. That is, the doctrinal revolt was inseparable from its existential import.[29]

Kierkegaard might also be called an existential reformer, notwithstanding his own caveats that he was not—and could not be—a reformer because he could never live up to Luther's heroism,[30] and was dubious about those who followed in the Reformer's wake without the same existential involvement.[31] However, if Luther *was* right, then the truth to which he bore witness, and the truth to which the Reformation as a whole bore witness, cannot be swept away under a neat category as though we could somehow move *beyond* it, like a Hegelian *Aufhebung* en masse. Indeed, it would simply be too convenient—and perhaps too suspiciously Christendomian—to separate Luther's view of the Gospel into a "perspective" of the past, as we continue on at a safe distance from his aggravating light. Rather, "contemporaneity with Luther," to borrow a concept (albeit somewhat blasphemously) from *Practice in Christianity*—is Christianly essential, at least in regards to the *condition* Luther was proclaiming. That is, if Luther is right on the diagnosis and cure of sin, as Kierkegaard believed he was, we no longer have the diversionist luxury of assuming that his condition was *only* his. Even if his thunderous experience *was* idiosyncratic of the anguished conscience *ad absurdum*, this does not remove *us* from facing the

---

[28] Owen Chadwick, *The Reformation* (London: Penguin, 1979), 443-4.

[29] "Luther's inner certainty depended on identifying his cause with Christ's." Roper, *Martin Luther*, 189.

[30] Kierkegaard, *Judge for Yourself!*, 211-13.

[31] "It has often been said that a reformation should begin with each man reforming himself. That, however, is not what actually happened, for the Reformation produced a hero who paid God dearly enough for his position as hero. By joining up with him directly people buy cheap, indeed at bargain prices, what he had paid for so dearly." Søren Kierkegaard, *The Present Age*, trans. Alexander Dru (London: Collins, 1962), 63.

potential implications of our state *coram deo*, nor for how we interpret Kierkegaard's appropriation of it.

What Hugh Pyper says of Kierkegaard could also be said of Luther: "What he burns to communicate is good news, while knowing that the majority of his hearers cannot tell good news from bad and have a tendency to mistake the disease for the cure and the cure for the disease."[32] As Pattison himself says in his work on Kierkegaard's discourses:

> The Christian communicator must be indirect in so far as he must meet his "audience" where they are, in the aesthetic and the babel of hermeneutic ambiguity. But it is never simply his intention to leave them there. His aim is rather to bring them to a point at which they will be appropriately receptive to the kerygmatic imperatives of the gospel.[33]

Evidently, Pattison does not want to minimize Kierkegaard's kerygmatic witness, even as he remains critical of the Reformational moorings in which it is often seen. But he primarily wants to stress the possibilities inherent in the hearer, as forming part of a revised view of the Kierkegaardian kerygma. Elsewhere Pattison points to the mode of the "subjunctive" in the discourses (lying somewhere between the "indicative" and the "imperative") as a way to guarantee the hearer's freedom in the midst of proclamation: "The ideality of the subjunctive…concerns what *may be* and, specifically, what may be a possibility for subjective appropriation…The subjunctive does not present its subject matter as simple fact, but makes the narrated facts available as ideal existential possibilities elicited from history."[34] This evokes an important distinction between the hearer of the Gospel and their sinfulness.

---

[32] Hugh S. Pyper, *The Joy of Kierkegaard: Essays on Kierkegaard as a Biblical Reader* (Sheffield: Equinox, 2011), 1.

[33] George Pattison, "The Theory and Practice of Language and Communication in Kierkegaard's *Upbuilding Discourses*," in *Kierkegaardiana* 19, ed. Joakim Garff, Arne Grøn, et al. (Copenhagen: C. A. Reitzels Forlag, 1998), 81-94 [86].

[34] George Pattison, *Kierkegaard's Upbuilding Discourses: Philosophy, theology, literature* (London: Routledge, 2002), 157.

Between Sin and Redemption

In *Philosophical Fragments* the idea of "the Socratic" is distinguished against the decisive "moment" of Christian revelation.[35] For the Socratic hearer it is supposed that the truth must merely be "recalled" in order to be grasped. They are what Pattison might call "privileged." However, the hearer of the Gospel recognizes that they cannot recall anything whatsoever since they begin in a state of fundamental "error."[36] They are bound within this error and must be radically "liberated" and "delivered" by a Saviour.[37]

Kierkegaard often makes the key distinction between what we might call the *act* of sin and the *condition* of sin:

> Fundamentally, the relation between God and man is in this, that a man is a sinner, and God is the Holy One. Confronting God...a man is not a sinner in this or that regard, but in his being he is sinful, not guilty in this or that, but guilty essentially and absolutely.[38]

Pattison claims that although we are tempted *by* sin, we are "free to resist and free to orient ourselves towards the good, to will it, and to

---

[35] See Søren Kierkegaard, *Philosophical Crumbs*, trans. M. G. Piety (Oxford: Oxford University Press, 2009), 88-110, 125-39.

[36] "If the teacher is to be the occasion that reminds the learner, then he cannot contribute to the learner's remembering that he really knows the truth, because the learner is actually in a state of error." Kierkegaard, *Philosophical Crumbs*, 92.

[37] Kierkegaard, *Philosophical Crumbs*, 95. For a nuanced account of Kierkegaard's Christocentric hamartiology in light of the place of sin within the purposes of redemption, see Jason A. Mahn, *Fortunate Fallibility: Kierkegaard and the Power of Sin* (New York: Oxford University Press, 2011).

[38] Kierkegaard, *Gospel of Sufferings*, 89. The effect of the sin-consciousness of the person before God is also mentioned in an 1850 journal entry: "original sin as guilt is also an expression of God's using his standard; for God sees everything in uno; and therefore the merely human understanding finds it so difficult." Kierkegaard, *Journals and Papers*, 1:525, 207. This refers to the notion that the more God (as the superior one) loves the sinner, the more unhappy the sinner becomes—even if God lays down his standard (i.e. who he is, in the sense of a "flag") in order to love us. The more he loves us, the more the difference (his superiority) is accentuated; and thus, the more "difficult" it is for us, the more we suffer as a result of God's love.

pray for it."[39] If indeed this "we" includes all human beings, it must be asked—in light of Kierkegaard's apparent definition of the *ontological* entrapments of sin in light of the Pauline imperative of Ephesians 2:1-5 (dead in sin, made alive in Christ)—on what grounds are we free to overcome the problem of sin by ourselves? For Kierkegaard, as for Calvin,[40] the raising of Lazarus was a perfect analogy of the sinner's redemption. Indeed, in an 1849 journal entry, Kierkegaard relates this stark difference to the suppression of the ideal in Christendom: "What it means actually to be Christian is seen here (John 12:10): the Jews wanted to kill Lazarus—because Christ had raised him from the dead. So dangerous it is to be raised from the dead—by Christ!"[41]

As Kierkegaard concludes his introduction to *Sickness Unto Death*: "Only the *Christian* knows what is meant by the sickness unto death."[42] This is precisely because the Christian has learned to fear God in the confrontation—and forgiveness—of their sin. This also assumes, of course, the paradox Kierkegaard refers to frequently, that original sin and individual guilt are complexly conflated, and may only be engaged via faith.[43] For Kierkegaard, the fundamental difference between paganism and Christianity is that Christianity knows what sin actually is.[44] So clear is Kierkegaard on the radical doctrine of sin that he claims it would be a terrible slight on Christianity if paganism's definition of sin were shown to be in agreement with its own.[45] It is this radical

---

[39] Pattison, "Kierkegaard, Freedom, Love," 2.

[40] John Calvin, *Commentaries*, trans. Joseph Haroutunian (Philadelphia: Westminster, 1958), 395.

[41] Kierkegaard, *Journals and Papers*, 3:2866, 268.

[42] Kierkegaard, *Sickness Unto Death*, 8.

[43] "That 'Original Sin' is 'guilt' is the real paradox. How paradoxical is best seen as follows. The paradox is formed by a composite of qualitatively heterogeneous categories. To 'inherit' is a category of nature. 'Guilt' is an ethical category of spirit. How can it ever occur to anyone to put these two together, the understanding says—to say that something is inherited which by its very concept cannot be inherited. It must be believed. The paradox in Christian truth always involves the truth as before God. A superhuman goal and standard are used—and with regard to them there is only one relationship possible—that of faith." Kierkegaard, *Journals and Papers*, 2:1530, 194.

[44] See Kierkegaard, *Sickness Unto Death*, 89.

[45] Kierkegaard, *Sickness Unto Death*, 89-90.

disjunction between the Christian and non-Christian that is labelled by Pattison as the "extreme" Augustinian-Protestant view of sin.[46] Unsurprisingly, this also manifests in a de-radicalized account of redemption *from* this sinful condition too, whereby Pattison argues that Kierkegaard's doctrine inclines more towards "recreation" than "satisfaction" of sin *per se*.[47] On Kierkegaard's frequent use of the term "satisfaction," Pattison sees this as related to God's love, not his wrath.[48] This reflects something of a common view in western academic theology today whereby divine wrath is often entirely ignored within theological discussions of redemption.[49] In Pattison's case, he seems to have expressed a false dichotomy of divine love over against divine justice. In doing so, however, this would seem to render the "requirement" of satisfaction something of a farce. That is, God might have simply *chosen* to love in spite of the sin of his beloved rather than requiring satisfaction of sin *in order that* he might be reconciled to his beloved.

---

[46] Pattison, *Kierkegaard and the Theology of the Nineteenth Century*, 124.

[47] Pattison, *Kierkegaard and the Theology of the Nineteenth Century*, 81.

[48] See Pattison, *Kierkegaard and the Theology of the Nineteenth Century*, 157-60; Pattison, *Kierkegaard and the Quest for Unambiguous Life*, 216. Pattison's argument here is not wrong in its illustration of the colourful variety within Kierkegaard's account, but rather in assuming that Kierkegaard's emphasis on love thereby necessarily excludes the category of God's judgement simultaneously.

[49] At an academic theology conference on the subject of eternity at the University of Aberdeen in 2015 the final session involved an anonymous Q&A box which had been set out for the panel of plenary speakers to discuss. One of the questions slipped into the box was the cause of great amusement as it highlighted a topic which had, up to that point, rather curiously, not been mentioned *at all* throughout the entirety of the conference. The question simply stated: "Eternal death and hell, anyone?" It is one thing for contemporary academic theology to nuance the various unreflective expressions of divine wrath in previous eras of the Church, but another thing entirely to eliminate (deliberately or otherwise) the concept of divine wrath from the theological conversation *per se*. This reflects the wider problem of the general embarrassment within the modern theological academy towards those attributes of God which simply cannot hope to gain a hearing in contemporary western society. See Philip G. Ziegler, ed., *Eternal God, Eternal Life: Theological Investigations into the Concept of Immortality* (London: T&T Clark, 2016).

For Kierkegaard, the sinful condition is so severe that even the conviction of human depravity itself is dependent upon radical revelation: "there must be a revelation from God to teach man what sin is and how deeply it is rooted."[50] And yet, perhaps like the Reformers and like Augustine, Kierkegaard's expression of redemption is equally as radical as his expression of depravity: "the Atonement wants to eliminate sin so completely as if it were drowned in the sea."[51] One is able to apprehend the gift of this Atonement only by faith, referred to in *The Concept of Anxiety* as "the inner certainty that anticipates infinity."[52] For Kierkegaard, the inner certainty of faith anticipates and expects much from God in eternity because it has eschewed the false foundation of doubt.

Between Disconsolate Doubt and Reflective Radicality

The antithesis to Kierkegaard's radical proclamation of this Gospel is the attitude of deliberative doubt. This is a particularly urgent problem in modernity, wherein doubt becomes the unquestioned foundation prior to faith. Kierkegaard calls out the sinner's subtle way of attempting to bypass their sinfulness by assuming a kind of neutral starting-point by which they may judge God's revelation: "If the starting-point be doubt, then long, long before the end God is lost to us…If, on the other hand, a sense of sin be the starting-point, then the starting point of doubt is made impossible, and so there is joy."[53]

---

[50] Kierkegaard, *Sickness Unto Death*, 96; see also Fremstedal and Jackson's neat summary: "Because of human guilt and sinfulness, Kierkegaard holds that we are neither capable of realizing moral virtue nor eternal happiness by our own unaided powers; we are only capable of realizing our incapability and of choosing whether or not to accept divine grace." Roe Fremstedal and Timothy P. Jackson, "Salvation/Eternal Happiness," in Steven Emmanuel, William McDonald and Jon Stewart, eds., *Kierkegaard's Concepts, Tome VI: Salvation to Writing* (Farnham: Ashgate, 2015), 1-8 [3].

[51] Kierkegaard, *Sickness Unto Death*, 100.

[52] Kierkegaard, *Concept of Anxiety*, 157.

[53] Kierkegaard, *Gospel of Sufferings*, 82.

Doubt, for Kierkegaard, becomes an attitude of presumptuousness before God.[54]

In the discourse, "The Care of Indecisiveness, Vacillation, and Disconsolateness" (a reflection on Christ's call that we cannot serve two masters), Kierkegaard says: "the Christian, free from care is never *indecisive*—he has faith; never *vacillating*—he is eternally resolved."[55] This is put in stark contrast to the pagan, who epitomizes Kierkegaard's critique of endless deliberation: "Perhaps one thinks that the longer a person deliberates the more earnest his decision becomes. Perhaps—if it does not entirely fail to come."[56] To an extent, modern Christendom itself epitomized the choice to privilege doubt over decision, becoming what Kierkegaard called "the slave of indecisiveness."[57] Faith, on the other hand, chooses God and "refuses to hear about anything else."[58] One can see, of course, as Pattison aptly observes, how easy it was for Kierkegaard to become co-opted into the "decisionistic" thinking of the twentieth century via controversial thinkers such as Emanuel Hirsch.[59] Kierkegaard, though certainly responsible for much of his interpretative litter, cannot be faulted for readings which are so violently selective of the grounds for which his strong emphases on "decision" were made (namely, Christ as the qualitative "content" of the Gospel). To see his reflections as "unnuanced" would itself seem to be an ironically simplistic approach. What Kierkegaard offers is not an ignorance of complexity in the midst of action but a rather profound knowledge of its inner workings, tensions, and implications. He is also aware, in a deeply important way, of the perils of calling for "complexity" when

---

[54] Presumptuousness, of course, is the very thing one might often assume to be the "problem" with radically decisive faith.

[55] Søren Kierkegaard, *Christian Discourses* and *The Crisis in the Life of an Actress*, ed. and trans. Howard V. Hong and Edna H. Hong (Princeton: Princeton University Press, 2009), 85.

[56] Kierkegaard, *Christian Discourses*, 88.

[57] Kierkegaard, *Christian Discourses*, 89.

[58] Kierkegaard, *Christian Discourses*, 88.

[59] Pattison, *Kierkegaard and the Quest for Unambiguous Life*, 86-114; see also Matthias Wilke, "Emmanuel Hirsch: A German Dialogue with 'Saint Søren,'" in Stewart, *Kierkegaard's Influence on Theology* I, 155-184.

this becomes simplistically accepted as the guiding mantra.[60] Kierkegaard, especially in his discourses, is encouraging the reader towards critical reflection precisely in relation to the ideology of critical reflection.

Commenting on the preacher in Ecclesiastes, a book which fascinated Kierkegaard and in many ways epitomized his own dialectical-but-decisive approach:

> He speaks not as one who wishes, not as one who longs, not as one who swoons, but he speaks to the young with the power of conviction, with the authority of experience, with the trustworthiness of assured insight, with the joyful trust of bold confidence, with the emphasis of earnestness, with the concern of the admonition.[61]

It might be tempting to imagine Kierkegaard was speaking indirectly here, especially given the hermeneutical complexity of Ecclesiastes itself, and Kierkegaard's own critique of preachers. Countering this, Will Williams observes:

> While Kierkegaard can undoubtedly make potent use of humor and irony, I believe it is a mistake to read him as a thoroughgoing ironist at every turn. Kierkegaard uses the Preacher [of Ecclesiastes] non-ironically as a genuine authority on wise living. If one attempts an inappropriately ironic reading of the Preacher in order to generate ambiguity and so to escape the moral

---

[60] If Hirsch could read Kierkegaard as a Romantic who enabled him to see the decisive action of National Socialism as a theological good, one must counter this with interpreters like Bonhoeffer, a great reader of Kierkegaard who saw in him precisely the opposite dynamic and a means by which individual decision (not passive vacillation to the Zeitgeist) was precisely necessarily in resisting the same ethical evils, which had been so seductively veiled within the tidal wave of *Völkisch* cultural energy. For an account of Kierkegaard's influence on Bonhoeffer, see Christiane Tietz, "Standing 'in the Tradition of Paul, Luther, Kierkegaard, in the Tradition of Genuine Christian Thinking,'" in Stewart, *Kierkegaard's Influence on Theology* I, 43-65. See also Matthew D. Kirkpatrick, *Attacks on Christendom in a World Come of Age: Kierkegaard, Bonhoeffer, and the Question of "Religionless" Christianity* (Eugene: Pickwick Publications, 2011).

[61] Kierkegaard, *Eighteen Upbuilding Discourses*, 238.

earnestness of a passage, Kierkegaard locates the fault in the reader and not in the author.[62]

This chimes in well with Kierkegaard's view of doubt as the temptation for the sinner to circumvent their sinfulness, and indeed their need of the Gospel. This is precisely what also concerned "the preacher," who —as Kierkegaard notes—spoke not with mere wishfulness but with "bold confidence."

To speak with boldness is to echo the Apostle Paul's prayerful plea: "that words may be given to me in opening my mouth boldly to proclaim the mystery of the gospel...that I may declare it boldly, as I ought to speak." (Ephesians 6:19-20). Kierkegaard's desire to heed the realities of "New Testament Christianity"[63] makes a rhetorical comparison with what has become known as "Pauline apocalyptic" particularly interesting.[64] Paul is often seen as having been eclipsed by James in Kierkegaard's writings, but in fact he and his writings appear far more abundantly than references to James across the authorship.[65] His employment of Pauline themes is numerous, but it is evident from Kierkegaard's genius/Apostle distinction that Paul has particular interest for him as a bringer of revelatory authority.[66] Something *happened* to Paul which affected how one ought to hear what he says.

---

[62] Will Williams, "Ecclesiastes: Vanity, Grief, and the Distinctions of Wisdom," in Lee C. Barrett and Jon Stewart, eds., *Kierkegaard and the Bible, Tome I: The Old Testament* (Farnham: Ashgate, 2010), 179-94 [181, n. 11].

[63] See, for example, Kierkegaard, *Journals and Papers,* 2:1807, 296; 3:2379, 31; 4:4499, 324.

[64] For an example of a Kierkegaardian implementation within this emerging theological movement, see Philip G. Ziegler, *Militant Grace: The Apocalyptic Turn and the Future of Christian Theology* (Grand Rapids: Baker Academic, 2018), 153-68.

[65] See Lori Unger Brandt, "Paul: Herald of Grace and Paradigm of Christian Living," in Lee C. Barrett and Jon Stewart, eds., *Kierkegaard and the Bible, Tome II: The New Testament* (Farnham: Ashgate, 2010), 189-208. See also Cyril O'Regan's comments on the influence of a Pauline vision on Kierkegaard in "The Rule of Chaos and the Perturbation of Love," in Paul Martens and C. Stephen Evans, ed., *Kierkegaard and Christian Faith* (Waco, TX: Baylor University Press, 2016), 131-56 [154].

[66] See Søren Kierkegaard, *Without Authority*, ed. and trans. Howard V. Hong and Edna H. Hong (Princeton: Princeton University Press, 1997), 91-106.

SØREN KIERKEGAARD: THEOLOGIAN OF THE GOSPEL

His encounter with Christ is truly dramatic, beginning as it does somewhat violently and ending in temporary blindness (Acts 9:3-9). This is not a mere historical curiosity but, like Lazarus' resurrection, is also a picture of what happens when sin is confronted by liberating love in its most supreme form.[67] This is a supremely chastening liberation, and yet it is one that could lead Paul to "rejoice" in all things (Philippians 4:4) despite the avalanche of suffering which would confront him in fulfilment of his revelatory calling (2 Corinthians 11:23-30).

It is the combination of radical revelation and Paul's willingness to suffer rejoicingly that Kierkegaard finds so inspiring as an antidote to Christendom's insipidness.[68] Kierkegaard's task as a Christian author from beginning to end was indeed to follow Paul's lead as the herald of a Gospel that was both dialectical and radically undilutable. The radicality of sin was precisely what Kierkegaard believed had been "diluted" out of Christendom:

> The consciousness of sin shuts my mouth so that in spite of the possibility of offense I choose to believe. The relationship has to be that penetrating. Christianity repels in order to attract. But Christianity has been diluted, the aspect of Christianity which, so to speak, turns a man upside down, has been diluted, and therefore the impetus of sin-consciousness is not needed to drive one into it—that is, it is all sentimentality.[69]

Try telling Paul that we may free ourselves from the bondage of sin-consciousness. He might respond, paradoxically—as indeed would Kierkegaard—that it is *for freedom* that Christ has set us free (Galatians 5:1) and that to submit again to a yoke of slavery (be it slavery to the self-contained ego *or* slavery to the crowd) is to step back into a life

---

[67] See again Calvin's connection between the raising of Lazarus and the radically activating power of the Gospel. Calvin, *Commentaries*, 395.

[68] See Søren Kierkegaard, *Upbuilding Discourses in Various Spirits*, ed. and trans. Howard V. Hong and Edna H. Hong (Princeton: Princeton University Press, 1993), 315.

[69] Kierkegaard, *Journals and Papers,* 6:6261, 64.

which is abundantly *less* than the life abundant that Christ's sacrifice secured for us.

But it is not only "for freedom" that we are set free, but also "from freedom," as Kierkegaard well knew—that is, from notions of freedom which conform precisely to this world;[70] the questionably "radical" freedom which might refuse to bow the knee to Christ's lordship, which might see radical discipleship as giving oneself away in vain,[71] which might refuse to be transformed by the liberating love and power of the Spirit (Romans 12:1-2) but rather insist on the fetishization of one's individual existential rights above all.[72] All such moves render the preaching of the cross all the more foolish (1 Corinthians 1:18) to the modern self-understanding, and render Kierkegaard's voice all the more important as one who continues to preach such apparent foolishness in the footsteps of Paul. Indeed, it is precisely in *not* removing the veil of Kierkegaard's Gospel radicality—in all its thoughtfully deliberate offensiveness—that we retain his most vital and most nuanced contribution to modern Christian thought (however alarming that may appear to many proponents of modern Christian thought).

The Nuance of Radicality

Pattison certainly sees Kierkegaard's later period (beyond 1851) as offering "a much less dialectical and nuanced view."[73] To be sure, the period that led to the "Attack" literature had a polemical slant, but it is

---

[70] See Kierkegaard's critique of the false deification of the concept of freedom in light of the 1848 European revolutions. Kierkegaard, *Journals and Papers*, 2:1261, 67-9.

[71] See Jean-Paul Sartre, *Being and Nothingness: An Essay on Phenomenological Ontology*, trans. Paris Gallimard (London: Routledge, 2003), 636.

[72] See Hauerwas' critique of "the unlimited scope of rights language" in contemporary political discourse. Stanley Hauerwas, *The Work of Theology* (Grand Rapids: Eerdmans, 2015), 196-98.

[73] Pattison, *Kierkegaard and the Theology of the Nineteenth Century*, 105, n. 3. See also Sylvia Walsh, *Living Christianly: Kierkegaard's Dialectic of Christian Existence* (Philadelphia: Pennsylvania University Press, 2006), 159-60.

not as though we are left in ignorance as to why Kierkegaard's approach changed. He offers reams of reflection not only in his various "total" interpretations of his authorship but also especially in his journals, whereby we see the contemplative agony that lay behind his careful change in emphasis.[74] To simply label his attack period "unnuanced" is almost to act as though this other reflective material simply doesn't exist.

As is well known, Kierkegaard thought long and hard about how and why he would choose to communicate in particular ways at particular times during his life, based on numerous factors.[75] Although his later work took a decisive turn towards a more radical emphasis it is not as though there was a substantial change in his fundamental understanding of the efficacy of sin, the incapacity of humanity, and the human need for divine deliverance. These were already present in his theology even during the earlier writings, albeit sometimes veiled. This radicality itself need not be seen as unreflective. Kierkegaard is just as dialectical in the attack literature as in the pseudonymous literature; he has merely chosen the one thing needful to the moment, at that particular time and in that particular place, taking into account all the complexities of Danish public life and what it would entail to challenge Christendom's lethargy most effectively.

One must also say, of course, that Kierkegaard saw the gravitation to reflective nuance as itself something of a temptation, precisely by imprisoning the self in a myriad of perpetually dialectical options. His critique of what we might call cultures of incessant reflection offers a sharp point of contact with our own contemporary digital existence, as Sheridan Hough aptly notes: "what Kierkegaard calls the 'prison' of reflection is nothing more than the infinite availability of yet another point of view, opinion, or aspect of the notion at hand. Consider the endless Web-parade of images and

---

[74] See the section, "a Theology of (In)direct Communication" in Aaron Edwards, "Kierkegaard as Socratic Street Preacher?: Reimagining the Dialectic of Direct and Indirect Communication for Christian Proclamation," *Harvard Theological Review* 110:2 (2017), 280-300 [287-91].

[75] For one of many possible examples, see Kierkegaard, *Judge for Yourself!*, 215.

opinions, its torrential, quenchless, and indeed senseless variety."[76] In a world still coming to terms with what this culture does to our thought, Kierkegaard's riposte to incessant reflection—particularly on the note of theological decisiveness—risks being drowned out for its uneasiness within contemporary academic modes of practice.

What is easily forgotten is just how thoroughly modern is the problem of conceiving of the "appropriate" tenor for theological discourse. This is a trait that was frequently challenged by the late John Webster, who began one memorable essay with the following unapologetic caveat:

> What follows is half-way between a theological essay and a homily; but we should not be particularly troubled by its homiletic tone. The clear distinctions which some members of the academic theological guild draw between proclamation and critical reflection are part of the pathology of modern theology; our forebears would have been distressed by the way in which theology has succumbed to the standardization of discourse in the academy and the consequent exclusion of certain modes of Christian speech, and we should probably worry more about what Bernard or Calvin might think of us than about the way in which our *wissenschaftlich* colleagues may shake their heads.[77]

We might certainly add Kierkegaard to the chorus of Bernard, Calvin, and Webster, that a homiletic tone does not mean an absence of reflective thought, not least when we consider that the content of theology is inseparable from its kerygma. That is, as Kierkegaard well knew, "the Gospel" is not the kind of content that can be spoken of abstractly, devoid of a kerygmatic imperative. This does not necessitate a sacralisation of "homiletic tone" *per se*. Anyone who has ever marked a first-year undergraduate essay knows of the need for an iconoclastic "stripping of the pulpits" too, wherever a bombastic or explosive rhetoric seeks to hide—as though via a questionable fig-leaf—the

---

[76] Sheridan Hough, *Kierkegaard's Dancing Tax Collector: Faith, Finitude, and Silence* (Oxford: Oxford University Press, 2015), 18.

[77] John Webster, "Christ, Church, and Reconciliation," in *Word and Church: Essays in Christian Dogmatics* (London: T&T Clark, 2016), 211-30 [211].

absence of thoughtful argumentation. In another sense, Kierkegaard was also the greatest critic of the pulpiteering voices of Christendom who sought to proclaim Christianity in words alone.[78] But such abuses do not change a single iota about the fundamental and inseparable connection between theology and proclamation. This is something all too easily forgotten in contemporary academic settings which may promote deliberatively hazier perspectives of the many bygone theological voices who sought to embody the Gospel in appropriately strong words.

---

[78] See Kierkegaard, *Practice in Christianity*, 233-37.

10.

THE DIFFERENCE THE INCARNATION MAKES: THE CHANGING NATURE OF *FAITH* AND *OFFENCE* IN THE PSEUDONYMS OF SØREN KIERKEGAARD

Stephen Backhouse

Introduction

Incarnational theologians are right to pay close attention to Kierkegaard when attempting to articulate authentic faith. However, not every book in the Kierkegaardian canon speaks with the same voice. *Faith* develops throughout Kierkegaard's works in relation to the changing nature of what constitutes an *offence,* an idea that itself changes from pseudonym to pseudonym. This is not merely an indication of Kierkegaard's development as an author, but is a deliberate part of his scheme to use the different pseudonyms to represent the varieties of faith available to citizens of Christendom. The changes are linked to the self-professed Christianity of the purported author of the text. As the characters become more Christian they notably begin to have a sharper focus on Jesus Christ, the essential nature of the offence, and thus faith occasioned by the Incarnation. By way of demonstrating the changing nature of faith and offence in light of the Incarnation, this essay will provide a close reading of three of Kierkegaard's most important pseudonyms: the non-Christian Johannes de Silentio, the almost-Christian Johannes Climacus and the super-Christian Anti-Climacus.

In *Fear and Trembling (FT)* Johannes de Silentio only dimly apprehends the true locus of faith and offence. De Silentio couches "offence" in terms of the affront to civic morality that arises when an individual is set against the universal.[1] This is De Silentio's

---

[1] *Fear and Trembling* (attributed to Johannes de Silentio, 1843), trans. and ed. Howard V. Hong and Edna H. Hong (Princeton: Princeton University Press, 1983), 52-53, 55-56, 60-61, 66.

"teleological suspension of the ethical," and it is this faith demand that God presents to each individual that he finds so offensive.[2] Offence in *Fear and Trembling* serves the useful purpose of preventing a facile approach to faith. In keeping with De Silentio's purpose to understand (and possibly even acquire) faith,[3] he is concerned when people assume that they can easily "go beyond" faith.[4] Only when people are "horrified" by Abraham will they truly understand what is involved in, and required by, faith.[5] Yet de Silentio is not himself a man who has faith,[6] and as a result, his opinions about what is offensive are not much more informed than anyone else in Christendom.[7]

Johannes Climacus in *Philosophical Fragments* (*PF*) comes closer to the essential offence by appreciating the importance of inward appropriation of offence, and recognising that offence is inextricably bound up with individual's response to the God-Man.[8] However, Climacus intellectualises the offence, locating it in the sphere of reason and understanding. He describes the God-Man as the Absolute Paradox who is actively opposed to reason, seeking its downfall.[9] It is in the moment when the reason "collides" with the paradox that Climacus finds the offence.[10] Climacus calls this collision the "unhappy understanding," because the reason refuses to bow to the Paradox.[11] He sees that this refusal is bound up with human sin, and he describes sin as ignorance.[12]

---

[2] *FT*, 54-67, esp. 59-60.

[3] *FT*, 47-48. See also *FT*, 33, 51.

[4] *FT*, 121-22.

[5] *FT*, 52-53.

[6] *FT*, 48.

[7] *FT*, 55.

[8] *Philosophical Fragments* (attributed to Johannes Climacus, 1844), trans. and ed. Howard V. Hong and Edna, H. Hong (Princeton: Princeton University Press, 1985), 37, 39, 47, 49-54.

[9] *PF*, 47.

[10] *PF*, 39, see also 37, 47, 49, 50, 53.

[11] *PF*, 49. See also 39, 44-45, 46.

[12] *PF*, 50.

Viewed from Anti-Climacus' higher vantage point, it emerges that both Climacus and Johannes de Silentio have been concerned with lesser offences.[13] Anti-Climacus speaks of the continual *possibility* of offence,[14] emphasising that the essential offence is not a singular epistemological event, or a unique broach of public mores. Instead, the offence has to do with the constant struggle of man's will to obey God or not to obey God. Sin is properly understood as disobedience, a matter of the will and not of the understanding.[15] The God-Man presents man not with a problem to solve, but a command to obey. The location of the offence is thus shifted, and it is not defined in relation to the intellect, but instead to the ethical existence of the individual. *Sickness unto Death* (*SUD*) emphasises that the possibility of offence is always before man, because all of man's decisions are made before God.[16] Linking the essential offence to sin, and sin to the will, is the most significant development in *SUD* and it leads to Anti-Climacus' treatment of the offence in *Practice in Christianity* (*PC*).

In that book, the continual possibility of offence before God is kept alive through the idea of *contemporaneity*.[17] Significantly, here the language of an unknown being, Paradox and the God-Man is left behind and specific details pertaining to the person of Jesus Christ come to the fore. The reader is not invited to stand before some paradoxical idea of what it is for the finite to co-inhere with the finite. The reader is faced with the man who says, "come unto me and I will give you rest." For anyone standing contemporaneously with Jesus Christ, his demand for obedience will always be keenly felt. Anti-

---

[13] For Anti-Climacus' judgement on the "Johannes de Silentio" type, see: *The Sickness unto Death* (attributed to Anti-Climacus, 1849), trans. and ed. Howard V. Hong and Edna, H. Hong (Princeton: Princeton University Press, 1980), 83, 89, 94 and *Practice in Christianity* (attributed to Anti-Climacus, 1850), trans. and ed. Howard V. Hong and Edna, H. Hong (Princeton: Princeton University Press, 1991), 111; On the type of thought Climacus represents: *SUD*, 83, 95, 130-31 and *PC*, 106, 136.

[14] On offence as *possibility*: *SUD*, 83-87, *PC* 139-44.

[15] *SUD*, 87-96.

[16] *SUD*, 85-87.

[17] *PC*, 62-66, 99-108, 144.

Climacus describes Christ as the "sign of contradiction"[18] that gives rise to the two forms of "essential offence."[19] These two forms are the ethical aversion faced when *this* lowly man claims to be God, and when *God* claims to be this lowly man.[20] Only the one who is contemporaneous with Christ will face the possibility of offence. Only by facing the offence can authentic faith result.[21]

Johannes de Silentio, Offence, and Social Morality

It is with Johannes de Silentio, the pseudonym that straddles the aesthetic and the religious stages,[22] that offence begins to take on shades of positive importance. Here, it moves from the generalised offence of common parlance, to *the* offence particularly situated in matters of faith. Although the actual word does not come up very much in the text (de Silentio uses the Greek σχάνδάλον),[23] the paradox of faith can be seen to be offensive in that it is "appalling," "shocking" and "horrifying."[24] Thus, in common with the later pseudonyms, De Silentio recognises that offence is a necessary component related to faith. However, unlike Climacus and Anti-Climacus, for whom offence provides the opportunity for individuals to come to faith, de Silentio's offence occurs only *after* faith has taken hold in the individual. Along with his society, de Silentio remains offended at what a person is led to do once he has faith. Thus, for de Silentio, offence is not a necessary

---

[18] *PC*, 124-28, 132, 134-36, 141.

[19] *PC*, 121.

[20] In *PC* Anti-Climacus calls the first an offence of "loftiness," 94-101; the second is the offence of "lowliness," 102–121.

[21] *PC*, 94, 101, 106, 136.

[22] See Climacus' assessment in the "Glance at Danish Literature," in the *Concluding Unscientific Postscript* (attributed to Johannes Climacus, 1846), trans. and ed. Howard V. Hong and Edna, H. Hong (Princeton: Princeton University Press, 1992), 259-62; and also Kierkegaard's view in *Point of View* (non-pseudonymous 1848/59), trans. and ed. Howard V. Hong and Edna, H. Hong (Princeton: Princeton University Press, 1998), 37.

[23] In his translator's introduction, Howard Hong notes that of the key phrases in Johannes de Silentio's lexicon, "offence" occurs least often. *Fear and Trembling*, p.xxxi.

[24] *FT*, 19, 30, 52.

prerequisite of faith. We find that for de Silentio the locus of offence lies in the demand that God makes upon an individual as a test of faith. That demand is constituted by the "teleological suspension of the ethical."[25] In other words, it is only when ethics, which de Silentio identifies as "social morality," is suspended and an individual is set against the universal that offence arises.[26] It is significant to note here that de Silentio does not differentiate himself from his society on this point. The offence of *Fear and Trembling* is an affront to the public and its code of ethics. Johannes de Silentio's repulsion is Christendom's repulsion.[27]

Johannes de Silentio's main goal in *Fear and Trembling* is to understand faith, and possibly even to acquire it for himself.[28] To that end, he is concerned with gaining a proper sense of what faith is, and what it is not, so that he and others in his society might properly recognise it when (or if) they ever find it. Offence serves his purpose in that it acts as an indication of the presence of authentic faith. Where the offence of the individual over the universal is, there faith will be also.[29] One of the biggest problems that he notices about his society is that by assuming everyone should "go beyond" faith, they have reduced its true value.[30] To protect faith then, he needs to keep a keen sense of what faith is in the mind of his readers. For de Silentio, it is the offence that accompanies faith that stops faith from becoming a mundane commodity. Abraham is, of course, the model Knight of Faith, and offence dogs Abraham every step of the way. "Let us then either cancel out Abraham or learn to be horrified by the prodigious paradox that is the meaning of his life, so that we may understand that our age…can

---

[25] *FT*, 54-67, esp. 59-60.

[26] *FT*, 55, 60-61, 66.

[27] Wanda Berry makes this connection in "Finally Forgiveness: Kierkegaard as 'Springboard' for a Feminist Theology of Reform," *Foundations of Kierkegaard's Vision of Community*, eds. George B. Connell and C. Stephen Evans (New Jersey: Humanities Press, 1992), 202.

[28] *FT*, 47-48. See also *FT*, 33, 51.

[29] *FT*, 55.

[30] *FT*, 121-22.

rejoice if it has faith."[31] That Abraham is often considered to be socially acceptable is a problem for de Silentio. Wherever Abraham is praised unreservedly, it means that no one recognises the moral difficulties surrounding true faith. De Silentio chastises Hegel and his followers for upholding a denuded version of Abraham's faith:

> But Hegel is wrong about faith; he is wrong in not protesting loudly and clearly against Abraham's enjoying honour and glory as a father of faith when he ought to be sent back to a lower court and shown up as a murderer.[32]

It is in this tension that he finds one aspect of the problem of faith, calling to mind the "prodigious paradox" that "makes murder into a holy and God-pleasing act."[33] Johannes de Silentio always keeps Abraham-as-murderer in view alongside Abraham-as-Knight-of-Faith, and his orations in praise of Abraham are tempered by the sobering thought that, humanly speaking, Abraham was an awful man.

> The ethical expression for what Abraham did is that he meant to murder Isaac; the religious expression is that he meant to sacrifice Isaac—but precisely in this contradiction is the anxiety that can make a person sleepless, and yet without this anxiety Abraham is not who he is.[34]

Johannes de Silentio realises that his harsh view of the demands of faith will repulse many people, but then again, faith should not be changed merely to enable easier acquisition. If de Silentio can get people at the very least to admit that they do not have faith, then that is no small success on his part.[35] The opposite of the cultured smug citizen of Christendom who assumes he has faith is the fanatic. However, in his opinion this is no better. The fanatic listens to the preacher expounding on Abraham as the father of faith and then attempts literally to emulate

---

[31] *FT*, 52-53.
[32] *FT*, 55.
[33] *FT*, 53.
[34] *FT*, 30.
[35] *FT*, 56.

the teaching by "sacrificing" his own son.[36] De Silentio recognises that there is a hypothetical danger that his writing might encourage such a murderous act, but then promptly assumes that there is no one in his age who is capable of having even that much passion.[37] In any case to move away from such a misinterpretation, de Silentio makes it very clear that it is faith he is promoting, and not killing. "It is only by faith that one achieves any resemblance to Abraham, not by murder."[38]

Johannes de Silentio prevents any one particular act becoming normative for faith by individualising the demands of faith. Abraham's (attempted) sacrifice of Isaac is *Abraham's* test of faith, it is not the picture for *all* faith.[39] De Silentio is not equating the offence of faith simply with the horror of murder. Faith is a matter that concerns God and each individual, and so the demands of faith will change according to each person.[40] Of course Abraham's actions are offensive, but de Silentio generalises the offence of faith by going behind the singular act of murder. The acts may change, but what remains is the offence of the teleological suspension of the ethical. For de Silentio, it is always offensive when an individual is set against the universal, the individual agent placed higher than the rest of society. This is what he means by the teleological suspension, and he deals with this aspect of the demand of faith in the first of three *problemata* in *Fear and Trembling*. In *Problema I* he states that "the ethical is the universal,"[41] and then that "Faith is namely this paradox that the single individual is higher than the universal."[42] Finally, de Silentio comes back to ethics, rounding out his definition when he explicitly identifies the ethical/universal with "social morality."[43] Thus, when an individual is set against the universal, what happens for that individual is effectively a suspension

---

[36] *FT*, 28-29.

[37] *FT*, 31.

[38] *FT*, 31.

[39] *FT*, 59-60.

[40] See *FT, "Problema* I," 54-67.

[41] *FT*, 54.

[42] *FT*, 55.

[43] *FT*, 55.

of the moral glue that holds society together. For the person with faith, there is no higher law than God, a fact that should make any society uncomfortable. It is this hard teaching that de Silentio recognises will repulse so many people, and in his opinion, rightly so.[44] It is not his intention to make faith palatable or easy.

The offence of *Fear and Trembling* is felt as an offence against public morality and the "right thinking" of the community. However, de Silentio does not expect that his Knights of Faith will actively make their offensive ways known to the public. That the Knight lives above social morality, and hence is socially repugnant, does not at the same time make him an activist or a social rebel. This is demonstrated by the way de Silentio makes fun of those "assistant professors" (his common term of abuse for the academic and clerical chattering classes that plagued Danish society) who assume that anything of value must be publicly debated and judged by the result.[45] They expect that any hero of faith worth his salt will shout confidently to his contemporaries, thus justifying his existence.[46] Instead, we see that the Knight does not go about forcing society to be offended at him. He is culturally invisible like the humble "tax-collector" who goes about his daily business secure in his faith,[47] and like Abraham, who hides his shocking relationship with God by remaining silent.[48] For de Silentio this silence of Abraham is offensive in its own right, both ethically and aesthetically. Ethically, the act of remaining silent throughout the ordeal is insulting to Sarah and Isaac, an offence because it "bypassed" what was for Abraham the highest expression of the ethical—family life. [49] Aesthetically, the silence ruins the beautiful poetic tragedy that Abraham could have enjoyed if he were a mere Tragic Hero rather than a Knight of Faith. Not being able to explain his trial to others means

---

[44] *FT*, 56.

[45] *FT*, 62-63.

[46] *FT*, 62.

[47] *FT*, 38ff.

[48] *FT*, 82ff.

[49] *FT*, 112.

that Abraham cannot attract any empathy or universal sympathy.[50] Note that even here, the offence of Abraham's silence, like the more general offence of the ethically suspended Knight of Faith, is primarily directed "outwardly," its effects not felt by the Knight but by the people around him.

In *Fear and Trembling,* the Knight may not actively court social comment, but nonetheless his very existence stands in opposition to social morality. When Johannes de Silentio reflects on Abraham, he encounters the paradoxical tension that signifies the presence of authentic faith. "Although Abraham arouses my admiration, he also appalls me."[51] Yet de Silentio is not himself a Knight, he cannot make the double movement of faith and resignation.[52] As a result, he does not stand apart from the rest of Christendom. He is, at best, a more accurate observer than are the others; but like the assistant professors that he criticises, Johannes de Silentio is condemned to dwell on a phenomenon of which he personally knows nothing. It is Johannes Climacus, with his notions of the Absolute Paradox and the offence against reason, who is able to improve on Johannes de Silentio's blind groping.

Climacus, Offence, and Reason

For Johannes de Silentio, offence against the public order turns out to be a consequence of an individual's faith. There is no indication that for de Silentio offence at the faithful person was of a different class than the sort of moral indignation that anyone in civilised Christendom would feel when their cultural sensibilities had been affronted. This is not the case with Johannes Climacus. He is not a Christian, but gives as his stated aim the subjective quest to discover how he might become a Christian.[53] Kierkegaard allows Climacus to come closer than Johannes de Silentio did to personally appropriating authentic Christianity. As a

---

[50] *FT,* 112-114. Abraham's silence as indirect communication will be considered in the following chapter.

[51] *FT,* 60.

[52] *FT,* 48.

[53] *CUP,* 17.

result, Climacus also apprehends more clearly the true nature of offence. He is not offended at the outward consequences of faith, rather he is offended at the object of faith. As a result, we will see that Climacus goes part way to discovering the "inward" implications of the offence for the individual.

It is with Climacus that we are introduced to the Absolute Paradox, which is the problem of the God-Man.[54] Climacus is not concerned overmuch with the actual earthly life of the God-Man, and he is vague about the details: "I shall merely trace [the idea] in a few lines without reference to whether it was historical or not."[55] Instead, Climacus devotes his time to the "idea about the different."[56] He is interested in the intellectual challenge that the paradox of the "known" coexisting with the "unknown" offers to human reason.[57] For someone like Climacus, it seems that the apparently insurmountable barrier that stands between himself and Christianity is the vast qualitative difference that exists between these two concepts. In *PF*, Climacus indulges in some metaphysical psychology.[58] Climacus describes the understanding as suicidally searching for its own downfall, surmising that reason always wants to "discover something that thought itself cannot think."[59] As a result, thought is always due for a collision with the ultimate Unknown, which Climacus also calls *the god*.[60] At the same time reason gropes blindly, attempting to understand what cannot be understood and mistaking what it finds with what it already knows. Climacus describes this situation as reason confounding like with unlike, and he gives as an example the idea of a devout worshipper who

---

[54] *PF*, ch. III, 37-48.

[55] *PF*, 45.

[56] *PF*, 45.

[57] *PF*, 39, 44-45, 46.

[58] *PF*, 37-39.

[59] *PF*, 37.

[60] *PF*, 39. Emphasising his connection to Platonic-Socratic thought patterns, and his attempt to separate the essential ideas from their Christian "clothing," Climacus usually speaks of "the god" using *Guden*, a noun with a definite article, as opposed to the more common Christian appellation "God" (*Gud*). This usage is unique to Climacus within the authorship. See *PF*, 278 n.13.

can't help but wonder if what he is praying to is a construct of his own imagination.[61] Stumbling reason eventually crashes into a terrible conundrum that Climacus dubs the "Absolute Paradox":

> ...the same paradox has the duplexity by which it manifests itself as the absolute—negatively, by bringing into prominence the absolute difference of sin and, positively, by wanting to annul this absolute difference in the absolute equality.[62]

It is these two functions, the negative and the positive, that Climacus finds so appalling. "Thus the paradox becomes even more terrible."[63]

The Absolute Paradox is, for Climacus, an explicit offence to reason, seeking reason's downfall.[64] Climacus, agreeing with the "Socratic principle," identifies sin with ignorance and error.[65] It is sin that is the cause of the absolute unlikeness, and also the cause of the confusion between like and unlike.[66] We see that sin, conceived of as misunderstanding, shadows every step that human reason takes. Sin is integrated with the understanding to the point where the paradox's challenge to sin is felt as a challenge to reason itself.[67] Faith will only occur when there is a "happy encounter" between reason and the paradox.[68] Climacus is clear that this happens only when reason "steps aside," allowing the paradox to reign in the mental life of the individual.[69] If reason does not rescind the throne, then the relationship with the paradox will be unhappy. Climacus has already named this event. "If the encounter is not in mutual understanding, then the relation is unhappy...we could more specifically term [this] *offence*."[70]

---

[61] *PF*, 45.

[62] *PF*, 47.

[63] *PF*, 47.

[64] *PF*, 47.

[65] *PF*, 50. Climacus here refers to Xenophon, *Memorabilia* III, 9, 5.

[66] *PF*, 47.

[67] *PF*, 47-48.

[68] *PF*, 59.

[69] *PF*, 59.

[70] *PF*, 49, original emphasis.

It is in the Appendix to Chapter III of *PF* entitled "Offence at the Paradox (An Acoustical Illusion)" that Climacus fully expounds on the relationship between offence and the paradoxical object of faith.[71] Here offence in the face of the paradox may take the form of mockery, denial or dumb suffering,[72] but all forms share one common factor: "Offence does not understand itself, but is understood by the paradox."[73] To elaborate on what this means, Climacus develops his idea of the "acoustical illusion."[74] Like an echo, or a mirror image in a funhouse, human reason can only respond to the original impulse imparted by the paradox. In a passage that bears a striking resemblance to Socrates's description of the cave dweller confused by the juxtaposition of light and shadow,[75] Climacus tells how reason thinks that when it pontificates about the Unknown its judgements are original, but this is only an illusion, for all judgements have been made first by the Unknown itself.

> The one offended does not speak according to his own nature but according to the nature of the paradox, just as someone caricaturing another person does not originate anything himself but only copies the other in the wrong way.[76]

Reason crashes up against the Absolute Unknown, the paradox of like with unlike, and declares that it is absurd.[77] But the paradox has pre-empted these observations. According to Climacus, whatever human reason says about itself and about the paradox, the paradox has already discovered and claimed as its own.[78] Everything the offended understanding says about the paradox, it has actually learned from the paradox, "even though, making use of an acoustical illusion, [offended

---

[71] *PF*, 49-54.

[72] *PF*, 50.

[73] *PF*, 50.

[74] *PF*, 49.

[75] Plato, *Republic*, trans. Benjamin Jowett (Oxford: Clarendon Press, 1936), 515b.

[76] *PF*, 51.

[77] *PF*, 52.

[78] *PF*, 52, 53.

understanding] insists that it itself has originated the paradox."[79] It is in this way that Climacus can understand the presence of offence as the paradox's proof: "[offence] can be regarded as indirect testing of the correctness of the Paradox...."[80]

Johannes de Silentio's offence was a human invention, born of social morality. Climacus asserts that it is false when human reason "insists that it itself has originated the paradox."[81] Instead the offence is much more integral to the object of faith than the previous pseudonym supposed: "No, the offence *comes into existence* with the paradox."[82] Climacus describes the "coming into existence" as "the moment."[83] The moment is the time of decision when faced with the demands of the paradox.

> *The moment* is actually the decision of eternity! If the god does not provide the condition to understand this, how will it ever occur to the learner?...without this we come no further but go back to Socrates.[84]

The moment is non-Socratic because it does not involve any immanent knowledge that resides within the individual. As a teacher, Socrates was the "occasion" who dealt with the type of knowledge that required only that the teacher unlock the student's latent potential.[85] Here, Climacus' moment represents an altogether new form of teaching, that of the transcendent Teacher who makes proposals that the learner would have had no way of discovering on his own. "If the god does not provide the condition to understand this, how will it ever occur to the learner?"[86] The moment marks the point in time when one apprehends the paradox. "If the moment is posited, the paradox is there, for in its most

---

[79] *PF*, 53.
[80] *PF*, 51.
[81] *PF*, 51.
[82] *PF*, 51, original emphasis.
[83] *PF*, 58.
[84] *PF*, 58, original emphasis.
[85] *PF*, 11, 58.
[86] *PF*, 58.

abbreviated form the paradox can be called the moment."[87] In the moment, we can see that the paradox goes on the offensive. The paradox turns reason into absurdity.[88] It attacks human understanding, turning everything on its head. Through the moment the learner becomes untruth, he who knows himself becomes confused, and self-knowledge becomes the consciousness of sin.[89] However, to describe the many possible shades of offence is not Climacus' aim. He sums them all up by maintaining that "all offence is *in its essence a misunderstanding* of the moment, since it is indeed offence at the paradox, and the paradox in turn is the moment."[90]

Here Kierkegaard has once again led one of his characters into a trap. Johannes de Silentio claimed to understand faith.[91] Yet because he does not have faith, Johannes de Silentio does not end up truly understanding faith after all. Likewise, Climacus is a self-proclaimed "outsider"[92] who is mistaken in his belief that he understands Christianity. In *Concluding Unscientific Postscript* (*CUP*), Climacus rightly points out that it is only the individual of Religiousness B who can recognise the true offence,[93] but Kierkegaard, the "master of irony,"[94] does not let Climacus fully understand what that offence is. It will take Anti-Climacus to demonstrate the connection between authentic Christianity and the essential offence.[95] We can see that Climacus is a character who still inhabits the state of Religiousness A, although he has some awareness of Religiousness B. Despite Climacus'

---

[87] *PF*, 51.

[88] *PF*, 52.

[89] *PF*, 51.

[90] *PF*, 51, emphasis added.

[91] *FT*, 69, 119. See also the "Epilogue," 121-23.

[92] *CUP*, 16.

[93] *CUP*, 585.

[94] Kierkegaard's MA thesis was later published as *The Concept of Irony* (non-pseudonymous 1841). Trans. and ed. Howard V. Hong and Edna H. Hong (Princeton: Princeton University Press, 1989). Occasionally, with his own tongue in cheek, he referred to himself as a master of irony. See *Point Of View*, 66-67.

[95] See below. *PC*, 94, 101, 106, 136.

disparagement of speculative philosophy,[96] he has not himself left speculation's thought patterns of immanence behind. Although the upshot of *PF* and *CUP* seems to be a set of works that is written against speculative thought and the pride of reason, whatever content Climacus imbues in the moment and the offence, he does so largely only by defining them in reference to the intellectual realm of the understanding. An acoustical illusion of sorts affects Climacus, for he is so concerned with combating speculative philosophy that he does not see that he himself is trapped in the same realm. Climacus makes light of those preachers and assistant professors who use apologetic arguments to "prove" the truth of Christianity, or otherwise promote its relevance to systematic thought.[97] Yet in identifying sin with error,[98] repulsion with proof for the presence of the paradox[99] and offence with misunderstanding,[100] Climacus does not really come any nearer to the true locus of Christian faith and its offensive nature.

For the non-Christian Climacus, offence (along with despair) makes up the "Cerberus pair who guard the gates to becoming a Christian."[101] Rejecting offence is a "one time only" epistemological event that defines and begins a life of faith. Later in *CUP*, Climacus writes that "the narrow gate to the hard way of faith is offence, and the terrible resistance against the *beginning* of faith is offence."[102] He sees the offence as the initial, cataclysmic moment in which the understanding is defeated by the paradox. It has been shown how Climacus identifies the moment as the paradox, and *the* paradox as the Absolute Paradox of the God-Man, a historical point upon which everything else turns.[103] Yet compared to the "clothing" that Anti-Climacus will put on all of this, Climacus' "point in history" is

---

[96] *PF,* 10, 43, 73, 109-10, and esp. *CUP*, 14-15, 50-57, 215-59.

[97] For example *PF,* 43; *CUP*, 14.

[98] *PF*, 50, 293.

[99] *PF*, 51.

[100] *PF*, 51.

[101] *CUP,* 372

[102] *CUP*, 585, emphasis added.

[103] *PF*, 51, 58.

strangely devoid of much substantive content. God is always "the god," the "God-Man" is never named as Jesus Christ, and the moment is abstracted away from any recognisable historical event. We see from Climacus' emphasis on the intellectual concept of offence that he is indeed concerned mostly with the paradox in its most abbreviated form. Climacus is more interested in talking of a moment in which reason collides with the paradox, than of the real life that is lived in "lowliness" and "loftiness" that Anti-Climacus will bring to the category of offence. The picture that Climacus leaves the reader with is, for the most part, a moment of metaphysical and conceptual difficulties (i.e. the "known" with the "unknown"[104]), a doctrine that understanding cannot get into its head.[105] It is not "timeless," but it is bereft of any specific temporal reference point that this moment could be anchored to. Only towards the end of *PF*, and in certain points in *CUP* is there some suggestion of providing earthly/historical content.[106] Here, Climacus writes about the god in human form who was born, grew up, had disciples and was a servant etc. Significantly, however, it is not the facts of a concrete human life that give rise to the offence as they will for Anti-Climacus.[107] Instead Climacus is left stuck at the stage of discursive reason, offended at the paradox as a thought that thought cannot think.

Anti-Climacus and the Essential Offence

With the offence of Anti-Climacus, not only is a development from the previous pseudonyms evident, but from one Anti-Climacus book to the next the idea takes firmer shape as well. *Sickness unto Death* marks a midway point between Climacus and the full development of the essential offence in *Practice in Christianity*. As in *PF*, offence in *SUD* is mainly dealt with in asides to the main work.[108] However, unlike the intellectual content of Climacus' offence (or of Johannes de Silentio's

---

[104] *PF*, 39, 44-45, 46.

[105] *PF*, 45, 53.

[106] For example *PF*, 93 and *CUP*, 217.

[107] *PC*, 94-121.

[108] *SUD*, "Appendix," 83-87; 113-131.

concern with civic morality for that matter), in *SUD* Anti-Climacus' offence tends to focus on the attendant problems of man's will, and his desire to hold onto his sin.[109] As such, the offence becomes directed more towards God than towards public morality or individual reason, and it is given a deep ethical content that is absent from both Johannes de Silentio's and Climacus' understanding.[110] *SUD* identifies three levels of this offence ("lowest," "middle" and "highest"),[111] all of which are fundamentally sins of defiance undertaken before God.[112] The notion of continually existing in the presence of God, and of the offence as involving willful disobedience is expanded in *Practice in Christianity*. The possibility of the essential offence becomes the central motif that runs throughout the whole book, intimately connected as it is with *contemporaneity*.[113] Anti-Climacus finds the highest concentration of the offence to revolve around what is most important for authentic Christianity—the person of Jesus Christ. Only the person who is contemporaneous with Christ will face the possibility of offence at the instance of a lowly man who claims to be God.[114] Only the person who faces this possibility and chooses to obey Christ's invitation to "come to me"[115] rather than be offended at him can be said to have authentic faith.[116]

Kierkegaard's readers often tend to ignore the particular use that each pseudonym makes of certain concepts in favour of producing a unified "Kierkegaardian" view. As a case in point, to my knowledge it has never been noted in the secondary literature how Climacus and Anti-Climacus differ in their syntax when discussing the offence. Throughout his writings, Climacus overwhelmingly talks of an unqualified "offence." Conversely, Anti-Climacus almost exclusively

---

[109] *SUD*, 87-100.

[110] *SUD*, 83, 85-87 89, 94-95; *PC*, 111, 120-21, 126, 128, 132.

[111] *SUD*, 129-31.

[112] *SUD*, 85-87.

[113] *PC*, 62-66, 99-108, 144.

[114] *PC*, 94-101, 102–121.

[115] Matthew 11:28; *PC*, no. 1, 3-69.

[116] *PC*, 94, 101, 106, 136.

speaks of the "*possibility* of offence." The discrepancy is important for it underlies the fundamentally different approaches that the two pseudonyms take towards the offence. For Climacus, the offence is a singular event,[117] while for Anti-Climacus, it is a live option at all times, and the possibility of offence must always be maintained.[118] The "singular event" compared to the ongoing "possibility" also reveals the different places where the two characters find the locus of the offence. It is proposed that Climacus represents the type of individual who does not recognise the offensiveness of the lived life of an actual individual man who is God. It has been shown that for Climacus the offence occurs only with reference to reason and to the comprehension (or not as the case may be) of an intellectual puzzle. Anti-Climacus, on the other hand, will come to find the core offence in the propensity of sinful man to take umbrage at the ethical implications of a person who is God, or a God who is a person.[119]

Although his "offence" is centred on the ethical, it is not the case that Anti-Climacus here returns to Johannes de Silentio's offence of civic morality. The great offence for Anti-Climacus occurs ethically for the individual subject who faces the possibility of perfect holiness bound by the suffering of utter lowliness.[120] Johannes de Silentio located the offence in the place where the faithful Knight transgresses against social morality.[121] Upon inspection it emerges that Anti-Climacus is not concerned with the "do's" and "don'ts" of mere public mores that make up Johannes de Silentio's "morality," but rather with the deeper realm of what is perhaps best termed "ethics." The distinction between *morality* and *ethics* is not one that Kierkegaard or any of his pseudonyms makes explicit, and for that reason it is acknowledged that employing such a distinction can prove to be problematic. Nevertheless, that there is a difference is apparent from the alternate uses that the pseudonyms make of the same words.

---

[117] *PF,* 51, 58; *CUP*, 372, 585.
[118] *PC,* 110, 139.
[119] *PC,* 94-101, 102-121.
[120] *PC,* 120-21, 126, 128, 132.
[121] *FT,* 55, 60-61, 66.

Johannes de Silentio's "ethical" refers to a social morality that is vastly different from Anti-Climacus' "ethical." Without inventing a new term or using a consistently recognisable phrase, Anti-Climacus nevertheless alludes to the different levels of "ethical" throughout his books. In *Sickness unto Death,* for example, the "Christian ethicist" apprehends a higher ethics than other thinkers, because the Christian begins with the presupposition of sin.[122] Anti-Climacus later refers to men who have an inkling of ethics and the religious, but who frame their thoughts according to metaphysics and aesthetics.[123] To dwell on such topics Anti-Climacus says is a distraction away from the truly ethical.[124] From this can be inferred a renewed interest in properly[125] understanding the "ethical" that is now separated from the "universal" concerns of the previous philosophers and ethicists. The Christian way "reshapes all ethical concepts and gives them one additional range."[126] In *PC*, Anti-Climacus applies this higher understanding of ethics directly to the offence. He disparages "natural man" who, endeavouring "to attain a certain civic justice," has merely a "provisional category" for the offence.[127] Only with Christianity, he says, will the real possibility of offence arise.[128] Both the "moral indignation" of the respectable citizen like Johannes de Silentio, and the "intellectual challenge" faced by Climacus, pale in comparison with the possibility for deep-seated repulsion that Anti-Climacus claims Christ is courting when he says, "Blessed is he who is not offended at me."[129]

---

[122] *SUD*, 89.

[123] *SUD*, 94.

[124] *SUD*, 94.

[125] For Anti-Climacus, "properly" means "Christianly" and "individually." See *SUD,* 83 and 85.

[126] *SUD,* 83.

[127] *PC*, 111.

[128] *PC*, 111.

[129] *PC*, 70, quoting Matthew 11:6.

Offence in *Sickness unto Death*

The possibility of offence in *SUD* suggests an ever-present factor, lived out every day. Climacus was concerned with the incomprehensible concept of the God-Man composite.[130] Anti-Climacus focuses on the offence that has ethical significance for a whole life, i.e., a life comprising the mundane choices of daily living as well as the singular epiphanies of reflection. By doing so he effectively shifts from *a* moment to the continual possibility of many moments. When Anti-Climacus writes that the offence is "Christianity's weapon against all speculation,"[131] we are not being invited to view this conflict in the same way that Climacus does. For Climacus, the battle consists in the moment of opposition between comprehension and faith. Those who choose to enthrone reason cannot have a happy understanding with the Absolute Paradox and so are offended.[132] Climacus does not himself claim to be offended, however, but continues to live at the place where the paradox remains incomprehensible and the understanding refrains from making a decision.[133] Anti-Climacus will have none of this, for from his perspective, withholding judgement is also a form of offence, and people like Climacus are as offensive as the "speculators" he is attempting to write against. To see that this is so, we must consider Anti-Climacus' three types of offence. In the final chapter of *SUD*, Anti-Climacus details "three forms of the offence" which are fundamentally related to the paradox.[134] The lowest form is that of the person who negatively states that he has no opinion, who does not believe and who does not care about Christ.[135] The highest is a "positive" form of offence: the active denial and denunciation of Christ,

---

[130] *PF*, 39, 44-45, 46.

[131] *SUD*, 83.

[132] *PF*, 49, 59.

[133] *CUP*, 617-23.

[134] *SUD*, 129-131. Note that in contrast with Climacus (cf. *PF*, ch. III), Anti-Climacus always readily identifies true religion with Christianity and names the Absolute Paradox as Christ. See for example *SUD*, 126.

[135] *SUD*, 129-30.

his work, his message and his existence.[136] The middle offence is the "negative but passive form."[137] Although he does not state so openly, it seems that here we find Anti-Climacus' judgement on the mistaken position of his brother. Of the middle form of offence Anti-Climacus writes:

> It definitely feels that it cannot ignore Christ, is not capable of leaving Christ in abeyance and then otherwise leading a busy life. But neither can it believe; it continues to stare fixedly and exclusively... at the paradox.[138]

Refraining from deciding is no less offensive to God than apathetic ignorance or active opposition, not matter how much interest and respect one claims to have for the paradox.

Anti-Climacus imbues all three levels of his offence with an ethical quality that Climacus does not recognise. Climacus claims that offence is the "unhappy understanding" between the paradox and reason.[139] Anti-Climacus refers instead to these offences as variations of "unhappy admiration," an envy directed towards God that grows from man's sinful aversion to holiness.[140] Both pseudonyms have problems with speculative philosophy, but it is Anti-Climacus who most clearly understands the inappropriateness of it for true Christianity, because he presupposes the sinful corruption of man's reason.[141] Speculative philosophy "universalises individual human beings imaginatively into the race."[142] In other words, the corruption that comes from this pattern of thought is to subsume into the "herd" what should be experienced individually. It has clouded the fact that

---

[136] *SUD*, 131.

[137] *SUD*, 130.

[138] *SUD*, 130-31.

[139] *PF*, 49.

[140] *SUD*, 85-86.

[141] *SUD*, 83. In his examination of "sin" in *SUD*, Ricoeur refers to the "psychology of evil." "Kierkegaard and Evil," *Modern Critical Views: Søren Kierkegaard*, ed. Harold Bloom (New York: Chelsea House Pub., 1989), 49-59.

[142] *SUD*, 83.

individuals make their choices "before God"[143] and has reverted to paganism, essentially by making a 'god' out of humanity in general.[144] To emphasise the continuing possibility of offence is to remember that all moments occur before God, and indeed, all offences are committed against God. The individual man cannot hide in the crowd and so avoid his responsibility for sin, for it is only an *individual's* offence against God that "actually makes sin into sin."[145] Sin, for Anti-Climacus, consists in the fact that each man wills not to understand what is right, not merely that he does not understand it, or is part of a culture that has not taught him properly.[146] In *PF*, sin was error and misunderstanding.[147] In *SUD*, "interpreted Christianly, sin has its roots in willing, not in knowing, and this corruption of willing embraces the individual's consciousness."[148] The location of the offence thus makes an "Augustinian" shift, and it is not defined in relation to reason's understanding, but instead to the ethical existence of the individual.[149]

> Thus offence is related to the single individual. And with this, Christianity [makes] every man a single individual, an individual sinner; and here everything that heaven and earth can muster regarding the possibility of offence…is concentrated—and this is Christianity.[150]

Offence in *Practice in Christianity*

With its discussion of sin and offence, *SUD* lays the foundations for Anti-Climacus' specifically Christian understanding of offence in his

---

[143] *SUD*, 85-87.

[144] A common theme. See *SUD*, 87, and especially 116-17. Also *PC*, 81-82.

[145] *SUD*, 87.

[146] *SUD*, 90, 93, 95.

[147] *PF*, 50.

[148] *SUD*, 95.

[149] In the *Confessions*, Augustine asks, "'What is iniquity?'…It is the perversity of the will, twisting away from the supreme substance, yourself, O God…." *The Confessions of St. Augustine* trans. John K. Ryan (New York: Image Books, 1960), VII.16 (p. 175). See also VII-VIII.

[150] *SUD*, 122.

most important book. Like an underground stream that bursts into the open in full flow, the offence that until now has only been seen in appendices is taken up by Anti-Climacus in his next book as its central theme. In *Practice in Christianity*, the possibility of offence is "present at every moment"[151] and is not, as Climacus sees it, a singular moment that only happens at the beginning of the Christian life.[152] More so even than *SUD*, what is most striking about the offence in *PC* is that it is "ethical," not epistemological. In *PC* Anti-Climacus emphasises the "lowliness" and "loftiness" of the God-man.[153] For Anti-Climacus, the Incarnation as an historical event involving an actual life lived on earth is far more offensive than the reason-confounding concept of the Absolute Paradox. Thus, Anti-Climacus' offence is an offence of the truly ethical,[154] informed by his vision of authentic Christianity. It is not an offence of Climacus' intellect, or of Johannes de Silentio's civic-moral sensitivity. We have seen that Climacus, obsessed with the moment when the understanding encounters the Unknown, has concluded that the offence lies with the inability of reason to comprehend the incomprehensible, and its stubborn refusal to bow to the mystery of the paradox.[155] Anti-Climacus thinks that the intellectual categories of "doubting" and "understanding" are too shallow when it comes to the heart of the matter.[156] He moves beyond trying to comprehend the God-man composition, saying that those who try to fête its profundity are merely performing tricks.[157] The real essence of the offence is not in trying (or failing) to understand the composite; it is the composite itself.

> the *situation* belongs with the God-man, the situation that an individual human being who is standing beside you is the God-man. The God-man is not the union of God and man - such terminology is a profound optical

---

[151] *PC*, 139.

[152] *PF*, 49, 51, 58-59; *CUP*, 372, 585.

[153] *PC*, 94-102; 102-121.

[154] *SUD*, 83, 85, 94.

[155] *PF*, 49-54.

[156] *PC*, 81-83.

[157] *PC*, 81.

illusion. The God-man is the unity of God and an individual human being. That the human race is or is supposed to be in kinship with God is ancient paganism; but *that* an individual human being is God is Christianity....[158]

Concurrent with the theme of offence is the theme of contemporaneity, where by metaphorically crossing the span of centuries, the would-be believer is removed from the "present age" and places him or herself next to Christ.[159] Climacus has discussed this at some length already,[160] but it is Anti-Climacus who draws out the significance of contemporaneity for the possibility of offence. With true Christianity, there can be no case of the so-called "second-hand disciple." "If you cannot bear contemporaneity...then you are not *essentially* Christian."[161] It is now that Anti-Climacus is able to add the most content to the category of offence. This content was certainly missing from Johannes de Silentio and Climacus. It is not even apparent in *SUD*. It is in *PC* that Anti-Climacus introduces the possibility of the essential offence as *only* occurring for those who see Christ as a contemporary,[162] that is for people who are able to apprehend that the challenge of the God-Man applies to them personally in inwardness and immediacy. Relegating Jesus to a point where he only exists historically does not make him "actual," that is, his demands do not impinge on anyone's immediate life.[163] Only that which is contemporary (that which is "for you"), is "actual" for an individual.

> The qualification that is lacking—which is the qualification of truth (which is inwardness) and of all religiousness is—**for you**. The past is not actuality—for me. Only the contemporary is actuality for me. That with which you are living simultaneously is actuality—

---

[158] *PC*, 81-82, original emphasis.

[159] For example, *PC,* 63 and 144.

[160] *PF,* ch. IV, "The Situation of the Contemporary Follower."

[161] *PC*, 65, original emphasis.

[162] *PC,* 106-107.

[163] *PC*, 63-64.

for you.[164]

In *PC* Anti-Climacus finds that the possibility offence occurs in two forms—that of loftiness and that of lowliness. With the "offence of loftiness" the individual must face the opportunity for moral indignation that *this* man (i.e. Jesus Christ) is, or is claiming to be, God.[165] With the offence of lowliness, the problem comes when one considers that God in all his majesty is *this* man.[166] Anti-Climacus identifies both as "forms of essential offence."[167] Significantly, both forms of offence can only occur for the one contemporaneous with Christ the God-Man.

The possibility for the "essential offence of loftiness" centres on the possibility that this individual man should be God, or when this man "speaks and acts as if he were God, declares himself to be God."[168] The possibility for the "offence of lowliness" comes when the "one who passes himself off as God proves to be the lowly, poor, suffering, and finally powerless human being."[169] We can see that both forms of offence presuppose three things about the individual approaching the Christian faith. First, they presuppose that the individual is standing in a contemporaneous relation to Christ. Secondly that the individual has an awareness of the majesty of God, and thirdly that the individual apprehends the qualitative gap between the life of God and the life of an individual man, an apprehension that itself presupposes an awareness of sin.

Anti-Climacus does not define either of these categories of essential offence in relation to reason. Indeed, Anti-Climacus insists that it is to Christendom's shame that the preachers have turned Jesus' life and actions into a logical proof for his divinity, for by taking away the possibility of offence at this lowly man who claims to be God, they

---

[164] *PC*, 64, original bold emphasis.
[165] *PC*, 94-102.
[166] *PC*, 102-21.
[167] *PC*, 121.
[168] *PC*, 94.
[169] *PC*, 102.

have taken Christ away as well.[170] Christendom thinks (as a delusion) that the God-man is directly visible.[171] The preachers point to miracles as evidence, forgetting that the Biblical accounts have Jesus himself putting no great stock in the persuasive effects of his actions.[172] For example, the gospels tell how when Jesus recounted a litany of his own healing miracles to John the Baptist's disciples, he ended the account by stating that the man who does not take offence on account of Christ will be blessed.[173] It is significant to Anti-Climacus that these demonstrations do not lead to faith, as if faith was a matter of proof and reasons, but that they instead lead to the possibility of offence.[174] "In order to believe," writes Anti-Climacus, "the person who believes must have passed through the possibility of offence."[175] At first glance this seems to echo Climacus' sentiments, but in actuality, Anti-Climacus' offence is so different from that of Climacus, that, in this respect, the two are almost opposites. The one who is potentially offended at the loftiness of *this* man being God can only do so if he or she is not looking at Christianity as set of propositions, but instead at Christ as a contemporary, and thus is already closer than Climacus is to authentic Christianity. Anti-Climacus' offence is not a blow to conceptual reasoning but instead a gut reaction to an affront, a repulsion at something that produces ethical unease. When discussing the impossibility of direct communication, Anti-Climacus talks of how Christ can only be a sign of contradiction.[176]

> If someone says directly: I am God; the Father and I are one, this is direct communication. But if the person who says it, the communicator, is this individual human being, an individual human being just like others, then this communication is not entirely direct, because it is not entirely direct that an individual

---

[170] *PC*, 94.

[171] *PC*, 95.

[172] *PC*, 95-97.

[173] Matthew 11:6.

[174] *PC*, 95.

[175] *PC*, 101.

[176] *PC*, 133-36.

human being should be God....[177]

When a particular lowly man invokes the divine by saying "Believe in me"[178], there is a direct statement coming from an *incognito* source, and it is this disjunction between the saying and the person saying it that produces the possibility of offence. One would not be offended if a being who was obviously God claimed to be God. For Anti-Climacus, the contradiction does not produce mental turmoil, as if it involved understanding proofs and propositions. Of this idea he says:

> What abominable, sentimental frivolity! No, one does not manage to become a Christian at such a cheap price! He [Christ] is the sign of contradiction, and by the direct statement he attaches himself to you only so that you must first face the offence of the contradiction, and the thoughts *of your heart* are disclosed as you choose whether you will believe of not.[179]

Climacus claims to understand that Christianity is not about doctrines,[180] yet his relation to Christianity hints at the fact that "doctrine" is the most accurate category for describing Climacus' approach to the offence. Climacus seems to think of Christianity as essentially a "doctrinal" position that one can either accept or reject. He says in *CUP*: "Although an outsider, I have at least understood this much, that the only unforgivable high treason against Christianity is the single individual's taking his relation to it for granted."[181] M. Hartshorne points out that here once again Climacus fundamentally misunderstands the Christian view; the true Christian (according to Anti-Climacus) would be concerned with Christ, the offensive God-man, not with Christianity. "Christianity in its authentic form it does not propose *itself* as a condition of salvation That would be idolatrous."[182]

---

[177] *PC*, 134.

[178] Mark 9:42.

[179] *PC*, 136, emphasis added.

[180] *CUP*, 379-81, 570.

[181] *CUP*, 16.

[182] M. H. Hartshorne, *Kierkegaard Godly Deceiver* (New York: Columbia University Press, 1990), 36.

The discussion on the offence of lowliness provides Anti-Climacus the opportunity to answer Climacus on this point, and to develop the notion of the essential offence as relating to a person's "lived" life.

> Christianity is no doctrine; all talk of offence with regard to it as a doctrine is a misunderstanding, is an enervation of the thrust of the collision of offence, as when one speaks of offence with respect to the *doctrine* of the God-man, the *doctrine* of Atonement. No, offence is related either to Christ or to being a Christian oneself.[183]

The concrete, day-to-day existence of an individual cannot be ignored. To be a Christian is to imitate Christ, which means, in the eyes of the world, to suffer every kind of evil, mockery and insult, and finally to be punished as a criminal. This, says Anti-Climacus, is part of the possibility of the offence of lowliness, that God should be abased in this way.[184] The possibility of offence is linked to a continuing life. It is present at every moment.[185] It is expressly not a point devoid of real physical and ethical content, to be mentally struggled over at an abstract early stage in an individual's process towards belief. Instead, Anti-Climacus talks of the sacrifice in life and blood that is made in order truly to be a Christian.[186] The real Christian offence, writes Anti-Climacus, is the remedy for all the petty and provisional offences that plague "natural man."[187] Climacus speaks only of reason; Anti-Climacus barely mentions it at all. Because he is standing in the presence of the source of the light, Anti-Climacus is able to differentiate between the lesser and the essential offences, a skill that Climacus does not share.

The argument that Kierkegaard ascribes to blind faith over reason is commonplace amongst the secondary literature. The attribution is rife in popular, introductory and academic discussion

---

[183] *PC*, 106, original emphasis.
[184] *PC*, 106.
[185] *PC*, 110, 139.
[186] *PC*, 144.
[187] *PC*, 111.

about Kierkegaard.[188] Yet each of these accusations is based on a reading of "Kierkegaard" that does not take into account the pseudonymous context, or which does so only in a cursory way. Only if Kierkegaard saw Christianity the way that Johannes de Silentio or Climacus sees it would he have a faith that exists only in opposition to reason. For Anti-Climacus, however, it seems that the opposite of offence is not "faith" as such, but obedience to the lowly man who says, "Come unto me."[189] Obviously, there is an element of faith involved in obeying someone, but the focus is shifted from the battle of the intellect to a battle of the will. The fideist must constantly define faith in opposition to reason. Anti-Climacus takes a different position in which the concerns of reason are transcended. The true Christian is not one who exists because of, or in spite of, reason alone, but one who exists in a life of willed obedience to the person of Christ.

Whether there is such a Christian at all is a question that lies behind Kierkegaard's last writings and his final Attack upon Christendom, where he finds the ultimate sign of obedience to be imitation of Christ.[190] Anti-Climacus provides hints of what that imitation might look like. At the beginning of the "Exposition" in *PC*, Anti-Climacus sketches out a third type of offence in addition to that of loftiness and lowliness.[191] This third offence is not related to the notion of the God-man as such, and Anti-Climacus does not dwell on it. Refusing to call it a form of essential offence, throughout the brief

---

[188] To list but a few examples: Karen Carr argues that Kierkegaard is an "anti-rationalist" and that, for Kierkegaard, Christianity is always a battle with reason in "The Offence of Reason and the Passion of Faith: Kierkegaard and Anti-Rationalism," *Faith and Philosophy* 13 (1996), 241; Gordon Kaufman accuses Kierkegaard of "unqualified fideism" in "Mystery, Critical Consciousness and Faith," *The Rationality of Religious Belief,* ed. William J. Abraham (Oxford: Clarendon Press, 1987), 57; Alastair MacIntyre paints a picture of a Kierkegaard who was trapped in an inescapable dilemma of basing truth on subjective passion in *After Virtue: A Study in Moral Theory* (Notre Dame: University of Notre Dame Press, 1984), 39-43.

[189] Matthew 11:28; *PC* 3-69, 94, 101, 106, 136.

[190] For example, see *The Moment and Other Late Writing* (non-pseudonymous, 1854-55), trans. and ed. Howard V. Hong and Edna, H. Hong (Princeton: Princeton University Press, 1998), 31, 42, 135, 148, 182, 292.

[191] *PC*, 85-94.

section Anti-Climacus continually downplays this type of offence at the expense of the more important "lofty" and "lowly" expressions, and it does not appear in the summation at the end of the chapter.[192] It is significant that Kierkegaard has Anti-Climacus talk about this offence at all, for it contains an apt description of the kind of criticism Kierkegaard would make under his own name in the next few years of his life. Anti-Climacus speaks of this offence is that of the man who collides with the established order.[193] Every time an authentic witness transforms truth into inwardness, he says, then the established order will be offended at him.[194] The offence appears to be that the individual is making himself higher than the herd, but this in fact is another acoustical illusion.[195] It is the established order that has said to itself that it is divine—and it is offended by the challenge to this divinity by the individual who stands apart.[196]

Conclusion

The developing nature of *faith* in the works of Kierkegaard cannot be long separated from the related theme of *offence*, which itself is intrinsically connected to the later Kierkegaardian focus on the *Incarnation*. Without the possibility of offence there can be no possibility for faith, and the possibility of offence is predicated upon one's posture towards the incarnate Christ. The transition of faith is the transition that causes one to face the possibility of taking offence at Jesus Christ, and also that of giving offence as one who necessarily stands counter to the world.

Kierkegaard's pseudonyms do not speak with the same voice when it comes to faith and offence. Johannes de Silentio's conception of offence is Christendom's conception. He is revolted by the awful murderous acts that the Knight of Faith may be required to do. For Johannes de Silentio, having a faith existence means existing as an

---

[192] *PC*, 85, 87, 93, 94, 120-21.

[193] *PC*, 85.

[194] *PC*, 86.

[195] *PC*, 88.

[196] *PC*, 86-88.

individual above the universal. Civic morality, the code of ethics that applies to all and is understood by all, is purposefully, or teleologically, suspended by God for each individual that relates to him. Thus, Johannes de Silentio sees the offence as that which goes against the laws of society, and as a result of faith.

Johannes Climacus reverses the relationship, introducing a greater offence that itself causes the lesser offences found in civil life. This essential offence stands as the gateway to faith, it is not a result of faith. Climacus' offence is not at the consequences of faith, but rather at the object of it. Climacus sees the essential offence as the Absolute Paradox's assault on human reason. The problem of the God-Man overshadows any lesser problem; it is this that the reason must assent to before Religiousness B can result. Climacus is not overly concerned with the actual life of the God-Man, and he takes pains in *PF* not to clothe the story of the Incarnation in any Christian trappings. Instead, Climacus looks at the intellectual stumbling block posed by the concept of the infinite residing in the finite, and he considers the metaphysical problem of reason coming up against a thought that thought cannot think. Climacus, following Socrates, identifies "sin" with ignorance, and he thinks of the Absolute Paradox as going on the offensive, actively seeking the downfall of corrupt human reason. Only if reason cedes the throne to the Paradox at this time can there be a happy relationship, a situation that Climacus identifies as "faith." The unhappy relationship, when reason resists the Unknown and refuses to bow, is the "offence." However, just as he has already done with Johannes de Silentio, Kierkegaard does not let Climacus the "Christian outsider" recognise the true locus of the offence. Climacus says that he is against philosophical speculators and assistant professors, yet he proves himself not to have escaped from the same confines by his insistence on treating Christianity as essentially a set of doctrines to assent to, and the offence/faith dichotomy as fundamentally residing in the sphere of human reason.

By contrast, Anti-Climacus hardly ever alludes to the offence against reason. His is a purer vision of essential Christianity, and in *Sickness unto Death* and *Practice in Christianity* he sees the offence as a matter of obedience to Jesus Christ, not assent to the intellectual problem of the God-Man. When Christ says, "Come to me," he is effectively saying he is God; the contemporaneous listener is faced with only two options: *either* believe and obey in faith, *or* refuse and become offended. As opposed to Climacus who seems to think of the offence as a "one-off" event at the beginning of the life of faith, Anti-Climacus insists that this possibility of offence must be kept alive at all times, in order to assure that true faith is not being clouded by delusions of grandeur. This offence is an ethical offence that runs deeper than the affront to civic morality that Johannes de Silentio represents. Anti-Climacus identifies two forms of the essential offence, the offence of loftiness and the offence of lowliness, both of which relate to the incarnate presence of divine holiness in lowly humanness. The deep ethical aversion is faced when the individual considers that supreme goodness is presiding with human sin, or that a lowly human is claiming to be divine. Anti-Climacus is insistent that it is only these two categories that constitute the essential offence, and, as such, they belong only to Christ. But he does briefly consider the possibility of a third type of lesser offence, that of the offence against the establishment. Even here, however, Anti-Climacus is keen to emphasise that it is Jesus who best embodies this offence. However, Anti-Climacus hints at, but does not develop, the possibility for followers to imitate Christ as a sign of offence themselves.

It is, of course, Kierkegaard who takes this mantle on under his own name during his final "Attack upon Christendom," where the pure vision of offence is developed into praxis.[197] Kierkegaard adopts for himself the role of the offensive individual acting as a sign against all of Christendom. The offence in the Attack builds on Anti-Climacus' essential offence of the individual man who is God, and makes the connection between that offence and the qualitative difference between Christendom and Christianity. Only the one contemporaneous with the incarnate Christ will be able to stand as the sign of offence in his

---

[197] The "Attack" marks the final phase of Kierkegaard's life and career when he publicly castigated the clergy and other citizens of Christendom for doing away with Christianity. It is not the title of a single work, but is instead made up of a series of polemical articles which originally appeared in the journal *The Moment* and in *The Fatherland* newspaper from 1854 until Kierkegaard's death in 1855.

society, in the same way that Christ was offensive to his. Kierkegaard unabashedly brings Jesus Christ into the fray, pointing out that Christ would be considered to be a philistine and barbarian in the cultured sophistication of Christendom. The implication for a Christ-imitator is that he or she too will be actively opposed to their surrounding culture. It emerges in the Attack that authentic Christianity is not just different from the world; in order for it to be authentic, it *must* be a minority religion necessarily opposed to the wider "host" society. By imitating and embodying Christ's offence, Kierkegaard moves into the realm of reduplication, using himself as a sign of contradiction, speaking directly yet, by his very offensive presence, provoking a choice from his listeners that has nothing to do with outward appearances. By imitating the incarnate Christ, Kierkegaard and other Christ-followers themselves become the sign of offence and the occasion for authentic faith.

11.

THE INVERSE DIALECTIC OF JEST AND EARNESTNESS IN KIERKEGAARD'S THEOLOGY

Sylvia Walsh

According to Kierkegaard's Christian pseudonym Anti-Climacus, "[t]he first condition for becoming a Christian is to become unconditionally turned inward" in earnestness (*Alvor*), which is a major concept in Kierkegaard's writings that is synonymous to certitude, inwardness, subjectivity, and faith in signifying the constituent of the eternal in a human being.[1] Declining to define or talk about earnestness in "the jest of abstraction," the pseudonym Vigilius Haufniensis associates it with disposition, not in the sense of a natural disposition or habit but as an "acquired originality," the object of which is always oneself, namely what it means to exist spiritually as a self, spirit, or concrete personality, and whoever lacks earnestness in that regard, Vigilius observes, is a "joker" (*Spøgefugl*), no matter how serious one may be about other things.[2] Jest (*Spøg*) is nevertheless a very important concept without which we cannot properly understand earnestness and the relation of human freedom and striving to the eternal and grace in Kierkegaard's theology. Speaking in the voice of the pseudonym Johannes Climacus, Kierkegaard suggests that it is impossible to understand earnestness if one does not understand jest and that it is important to understand in jest what jest is.[3] Both jest and earnestness are among the most frequently used terms in Kierkegaard's authorship,

---

[1] *PC*, 225; *CA*, 146, 151; *CD*, 237-38; *CUP*, 210, 224; *WL*, 190, 320; *JP*, 2:2112 / *SKP VB* 65; *JP*, 2:2113 / *SKP VB* 66; *JP*, 2:2114 / *SKP V* 227:5.

[2] *CA* 150.

[3] *CUP* 1:70-71, 139.

yet jest has been given very little attention in studies of his thought.[4] In an effort to give jest its due—or at least to move jestingly in that direction—this essay proposes to consider what jest is for Kierkegaard and how it informs his understanding of earnestness in a dialectical manner.

The concept of jest appears in almost all of Kierkegaard's works, beginning with *The Concept of Irony* (1841), where he identifies two forms of irony, the first and most common form being "to say something earnestly that is not meant in earnest," and the second, more rare form being "to say as a jest, jestingly, something that is meant in earnest."[5] The ironist is thus described as a person who is always making himself seem to be other than he actually is, hiding jest in earnestness and earnestness in jest.[6] The model or paradigm of such ironic jesting for Kierkegaard is the Greek philosopher Socrates (470/469-399 BCE), who according to the figures Quidam and Frater Taciturnus in *Stages on Life's Way* (1845) "was the most earnest man in Greece" yet concealed his earnestness in jest in such a way as to be able to see the most profound earnestness and the greatest jest at one and the same time.[7] In *Prefaces* (1844), a satirical jest in its own right, the pseudonymous author Nicholas Notabene describes Greek philosophy, by which he means Socrates, as being "like a god who walks about in human form and at every moment works a miracle with the humble everyday phrase, although in everything he still resembles an ordinary human being except insofar as that sadness…transfigures itself as a divine jest that rejuvenates his figure almost to the point of jocularity."[8] Speaking in his own voice in *Upbuilding Discourses in*

---

[4] See *Fundamental Polyglot Konkordans til Kierkegaards Samlede Værker*, compiled by Alastair McKinnon (Leiden: E. J. Brill, 1971), 925-28, 23-25; John J. Davenport, "Earnestness," *Kierkegaard's Concepts Tome II: Classicism to Enthusiasm*, ed. Steven M. Emmanuel, William McDonald and Jon Steward (Burlington, VT and Farnham, UK: Ashgate, 2014), 219-27; John Lippitt, *Humour and Irony in Kierkegaard's Thought* (London: Macmillan Press Ltd. and New York: Saint Martin's Press, 2000), 79-80, 82, 94, 124-25.

[5] *CI*, 248.

[6] Ibid., 256.

[7] *SLW*, 365-66, 415; see also *CUP*, 1: 88.

[8] *P*, 42.

Various Spirits, Kierkegaard describes Socrates' art as "paganism's supreme ingenuity" in working for the good by way of jest in order to prevent people from taking the earnestness of the good in vain.[9] Lacking any earnestness in themselves, however, they utterly failed to see the earnestness in Socrates' words and therefore chose to understand them only as jest. The pseudonym Johannes Climacus likewise regards Socrates as a jester (*Spøgfugl*) whose words sound like a jest yet express the highest earnestness.[10] But he also credits the style of the German theologian Gotthold Ephraim Lessing (1729-1781) with being a "mixture of jest and earnestness that makes it impossible for a third person to know definitely which is which—unless the third person knows it by himself."[11]

Jest appears in several different forms or senses in Kierkegaard's writings, sometimes simply as "innocent and God-pleasing jest," at other times in sharp contrast to earnestness.[12] More commonly, however, it appears in combination with earnestness as the unity of jest and earnestness, that is, both jest and earnestness at the same time, as in "earnest jest," "jesting earnestness," "divine jest," "holy jest," "devout jest," and "gracious jest."[13] For Kierkegaard, jest and earnestness are united only by that which is upbuilding or edifying.[14] The unity of jest and earnestness is thus operative in both an ethical-religious and Christian context as an expression of the inverse dialectic that informs his understanding of religiousness in general and Christianity in particular.[15] As defined in *Concluding Unscientific Postscript*, the formula for this dialectic is: "the positive is

---

[9] *UDVS*, 97.

[10] *CUP*, 1:87-88.

[11] Ibid., 69, 103; see also *SLW*, 440-41.

[12] *EUD*, 253; *LD*, 281-82; *C*, 178-79; *SLW*, 48, 55; *TDIO*, 10. 28.73.77; *WL*, 30, 98, 126, 184, 346, 353.

[13] *UDVS*, 124, 196; *CUP*, 1:101, 137, 138, 135, 462; *CD*, 9; *JP*, 2:1135; *JFY*, 186. See also *SLW*, 365, 440; *CUP*, 1:104, 290; *JP*, 4:4924.

[14] *KJN*, 2, JJ90 / *JP*, 4:4924.

[15] On inverse dialectic see Sylvia Walsh, *Living Christianly: Kierkegaard's Dialectic of Christian Existence* (University Park: The Pennsylvania State University Press, 2005).

distinguished by the negative."[16] In the religious sphere this means that "the positive is continually in the negative, and the negative is its distinctive mark."[17] In his journals Kierkegaard likewise states that "the formula for Christianity is that Christianity is always the positive that is recognizable by the negative."[18] That is, the positive spiritual qualities of faith, hope, love, joy, and consolation are given expression in and recognized by negative qualifications such as the consciousness of sin, the possibility of offense, dying to the world, self-denial, and suffering. In like inverse manner, earnestness is distinguishable by jest, or as Kierkegaard expresses it in *Christian Discourses*, one must learn to look at everything turned around, so that what appears to be only a meaningless jest is just the opposite, namely "the earnestness of eternity."[19]

The inverse dialectic of jest and earnestness is most thoroughly spelled out in *Concluding Unscientific Postscript* (1846), where it comes to the fore in the context of Climacus' definition of the ethical as becoming subjective, which in his view is the highest task assigned to a human being.[20] As Climacus understands it, the ethical constitutes "the most original element in every human being" and has "an irrefutable claim upon every existing individual," so that "whatever a person achieves in the world, even the most amazing thing, is nevertheless dubious" if one has not been ethically clear to and about oneself in choosing.[21] The ethical has its concreteness only in inwardness or earnestness. For Climacus, therefore, "true ethical enthusiasm consists in willing to the utmost of one's ability, but also, uplifted in divine jest, in never thinking whether or not one thereby achieves something. As soon as the will begins to cast a covetous eye on the outcome, the

---

[16] *CUP*, 1:432.

[17] Ibid., 524, 532.

[18] *KJN*, 8, NB25:32 / *JP*, 4:4680; *KJN*, 8, NB22:158 / *JP*, 4:4666; see also *JP*, 4:4696.

[19] *CD*, 150-51.

[20] *CUP*, 1:129, 138-39.

[21] Ibid., 134, 144.

individual begins to become immoral."[22] Inasmuch as God needs no human being yet can require everything of us "for nothing," since we are all unworthy servants in relation to the divine, the ethical individual, elevated in holy jest, says: "Let me be as if created for the sake of a whim," that is, in jest, yet "I shall with utmost strenuousness will the ethical," which is earnestness.[23] As Climacus understands it, then, jesting earnestness consists in developing oneself to the utmost of one's capability, perhaps even producing a great effect in the external world, while nevertheless understanding that the external means nothing either *pro* or *con* concerning one's ethical status before God: "The earnestness is his own inner life; the jest is that it pleases God to attach this importance to his striving, to the striving of one who is only an unworthy servant."[24] In the process of trying to fulfill this ethical requirement, however, one goes backward rather than forward in the effort to bring one's existence into conformity with the highest good or eternal happiness.[25] Or more accurately, one goes forward inversely by going backward, inasmuch as for Climacus "immersing oneself in something means to go forward," although backward in expression.[26] In striving inwardly to renounce one's finite existence in immediacy, worldliness, or relative ends for the sake of the absolute or eternal, one discovers that one is unable to transform oneself, for as soon as one has done it once, one must do it again and again, making progress chimerical and occasioning continuous suffering and the consciousness of guilt as the essential and decisive expressions of existential pathos respectively.[27] As Climacus describes this plight:

> The religious person lies in the finite as a helpless infant; he wants to hold on to the conception [of God] absolutely, and this is what annihilates him; he wills to do everything, and while he is willing it, the powerlessness begins, because for a finite being there

---

[22] Ibid., 135; see also 506.
[23] Ibid., 136-37.
[24] Ibid., 139. See also 78.
[25] Ibid., 527.
[26] Ibid.
[27] Ibid., 433, 526.

> is indeed a meanwhile. He wills to do everything; he wants to express this relation absolutely, but he cannot make the finite commensurate with it.[28]

How one relates to the suffering entailed in this existential plight is what determines the difference between a humorist and a religious personality and the corresponding forms of humor or jest which they exemplify. Climacus identifies two forms of humor that function as boundary categories on the border of the religious and within the religious. The first is between the ethical and the religious; the second is between immanent religiousness or Religiousness A and paradoxical religiousness or Religiousness B (Christianity). In the first form of humor the humorist understands suffering as belonging essentially to existence and thus feels the pain of suffering but does not comprehend its meaning and thus revokes it in the form of jest by making light of the existential plight and opting for retirement out of existence into the eternal by way of Platonic recollection on the basis of the presupposition that the eternal is immanent in everything.[29] The second form of humor, which Climacus calls "holy jest," functions as the incognito of the religious personality, who appears outwardly to be a humorist but inwardly is not inasmuch as the religious person exists in a relationship to God, whereas the humorist does not, and he or she understands that one is nothing before God and can do nothing of oneself.[30] Religiously, Climacus observes, "the task is to comprehend that a person is nothing at all before God or to be nothing at all and thereby to be before God, and he continually insists upon having this incapability before him, and its disappearance is the disappearance of religiousness."[31] This situation becomes comic or humorous to the religious individual "when to all outward appearances in the external world it seems that he is capable of a great deal."[32] "But if this jest is to be a holy jest and continue," Climacus observes,

---

[28] Ibid., 484.

[29] Ibid., 447-48, 451.

[30] Ibid., 505.

[31] Ibid., 461.

[32] Ibid., 462.

> it must at no moment disturb for him the earnestness that before God he is nothing and is capable of nothing, and the work of holding this fast, and the suffering of expressing it existentially. If, for example, Napoleon had been a genuinely religious personality, he would have had a rare opportunity for the most divine amusement, because seemingly to be capable of everything and then divinely to understand this as an illusion—indeed, this is jest in earnest![33]

The inverse dialectic of jest and earnestness comes into play here once again as Climacus points out that "the negative is the sign, because the greatest effort is distinguishable by one's becoming nothing through it."[34] Noting the contradiction between the Sunday preaching that declares a human being is capable of nothing at all while on the other six days of the week everyone, including the pastor, is capable of a great deal, Climacus suggests that "one of the two must be a jest; either what the pastor says is a jest, a kind of parlor game one plays at times," or the pastor is right and the rest of us are wrong.[35] But if the pastor is right, does this mean that one should not "undertake anything at all because all is vanity and futility?"[36] The answer, of course, is no, for in that case, Climacus observes,

> [one] will not have the opportunity to understand the jest, since there is no contradiction in putting it together with life's earnestness, no contradiction that everything is vanity in the eyes of a vain person. Laziness, inactivity, snobbishness about the finite are a poor jest or, more correctly, are no jest at all. But to shorten the night's sleep and buy the day's hours and not spare oneself, and then to understand that it is all a jest: yes, that is earnestness. Viewed religiously, the positive is always distinguishable by the negative—earnestness by the jest—that it is religious earnestness, not direct earnestness. To have the fate of many people in one's hand, to transform the world, and then

---

[33] Ibid.

[34] Ibid., 464.

[35] Ibid., 471.

[36] Ibid.

> continually to understand that this is jest—yes, that is earnestness! But in order to be capable of this, all the passions of finitude must be dead, all selfishness rooted out, the selfishness that wants to have everything and the selfishness that proudly turns away from everything. But that is just the trouble, and here is the suffering in dying to oneself, and although the distinguishing feature of the ethical is that it is so easy to understand in its abstract expression, it is so difficult to understand *in concreto*.[37]

Although Climacus uses the example of Christian preaching to make his point here, the expression of humor as the incognito of the religious person pertains specifically to Religiousness A or immanent religiousness, leaving open the question of how the inverse dialectic of jest and earnestness applies to Religiousness B or Christianity, which in his view is a forward rather than backward movement by virtue of a relation to the absolute paradox of the eternal in time as the point at which all Christian categories are situated.[38] To see how this dialectic operates more specifically in Christianity, therefore, we must turn to Kierkegaard's upbuilding and Christian works.

Let us begin by considering the first of three discourses in *Eighteen Upbuilding Discourses* (1843 and 1844)) based on the text, "Every Good and Every Perfect Gift is from Above," from James 1:17, which was one of Kierkegaard's favorite biblical verses. Although these discourses are intended to be broadly ethical-religious rather than specifically Christian in content, they are applicable to both forms of religiousness. The first discourse emphasizes that every good and perfect gift comes from God, who is "the one who does everything" in us.[39] God's gifts thus should be acknowledged and received with meekness, humility, joy, courage, faith, trust, thankfulness, courage, and love, which are themselves good and perfect gifts from God.[40] Admitting that we are neither good nor perfect in ourselves, so that even the love with which we accept God's gifts is impure due to the

---

[37] Ibid., 472.

[38] Ibid., 104.

[39] *EUD*, 46.

[40] Ibid., 36, 38, 41, 42-44, 45-46.

sinful change that takes place in everything received from God, Kierkegaard suggests that we love God truly only when we love him according to our imperfection, that is, with a love that is "born of repentance," which in his view "is more beautiful than any other love" inasmuch as "in repentance it is God who loves you."[41] It is in and through repentance, then, that we receive everything from God, even the thanksgiving which we presumably bring to him. Yet even that, Kierkegaard points out, is a *jest*, namely a receiving of something that God has given to us while granting us "the childlike joy" of regarding our thanksgiving as a gift to him from us.[42] Although repentance on our part is required in order to love God truly and to be receptive to his good gifts, the emphasis in this discourse and throughout the entire collection is clearly on God as the source and giver of all spiritual qualities, which are perfect in themselves. Thus they are not gifts to be perfected in or by us through a process of personal striving. On the contrary, in Kierkegaard's view a human being's highest perfection is to need God: "In a human being's relationship with God, it is inverted: the more he needs God, the more deeply he comprehends that he is in need of God, and then the more he in his need presses forward to God, the more perfect he is."[43]

Here again we see the inverse dialectic that governs Kierkegaard's understanding of ethical-religious existence in general and Christianity in particular. From an inverse perspective, perfection is not something we accomplish on our own but only by becoming convinced that we are "capable of nothing, nothing at all."[44] Outwardly, it may appear that we are capable of doing a great deal, but inwardly to comprehend one's total inability to do the good, Kierkegaard claims, "is the highest thing of which a human being is capable."[45] Yet even that is a misunderstanding inasmuch as in Kierkegaard's view "the human being is a helpless creature" in which "all other understanding

---

[41] Ibid., 45-46.
[42] Ibid., 46.
[43] Ibid., 303.
[44] Ibid., 307.
[45] Ibid., 308-9.

that makes him understand that he can help himself is but a misunderstanding, even though in the eyes of the world he is regarded as courageous."[46] God, by contrast, is capable of everything, while correspondingly our greatness and highest perfection consists precisely in being capable of doing nothing at all by ourselves.[47] Pointing to Moses as an example of a person whose greatness consisted in understanding that he was capable of nothing at all and his work was entirely the Lord's, Kierkegaard states: "Just as knowing oneself in one's own nothingness is the condition for knowing God, so knowing God is the condition for the sanctification of a human being by God's assistance and according to his intention," which is "to create in him a new human being."[48] A sense of one's own nothingness, then, is a prerequisite not only for a true knowledge of oneself and God but also for the new creation and sanctification of oneself as a human being, whose "exalted destiny" is to be "God's co-worker" in ruling over creation as his servant.[49]

In *Works of Love* (1847) the concept of jest is viewed strictly from a Christian perspective as it relates to Christian love, whose "most characteristic specification," Kierkegaard claims, is building up, so that "[w]herever upbuilding is, there is love, and wherever love is, there is upbuilding" inasmuch as both possess the quality of being able to give themselves completely and to be present in everything.[50] Noting that "to build up" is a metaphorical expression frequently used in Holy Scripture, Kierkegaard regards it as an "upbuilding jest" or earnestness "when someone humbly manages to be satisfied with the scriptural word instead of busily making new discoveries that will busily displace the old, when someone gratefully and inwardly appropriates what has been handed down from the fathers and establishes a new acquaintance with the old and familiar."[51] When love is understood from a biblical

---

[46] Ibid., 309, translation modified.

[47] Ibid., 310-11.

[48] Ibid., 311, 325.

[49] Ibid., 86.

[50] *WL*, 212, 214, 216.

[51] Ibid., 210.

and/or Christian perspective, Kierkegaard observes, one no longer plays "on humanity's childish stage, which leaves in doubt whether it is jest or earnestness," inasmuch as for the Christian "the one and only earnestness" consists in relating oneself to God in such a way as to become nothing before him in the infinite debt of love to other people and to God, who is Love itself.[52] It is only in self-denial that one relates oneself to God in a Christian manner, for it is only in self-denial that one holds fast to God and discovers that God exists.[53] For Kierkegaard, therefore, "the relationship of self-denial to God, or to relate oneself to God in self-denial, ought to be everything, ought to be the earnestness" with which one overcomes the illusion that one is capable of something and comes to understand instead that one is capable of nothing at all, whereas God the Omnipotent One is one's co-worker in and through whom one is able to do everything through divine assistance.[54] Earnestness is thus equated with inward self-denial and outward self-sacrificing unselfishness in the recognition that one's relationship to God is everything. Consequently, whether a person's works of love are finished or not "ought to be a jest," that is, "the God-relationship itself ought to be more important to him than the yield" in the "utterly earnest conviction that God is the one who is helping him."[55] Only by loving the neighbor in self-denial, then, can one achieve the highest, which for Kierkegaard is to become an instrument for God, "completely and wholly transformed into simply being an active power in the hands of God," which every human being can do if he or she so wills.[56]

In *Christian Discourses* (1848) Kierkegaard uses his favorite examples from nature, the lily and the bird, to elucidate the dialectic of jest and earnestness in Christianity. Noting that the Sermon on the Mount was preached at the foot of the mountain rather than on top of Mt. Sinai, where the Law was given to Moses, he observes that, in being referred to by Jesus in that sermon, the lily and the bird were

---

[52] Ibid., 102-103, 190, 264-65, 320.
[53] Ibid., 362, 364.
[54] Ibid., 86, 362-63, 365.
[55] Ibid., WL, 364-65.
[56] Ibid., 86, 279, 364; see also *CD*, 83-84.

present as well, making the Gospel sound as if it "ends up jesting."[57] For Kierkegaard, however, the earnestness of the Gospel "becomes all the more holy just because the lily and the bird are there" inasmuch as "it becomes that by way of the jest," although "it still remains a jest that the lily and the bird are there."[58] The lily and the bird are jestingly employed as assistant teachers by the Gospel to clarify what paganism is and what is required of the Christian. Being neither pagans nor Christians, nor opposed to either of these contending parties, the lily and the bird function as neutral or non-judgmental, non-condemnatory teachers of the difference between paganism and Christianity by doing nothing at all, living as they do in an unconcerned, carefree manner in total dependence upon God. Yet by their help we can get to know the cares of the pagans—and perhaps those of people in the pagan but so-called Christian country of Denmark and other places as well—which distinguish them from the true Christian, who lives like the lily and the bird without care by existing for God in total dependence upon him.

In *Practice in Christianity* (1850), the dialectic of jest and earnestness is seen as being essential to the art of indirect communication in Christianity.[59] It appears first of all in the communication of the God-Man as a sign of contradiction who combines in himself the qualitative contradiction of being the unity of God and an individual human being, which cannot be communicated directly because it is impossible for the recipient to determine whether the communication is in earnest or a jest. In this case, therefore, the earnestness of the communication lies not in the communication itself but in making the recipient self-active by drawing attention to itself in such a way as to show that it contains a contradiction that requires a response of either faith or offense on the recipient's part. To do that, the communicator must make him/herself into a nobody or nonperson, as it were, by continually placing the qualitative opposites of jest and earnestness together in such a way as to make the composite into a

---

[57] *CD*, 9.

[58] Ibid.

[59] *PC*, 125, 133.

"dialectical knot" which the recipient must untie him/herself through double-reflection and the choice of whether to believe or not.[60]

In *Judge for Yourself!* (1951/52) Kierkegaard returns to the example of the lily and the bird as an expression of the dialectic of jest and earnestness in the context of a discussion of Christ as the prototype for humankind, focusing this time on the text from the Sermon on the Mount for which the bird and the lily serve as illustrations, namely "No one can serve two masters" (Matthew 6:24). Christianity is once again contrasted to the merely human wisdom, sensibleness, or sagacity of the cultured age in his time, which views the requirement of the unconditioned of human beings as madness and a "ludicrous exaggeration" that no sensible person is capable of meeting or at most only to a certain degree. Kierkegaard suggests that Christ's life "must have been designed from the very beginning to express serving only one master" by fulfilling the unconditional requirement as a prototype for humanity.[61] Born in poverty and lowliness as an illegitimate child, he came and remained in the world in order to suffer and to use his powers of omnipotence to become nothing in the eyes of the world while at the same time drawing attention to himself as if he were "something utterly extraordinary" in wanting to establish a kingdom that is not of this world right smack in the middle of this world.[62] In order to keep the matter from becoming "all too earnest" and "deadly with anxiety" by asking people to look at him as the embodiment of the truth of his words, Christ diverts attention instead to the lily and the bird as symbols of what he signifies.[63] Ordinarily, Kierkegaard observes, to ask someone to consider the lilies and the birds would not be taken as the expression of earnestness on the part of the speaker but merely baubles and empty words.[64] When spoken by Christ, however, the words are an expression of earnestness, although an "earnestness toned down almost to a jest" by virtue of the ludicrousness of the lily

---

[60] Ibid., 133.
[61] *JFY*, 154, 160.
[62] Ibid., 160-61, 174-75.
[63] Ibid., 179.
[64] Ibid.

and the bird being our teachers.[65] "Yet it is not therefore a laughing matter—however odd it is that the sparrow has now become a professor," Kierkegaard states, "because the teacher's presence during the lesson means that no one dares to laugh."[66]

What do we learn by paying attention to the bird and the lily in this instance? Kierkegaard suggests that their instruction "is always plain, reliable, not vacillating in mood, but 'the same and about the same and always the same,'" namely the peace to be found in resting in God.[67] By resting in God the lilies and the birds are able to be happy today in carefree joy and thus to have their own "merriest jest" with sorrow by continually putting it off until tomorrow, which never comes. Moreover, they neither sow nor spin, leaving it to God in heaven to provide for their needs. Unlike the lilies and the birds, however, human beings do sew and spin. The main lesson we should learn from them, therefore, "is to understand that when human beings spin and sew it is nevertheless really God who spins and sews."[68] Using the example of a seamstress, Kierkegaard explains that this does not mean that she should not sew or become less diligent in her work but rather should understand that only when she is sewing does God sew for her, so that:

> by continually sewing she may continually understand that—what a gracious jest—it is God who sews, every stitch, so that by continually sewing she may continually understand—what earnestness!—that it is God who sews, every stitch. And when, instructed by the lily and the bird, she has understood this, then she has grasped the meaning of life, and her life has in the highest sense become meaningful.[69]

The lily and the bird not only teach us the meaning of life but also the meaning of work, which is also discerned inversely by "considering the matter upside down," namely that "work is not toil and trouble from which one would rather be free" but that "God has allowed human

---

[65] Ibid.

[66] Ibid.

[67] Ibid., 181.

[68] Ibid., 183.

[69] Ibid.

beings to be able to work in order to give them an enjoyment, a feeling of independence."[70] To illustrate this "godly understanding" of what it means to work, Kierkegaard concocts another example, this time a little child named Ludvig, who takes delight in believing that he is pushing the stroller himself on his daily ride when it is really his mother who is pushing it.[71] Being able to push it himself is comparable to being able to work, which when properly understood enables one to have pure delight and enjoyment. But Kierkegaard goes on to suggest that there is "an even higher godly understanding of work," namely that it is God who works when we work.[72] Thus, even when little Ludvig becomes an adult and is actually able to move the stroller himself, Kierkegaard suggests that he is still in the same situation as a child, namely that when the adult works it is really God who is working. But like the diligent seamstress, "the worthy, honest, God-fearing worker... becomes all the more industrious" so as increasingly to understand what a gracious jest and earnestness it is that God is her or his co-worker.[73] Kierkegaard thus concludes that we owe much to the lily and the bird, for when they were appointed to be our prototype and schoolmaster, "the Law was abrogated and jest was assigned its place in the kingdom of heaven," freeing us from "the strict discipline" of the Law.[74]

Does this mean, then, that the earnestness of imitating Christ is a jest? To this question Kierkegaard answers with a quick No, for two reasons: first of all because he thinks that it "would make the Gospel so easy that basically it would become poetry," which is exactly what the imitation of Christ is intended to prevent; and secondly because it would only be an expression of Jewish piety, not Christianity, inasmuch as "what is crucial in Christianity" is not manifested by the birds and lilies at all, namely to suffer for the doctrine, which is what constitutes

---

[70] Ibid., 184-85.
[71] Ibid., 185.
[72] Ibid., 186.
[73] Ibid.
[74] Ibid.

the true imitation of Christ.[75] In Kierkegaard's journals, however, a different point of view concerning this question is expressed. In an entry from 1849 he equates Luther's doctrine of faith with "the religiousness of manhood" (*Manddommens Religieusitet*) in contrast to the "childlike relation of equality" between the believer and Christ as the Exemplar in youth, a time when it seems possible to attain the ideal if one strives to the utmost of one's abilities.[76] As the youth develops into manhood, however, "God becomes more and more infinite" to the believer and he feels himself to be "farther and farther away from God," with the result that the ideal becomes "so infinitely elevated" that all one's efforts to resemble Christ are transformed "into an insane nothing or into a sort of God-fearing joke" in the faith that one is saved by faith alone.[77] And in another journal entry from 1852 Kierkegaard states:

> If imitation—even in its most extreme efforts—in earnest (i.e. before God) is to claim significance as something in the sense of being meritorious, it must be as a sort of a jest, something childish: what is in earnest is the atonement.... Yes, where something rigorous is required, that is where there can be talk of meritoriousness; but when everything is grace, meritoriousness is impossible—it is impossible to have merit in the face of grace.[78]

Indeed, for Kierkegaard, "the first thing you learn when you relate yourself to God in everything is that you have no merit whatever."[79] Thus, even when, out of joy and gratitude over the atonement, that is, over the fact that restitution for one's sins has been made by Christ, "an honest effort" at striving emerges, it is nonetheless to be regarded "almost as a jest—however honest and earnest it may be."[80]

---

[75] Ibid., 187.

[76] *KJN*, 6, NB, 14:41 / *JP*, 2:1135.

[77] Ibid. See also *KJN*, 8:NB, 22:57 / *JP*, 2:2140.

[78] *KJN*, 8, 25:67 / *JP* 2:1909.

[79] *WL*, 385.

[80] *KJN*, 6, NB, 14:42 / *JP*, 1:983.

What then should we conclude from this excursion into the inverse dialectic of jest and earnestness in Kierkegaard's theology? First and foremost, it is apparent that Kierkegaard is a dialectical thinker through and through, affirming both jest and earnestness, freedom and grace, divine agency and human agency, independence and dependence, continuous striving yet an incapacity to do anything at all on our own. Thus, to emphasize one of these terms to the exclusion or neglect of the other is to miss or misconstrue the thoroughly dialectical character of his theology. But it is also important to discern the inverse, indirect, paradoxical nature of Kierkegaard's dialectic. It is not just a matter of affirming both terms but of understanding how they are held together, which is not simply by discussing one term in one text and the other in another, depending on the particular rhetorical context and strategy being employed at the time. While it is true that Kierkegaard sometimes does discuss them separately in such a manner, the question remains as to how they actually fit together in human life. We have seen that Kierkegaard is consistent in his emphasis on our human nothingness and total inability to accomplish anything on our own in both ethical-religious and Christian contexts. But whereas the ethical-religious individual runs aground and gets no further along in actually establishing an absolute relation to the absolute than the nonreligious person who does not concern himself with such matters at all, in Christianity God works in and through us as his co-workers to accomplish the divine will in the world, with the result that, paradoxically, all our striving, in itself only a jest if understood as accomplishing something on our own, is actually God working within and through us, which constitutes the earnestness of eternity. Jest, then, is a crucial category for understanding the relation of human agency to divine agency and grace in Kierkegaard's theology. Not only does it serve to humble all our striving in relation to the divine, it testifies indirectly and inversely to the Christian conviction that God is and remains active in the world precisely in and through our earnest yet jesting efforts to serve the divine will in the imitation of Christ.

Contributors

Stephen Backhouse is Director of Tent Theology and Senior Lecturer in Political Theology at Westminster Theological Centre. He is the author of *Kierkegaard's Critique of Nationalism* (2011) and *Kierkegaard: A Single Life* (2016).

Lee C. Barrett is the Stager Professor of Theology at Lancaster Theological Seminary. He is the author of *Kierkegaard* (2010) and *Eros and Self-Emptying: The Intersections of Augustine and Kierkegaard* (2013).

Joshua Cockayne is Lecturer in Analytic and Exegetical Theology at the University of St Andrews. His forthcoming publication is entitled *Becoming Contemporary with Christ: A Kierkegaardian Account of the Christian Spiritual Life*.

Aaron P. Edwards is MA Programme Leader and Lecturer in Theology, Preaching, and Mission at Cliff College. He is the author of *A Theology of Preaching and Dialectic* (2018)

C. Stephen Evans is University Professor of Philosophy and Humanities at Baylor University. He is also a Professional Fellow at the Logos Institute, University of St. Andrews, and at the

Institute for Religion and Critical Enquiry, Australian Catholic University. His publications include *Kierkegaard: An Introduction* (2009) and *Kierkegaard and Spirituality* (2019).

David J. Gouwens is Professor Emeritus of Theology at Brite Divinity School. He is the author of *Kierkegaard as Religious Thinker* (1996).

G. P. Marcar is a Teaching Fellow in Theology and the Harold Turner Research Fellow at the Centre for Theology and Public Issues at the University of Otago.

Murray Rae is Professor of Theology and Religion at the University of Otago. He is the author of K*ierkegaard's Vision of the Incarnation: By Faith Transformed* (1997) and *Kierkegaard and Theology* (2010).

Andrew B. Torrance is Senior Lecturer in Theology at the University of St Andrews. He is the author of *The Freedom to Become a Christian: A Kierkegaardian Account of Human Transformation in Relationship with God* (2016).

Sylvia Walsh is Retired Scholar in Residence at Stetson University. She is the author of *Living Christianly: Kierkegaard's*

Dialectic of Christian Existence (2010) and *Kierkegaard and Religion: Personality, Character and Virtue* (2018)

Philip G. Ziegler is Professor of Christian Dogmatics at the University of Aberdeen. His recent publications include *Militant Grace* (2018) and *Dietrich Bonhoeffer: Theologian of the Word of God* (2018).

www.ingramcontent.com/pod-product-compliance
Lightning Source LLC
Chambersburg PA
CBHW050845230426
43667CB00012B/2155